Action Therapy With Families and Groups

Action Therapy With Families and Groups

Using Creative Arts Improvisation in Clinical Practice

EDITED BY

Daniel J. Wiener
and Linda K. Oxford

AMERICAN PSYCHOLOGICAL ASSOCIATION
WASHINGTON, DC

Published by
American Psychological Association
750 First Street, NE
Washington, DC 20002
www.apa.org

To order
APA Order Department
P.O. Box 92984
Washington, DC 20090-2984
Tel: (800) 374-2721; Direct: (202) 336-5510
Fax: (202) 336-5502; TDD/TTY: (202) 336-6123
On-line: www.apa.org/books/
E-mail: order@apa.org

In the U.K., Europe, Africa, and the Middle East, copies may be ordered from
American Psychological Association
3 Henrietta Street
Covent Garden, London
WC2E 8LU England

Typeset in Goudy by Stephen McDougal, Mechanicsville, MD

Printer: Sheridan Books, Ann Arbor, MI
Cover Designer: Berg Design, Albany, NY
Technical/Production Editor: Casey Ann Reever

The opinions and statements published are the responsibility of the authors, and such opinions and statements do not necessarily represent the policies of the American Psychological Association.

Library of Congress Cataloging-in-Publication Data

Action therapy with families and groups : using creative arts improvisation in clinical practice / edited by Daniel J. Wiener and Linda K. Oxford.
    p. cm.
  Includes bibliographical references and index.
  ISBN 1-59147-012-9 (alk. paper)
    1. Arts—Therapeutic use. 2. Movement therapy. 3. Improvisation in art—Therapeutic use. 4. Group psychotherapy. 5. Family psychotherapy. I. Wiener, Daniel J. II. Oxford, Linda K.
  RC489.A72A28 2003
  615.8'5155—dc21   2002154561

British Library Cataloguing-in-Publication Data
A CIP record is available from the British Library.

Printed in the United States of America
First Edition

CONTENTS

CONTRIBUTORS

Barbara F. Cooper, MPS, ATR-BC, Codirector, SuperKids, Ridgefield, CT; Adjunct Professor of Art Therapy, Pratt Institute, New York

Pamela Dunne, PhD, RDT-BCT, Professor of Theatre Arts and Dance, California State University, Los Angeles

Kimberly C. Galway, MA, RDT-BCT, Director, Goddard Riverside Community Center, New York

Steve Harvey, PhD, ADTR, RDT, RPT-S, Child and Adolescent Psychologist, U.S. Naval Hospital, Sigonella, Italy

Kate Hurd, MA, RDT, Assistant Director, Goddard Riverside Community Center, private practice, New York

David Read Johnson, PhD, RDT-BCT, Director, Institute for Developmental Transformation and Institute for the Arts in Psychotherapy, New York; Associate Clinical Professor, Department of Psychotherapy, Yale University School of Medicine, New Haven, CT

Hadar Lubin, MD, Codirector, Posttraumatic Stress Center, Yale University, New Haven, CT; Assistant Clinical Professor, Department of Psychiatry, Yale University School of Medicine, New Haven, CT

David Marcus, MA, CMT, NRMT, Music Therapist, Nordoff–Robbins Center, New York University; Founding Codirector, Creative Music Therapy Studio, New York

Ilo B. Milton, MPS, CSW-R, NCPsyA, ATR-BC, Adjunct Assistant Professor, Creative Arts Therapy, Pratt Institute, New York

Linda K. Oxford, MAR, MSSW, Adjunct Instructor, Counseling Program, Harding University Graduate School of Religion; Clinical Director of Agape Child and Family Services, Memphis, TN

Charlotte A. Ramseur, MSMFT, LMFT, private practice, New Haven, CT

Alan Turry, MA, MT-BC, NRMT, Codirector, Nordoff–Robbins Center, New York University, New York

Daniel J. Wiener, PhD, Professor, Department of Counseling and Family Therapy, Central Connecticut State University, New Britain

PREFACE

We identify ourselves primarily as systemic family therapists who both practice and train clinicians. In our work we make frequent use of action methods (therapy approaches involving physical movement and expressive arts techniques), as we find them extremely useful to achieve change.

The idea for this book arose out of discussions with colleagues and students regarding *Beyond Talk Therapy: Using Movement and Expressive Techniques in Clinical Practice* (Wiener, 1999). That book featured detailed descriptions of the use of action methods within case vignettes, mostly in the context of individual psychotherapy. The feedback centered on two needs: to learn more about action methods in the contexts of family and group therapy, and to gain a better understanding of how action methods contribute to otherwise-verbal psychotherapy.

About this same time we were copresenting workshops on action methods of couples and family therapy and had collaborated in writing a full-length case study that eventually became chapter 2 in this book. Our discussions of both the feedback described above and our teaching experiences coalesced in the desire to produce a work that offered in-depth conjoint case presentations featuring a diversity of action methods used with different client populations across a variety of problems. Accordingly, we solicited contributions from other experienced practitioners who use action methods in conjoint therapy.

Producing an edited book is obviously a collaborative effort that extends well beyond its authors. We would like to thank (in alphabetical order) Mario Cossa, Pamela Dunne (who also authored chapter 8), Joyce Hayden-Seman, Andrew Hughey, David Kipper, Debra Linesch, William More, Suzanne Peterson, Jim Rice, Barbara Rimer, Rebecca Rucker, Marcella Trevathan, David Waters, and Richard Whiting, who provided expert reviews of chapter contents and offered valuable editorial suggestions.

Action Therapy With Families and Groups

INTRODUCTION

DANIEL J. WIENER AND LINDA K. OXFORD

The purpose of this book is to provide a detailed introduction to use of *action methods*—therapy approaches involving physical movement and expressive arts techniques—in *conjoint treatment*—therapy conducted for more than one client, as in group, couples, or family therapies—by showcasing applications of a variety of action approaches in full-length case studies. The diversity of cases and methods featured is designed to inspire readers to seek more extensive training in action methods to expand their repertoire of clinical skills and to enhance their own and their clients' natural spontaneity, creativity, and resourcefulness.

This book should appeal to clinicians looking for fresh approaches to working with their clients and expanding their therapeutic options. Primarily written for mental health professionals and students (e.g., psychiatrists, psychologists, social workers, marriage and family therapists, professional counselors, pastoral counselors, psychiatric nurses, expressive arts therapists), the methods described will also offer inspiration and new perspectives to paraprofessionals and educators (e.g., chemical dependency counselors, guidance counselors, peer counselors, lay counselors, expressive arts teachers, relationship enhancement program instructors).

The term *action methods* refers to experiential techniques that use physical movement and creative, dramatic, or symbolic expression (e.g., dance and

3

movement, role-playing, improvisation, art, music, or rituals) in which the client engages at the direction of the therapist. Although the terms are often used interchangeably, *experiential therapy* refers to methods that focus one's attention and awareness on the here and now but do not necessarily involve the physical activity characteristic of action methods. Thus, all action methods of therapy are experiential, although not all experiential therapy involves action methods. In contrast to more widely used conventional "talk therapy" approaches, which are occasionally supplemented by other therapeutic activity, the action methods in the cases featured here are central to the conduct of the therapy, not merely adjunctive.

As noted above, *conjoint therapy* refers to concurrent clinical work with two or more clients and may include couples, family, and group psychotherapy. Relationships are the natural contexts in which individuals live and, to a large extent, shape their thoughts, feelings, and behaviors. One significant limitation of individual therapy is that individual change is difficult to achieve and sustain without a supporting change in those relationships that influence the individual's actions.

Psychotherapy, including conjoint therapy, has traditionally been conducted through the exclusive use of spoken language; consequently, facilitating therapeutic change has relied heavily on the verbal discourse between therapist and client system. Action interventions, when used, generally have been confined to "homework" assigned to members of the client system by the therapist. Yet, throughout the history of psychotherapy, there have been a variety of approaches developed that have gone beyond talk therapy: behavioral therapies of both the classical and operant paradigms, social milieu therapies, George Kelley's fixed role therapy, classical psychodrama, and contemporary body psychotherapies, to name but a few.

A major advantage of using action methods in conjoint therapy is the opportunity for experiential focus on those interaction patterns that have developed and maintained the problem. Although some therapists, notably family systems theorists, advocate changing the context in which the symptom occurs to resolve the presenting problem, the talk therapy approaches habitually used in conjoint therapy often serve to keep the system operating in familiar territory. Changing the context often requires moving from the comfortable and familiar arena of language to the relatively uncharted and novel terrain of action to present new possibilities and options to both therapists and their clients.

Because they invite therapist and client to enter and navigate unfamiliar and unexplored territory, action methods require some degree of improvising by both. Action methods challenge the spontaneity and creativity of therapist and client by confronting them with new situations and possibilities and promote in each the development of new skills, competencies, and "action insights" (Moreno, 1946) as new behaviors are tested and evaluated. Through these methods both therapist and client acquire increased self-confidence and competence in problem-solving and responding successfully to new demands. Both develop faith in their improvisational ability and decreased performance anxiety.

Action methods, which provide better ways of representing complex, multidimensional patterns than do verbal–sequential approaches, uniquely enhance conjoint treatment, which deals with ongoing relationships and interaction among clients. Language may even serve to obscure the fact that other ways of organizing and understanding experiences exist, because language is a means of constructing rather than reflecting reality (Fairclough, 1992). Talk therapy often encourages a focus on words and meanings and places disproportionate reliance on verbal communication skills to accomplish change in immediate relationship processes and patterns.

WHY ACTION METHODS?

Broadly, action methods provide clients and therapists new ways both of looking at problems and of discovering solutions to these problems. Because they operate simultaneously at cognitive, affective, and behavioral levels and appear to bypass habitual ego defense mechanisms, action methods can facilitate rapid learning and quickly produce significant systemic change in relationship and interaction patterns. Action methods are thus especially appropriate to skills training; role development and expansion; relationship enhancement; and short-term treatment with groups, couples, and families.

More specifically, action methods offer the following advantages over verbal-only approaches:

- They better engage those clients who process information predominately in the visual and kinesthetic modes (Bandler & Grinder, 1975).
- They "level the playing field" for clients (e.g., "play-age" children) who are at a distinct disadvantage in arenas that favor individuals with highly developed verbal and intellectual skills.
- They provide clients with alternative frameworks for their experiences through activity that engages the senses, often in novel ways. These other-than-verbal experiences and frameworks then can be compared with prior verbal representations to shift meanings and enrich awareness.
- They change the mode through which clients habitually express themselves. Although language can alter the meaning of an experience, enactment holds the power to alter the experience itself. "Action methods get clients to venture into the territory of experience, de-skilling clients who have come to [over-] rely on the maps of verbalization" (Wiener, 1999, p. xiii) and putting their verbalizations to the test of experience.

- They may facilitate resolution of psychological trauma in cases in which verbal approaches have proved unsuccessful. Research indicates that traumatic experiences are stored or encoded in the brain differently than are nontraumatic experiences (James, 1999; van der Kolk, 1996).
- They illustrate intangibles more clearly and concretely than can most other techniques. For example, interaction patterns and relationship structures can be visibly expressed through action methods in ways that make covert or unconscious processes overt and subject to conscious awareness and choice.
- They can dramatize role relationships and role perceptions, illustrating the transactional and systemic nature of family roles and permitting role expansion of each family member in interaction with the others.
- They can provide opportunities for couples, families, and groups to challenge and alter their stories, scripts, and myths, which can be concretely constructed and compared. This process may effect pervasive, substantive, and lasting changes in perception, behavior, relationships, and interactions.
- They can provide clients opportunities to experience, explore, and experiment with new behaviors and solutions in a safe, supportive setting where the consequences of failure and threats to their relationships are minimal.
- They may be used to develop rituals or rites of passage to deal with significant transitions in ways that are meaningful to all members of a relationship system and allow them to recognize and affirm their success in negotiating transitions as a couple or family.

EMPIRICAL SUPPORT

Quantitative research substantiating the efficacy of psychotherapy action methods is limited. Researchers wishing to produce rigorous outcome experiments are more inclined to study standardized approaches that more easily lend themselves to application with large client samples, accepted research design, and statistical interpretation of results, conditions infrequently met in the application of action modalities. Indeed, the requirements set by the major sources of grants for psychotherapy research mitigate against the likelihood of funding research designs that use unconventional treatment, do not use standard measurement protocols, or apply to specialized populations. Moreover, it appears that the majority of current practitioners drawn to modalities utilizing action methods are neither interested in nor trained in empirical research.

This is not to say, however, that the positive results attributed to action methods in psychotherapy are insignificant or unsubstantiated. Numerous case studies and qualitative research supporting the value of these techniques have led many in both the therapeutic and scientific communities to conclude that verbal therapy alone is ineffective with certain populations, such as young children or individuals with intellectual or cognitive deficits, and that action methods of treatment are much more likely to be successful with these clients. Furthermore, practitioners of several action methods have truthfully and reliably justified on a case-by-case basis the appropriateness and effectiveness of their interventions with clients to the satisfaction of both clients and providers of third-party reimbursement benefits (Wiener, 1999). In several expressive arts therapies, standardized measures of assessment have been developed that also permit the measurement of treatment outcomes; further, sufficient empirical support has been marshaled by music therapists to propose standardized reimbursement criteria (Standley, 2000).

LIMITATIONS AND CAUTIONS

It should not be assumed that the descriptions of action methods provided in this book provide sufficient training for otherwise-uninformed readers to apply these successfully or ethically to their own clinical work. These descriptions are themselves verbal representations of experience, which are an inadequate substitute for action in the form of experiential training and supervised practice. All too often, enthusiastic readers try out superficially learned action methods without adequate preparation, only to become discouraged when they fail to work. This unfortunate sequence then results in three possible negative perceptions: The reader concludes (a) that the methods do not work; (b) that he or she is insufficiently talented to apply them; or (c) that such advanced training is required for their successful use that he or she can never master them without dedicating himself or herself to lengthy, intensive training. In all three instances, the reader is likely to abandon further efforts to use action methods.

We assert (a) that these methods work, (b) that most practitioners have the aptitude to learn to use them successfully, and (c) that the extent of training necessary to use them ethically and effectively tends to be exaggerated. Although the most effective results can often be obtained only by practitioners with considerable experience and thorough theoretical grounding, the more widespread application of action methods in psychotherapy by adequately "cross-trained" practitioners affords an overriding benefit to clients. Such cross-training requires a less proprietary attitude on the part of "purists" and a willingness to educate the broader mental health practitioner population. Recently, programs for the cross-training of therapists within the expressive arts has begun (in the form of generic expressive arts therapy programs in place of an exclusive concentration in one particular approach, such as music therapy or art therapy) with the aim of broadening student competencies rather than attaining in-depth mastery of one particular method. Of course, we support the practice of all these action modalities and encourage interested practitioners to continue to seek further training in them.

ORGANIZATION AND SCOPE OF THIS BOOK

This coedited book presents a variety of action methods and their applications to family and group therapy, as demonstrated by eight case presentations. This in-depth treatment is intended to permit readers to grasp the significance and interrelationship of interventions in a context richer than is typically afforded by abbreviated case descriptions such as those found in journal articles. Rather than presenting specific action techniques isolated from clinical context, we have solicited fuller case presentations that provide the authors opportunities to explain their rationales for the choice, timing, and sequence of the interventions used.

In each of the case descriptions, the authors have either obtained appropriate permission from the clients represented or altered the case narratives sufficiently to protect the clients' rights to confidentiality. Case studies were chosen to represent the broad spectrum of client compositions encountered in family and group treatment: three-generational family systems, intact and blended (step-) nuclear families, multiple family groups, and theme-centered groups with a diversity of populations and presenting problems. Across these systems, the clients featured are diverse with respect to psychosocial functioning, therapeutic setting, and economic resources. Although the client population treated in each case is specific, many of the action methods described may be applied to conjoint psychotherapy across a broad range of populations. By presenting a diverse range of case examples we hope to demonstrate the versatility and advantages of these action methods in overcoming some typical constraints of traditional verbal-only approaches.

As noted earlier, a unifying theme that we discern across therapists' use of those action method approaches featured in this book is that of *improvisation*, acting with spontaneity rather than relying on pre-planned interventions or routine responses. For therapists, improvisation is a practice of developing interventions in-the-moment from whatever is offered by their clients; for clients, it is a way of attending to and acting on impulses in the now. In common with improvisation, action methods entail discovery in the present moment, a process not as controllable as verbal representation of prior, or even current, experience. While improvisation is not unknown in verbal-only therapy, the benefits of its practice within action approaches appear considerably more potent. The likely explanations for this are linked to some of the aforementioned advantages of action methods: their accessing of sense modalities, their lesser familiarity, and their experienced intensity.

We have asked that chapter authors adhere to a uniform format that facilitates comparisons across chapters. Following a brief overview of the featured approach, each author illustrates the application of action methods to a specific conjoint therapy case. Theory is described briefly and nontechnically and does not assume readers' familiarity with the approach. Interested readers are referred to source material for a fuller exposition of the theoretical foundations of each action method represented. Distinguishing characteristics of the featured action method may be learned from the intervention sequence and general progression of the case. Considerations specific to the case in question are highlighted by the choices made at key decision points by the author, who discusses the rationale behind his or her clinical choice and how he or she handled any special challenges or complications.

Action method interventions, when first introduced, are highlighted in italics. Case narratives are interspersed with separated italicized commentary concerning one or more of the following:

- observations made by the therapist, both during the therapy session and subsequently;
- specific descriptions of each method used as an intervention in the case;
- instructions for using each method described, including what it is designed to accomplish;
- general indications and contraindications in the use of each method;
- rationale for the use of a particular method with the case presented;
- discussion of the judgments used by the therapist in selecting a specific intervention at that particular point in the case;
- descriptions of any unexpected consequences of using the intervention and how this was handled by the therapist;
- discussion of how action and verbal elements were juxtaposed in the case; and
- discussion of the typical and atypical features of this case regarding the expectable outcome of or the clients' responses to the intervention.

The chapters also address

- ways of engaging clients in action methods so that they are invested in the treatment process and cooperative in following directives;
- aspects of the therapist's use of self in effective application of these methods; and
- empirical support, where available, for the efficacy of the methods used and questions or concerns for further research.

An appendix, compiled from resources supplied by chapter authors, contains information, where available, on references to foundational writings on theory and practice; key journals; names and contact information for professional associations; educational requirements for achieving professional competence; and contact information for professional training programs.

Obviously, the wide range of action methods for conjoint therapy far exceeds the scope of this book. We have presented only a small sampling of action approaches, sacrificing breadth for depth in the belief that fuller presentation of a selected few methods will allow readers a deeper experience of the rich possibilities afforded by action methods.

The eight chapters in this book have been organized into two parts, each beginning with a brief history of the use of action methods in that modality. Part I illustrates action methods in family (i.e., affiliative) therapy, whereas Part II features action methods in therapy with focused groups (i.e., nonaffiliative therapy). This order is designed to facilitate easy access to relevant chapters for those readers who work primarily as either family or group therapists and are seeking methods for working with these particular systems. It should be noted that some methods that are effective with nonaffiliative systems are less effective, or even contraindicated, with affiliative systems, a point expanded on in the last chapter.

Many readers will simply read this book in the order in which each chapter sequentially appears or will select from the table of contents the chapters that seem of particular interest or applicability. Others, interested in learning how action methods compare across different approaches and the implications of integrating action methods across therapeutic approaches, will find themselves alternating between comparable sections of different chapters. Because we have prepared this book expressly to offer action methods in fuller therapeutic context, we caution readers not to assume that they can benefit clients simply by extracting techniques from the index and applying these to other cases.

Part I consists of three chapters dealing with grief and loss, family reorganization, and the effects of trauma. In chapter 1, "Dynamic Family Play With an Adoptive Family Struggling With Issues of Grief, Loss, and Adjustment," Steve Harvey describes the struggle of a family to make peace with the loss of one child and incorporate another. Through a sequence of both spontaneous and directed play activities, interspersed with verbal therapy, the therapist coaches the family to play in ways that are diagnostically revealing, emotionally relevant, developmentally appropriate, and mutually healing. As a result, family members acknowledge their pain and affirm their support for one another.

Chapter 2, "Rescripting Family Dramas Using Psychodramatic Methods," by Linda K. Oxford and Daniel J. Wiener, describes a family's struggle to surmount their grief and successfully cope after the death of the family matriarch leaves the family without a functional head. Guided by a narrative therapy approach that reframes the family's internal conflicts as a collective struggle against an external antagonist, the therapist uses an array of psychodramatic techniques that go beyond linguistic intervention to separate the family experientially from the problem, mobilize their strengths and resources, and promote healthy and lasting reorganization.

In chapter 3, "Use of Ceremony in Multiple Family Therapy for Psychological Trauma," Hadar Lubin and David Read Johnson give detailed examples of how ceremonies orchestrated for multiple family groups successfully facilitate the healing and integration of traumatic family problems. Through the creation and enactment of call-and-response scripts, the therapists demonstrate the effectiveness of their approach with families dealing with foster placement and those containing Vietnam veterans with posttraumatic stress disorder.

Part II contains five chapters featuring group therapy approaches to the treatment of addictive and compulsive disorders, self-mutilation, substance abuse, autism, chronic mental illness, and career difficulties. In chapter 4, "Rehearsals for Growth Applied to Substance Abuse Groups," Charlotte A. Ramseur and Daniel J. Wiener describe the use of improvisational theater games in brief outpatient group therapy for clients with substance abuse problems. Through the therapist's continual creation of a supportive, low-risk climate, clients mobilize their emotional expressiveness and self-revelatory performances during the crucial early stage of recovery. Client participation in these groups results in significant improvement in their enjoyment of social interaction in a nondrug state, social skills development, and exploration of alternatives to dysfunctional social behavior.

In chapter 5, "Developmental Transformations in Group Therapy With Homeless People With a Mental Illness," Kimberly C. Galway, Kate Hurd, and David Read Johnson illustrate the uses of improvisational group play methods in working with a chronically impaired psychiatric population conspicuously lacking in social and economic resources. Their approach is conceptualized as restoring healthful developmental processes that have been arrested in these clients; their methods feature the highly active use of the therapist's self to model playful physical activity for the group and imaginatively utilize emergent, here-and-now impulses to overcome aversion and apathy while promoting integration, hope, emotional expressiveness, and prosocial behavior.

In chapter 6, "Group Art Therapy With Self-Destructive Young Women," Barbara F. Cooper and Ilo B. Milton demonstrate how the use of planned multimedia art project directives channels the self-destructive impulses of a group of eating-disordered, substance-abusing, and self-mutilating women into art-making. Overcoming intragroup competitiveness and the occasional destructive acting out of members, the therapist validates and supports group members toward improved social interaction, self-knowledge, and ego integration.

In chapter 7, "Using the Nordoff–Robbins Approach to Music Therapy With Adults Diagnosed With Autism," Alan Turry and David Marcus demonstrate in detail how the formidable challenges faced in the treatment of adults with severe autism are met by a structured yet improvisational group music therapy approach. Although the group members do not achieve breakthroughs in their social lives, their responses to one another in therapeutic group music-making display marked improvement in awareness of one another, responsiveness, spontaneity, and organization.

In chapter 8, "Narradrama: A Narrative Action Approach With Groups," Pamela Dunne introduces narradrama, her own unique integrated action methods approach. Drawing from several creative arts traditions and a narrative therapy theoretical framework, she uses a wide array of action methods and techniques to facilitate personal growth and successful problem resolution with a group of professionals whose lives have run into roadblocks.

CONCLUDING THOUGHTS

We believe that the further study and wider use of action methods in psychotherapy has the potential to invigorate the mental health field, provide effective treatment to a wider population than is currently served, and enhance the creative artistry and technical craftsmanship of therapists. We hope that this book stimulates the imaginations of readers and contributes to their realization of these potentials.

REFERENCES

Bandler, R., & Grinder, J. (1975). *The structure of magic: A book about language and therapy*. Palo Alto, CA: Science and Behavior Books.

Fairclough, N. (1992). *Discourse and social change*. Cambridge, England: Polity Press.

James, M. (1999). Symbolic functioning and alexithymia in Vietnam combat veterans diagnosed with posttraumatic stress disorder. *Dissertation Abstracts International*, 61, no. 01B, Accession No. AA19958870, p. 534.

Moreno, J. L. (1946). *Psychodrama* (Vol. 1). Beacon, NY: Beacon Press.

Standley, J. (2000). Music research in medical treatment. In C. Furman (Ed.), *Effectiveness of music therapy procedures: Documentation of research and clinical practice* (3rd ed.), pp. 1–64. Silver Spring, MD: American Music Therapy Association.

van der Kolk, B. A. (1996). *Traumatic stress: The effects of overwhelming experience on mind, body, and society*. New York: Guilford Press.

Wiener, D. J. (1999). *Beyond talk therapy: Using movement and expressive techniques in clinical practice*. Washington, DC: American Psychological Association.

I

ACTION METHODS IN FAMILY THERAPY

INTRODUCTION:
ACTION METHODS
IN FAMILY THERAPY

Action methods have a long tradition in family therapy. Satir (1967) and other experiential therapists initially imported action methods into family therapy from the humanistic psychology movement. Whitaker (Whitaker-Napier, 1978) immersed himself completely in the family system, engaging in physical interactions such as playing "horsey" with a young child or wrestling with a teenager. His methods, which he characterized as "atheoretical," were spontaneous, unconventional, and highly intuitive, and emphasized the importance of direct experience in facilitating change.

Duhl, Kantor, and Duhl (1973) are credited with introducing the influential family sculpting technique, in which members of the family arrange each other into tableaux representing different relationship patterns. Papp (1977) also used sculpting and choreography to facilitate awareness and change in the family system. Minuchin's (1974) work in Structural Family Therapy emphasized demonstrating to the family the new, more functional relationships being sought by changing seating arrangements or interaction patterns in the session. Strategic therapists such as Haley (1976) and Madanes (1981) extended these ideas through the use of action directives, in which families were given tasks to accomplish between sessions at home.

The Milan school introduced various forms of prescribed family rituals, which were designed to alter or disrupt family interaction patterns (Palazzoli, Cecchin, Prata, & Boscolo, 1978). Imber-Black, Roberts, and Whiting (1988) offer an excellent text on the use of therapeutic rituals in family therapy, though they concentrate on individual families. Narrative approaches have also utilized metaphorical, ceremonial, and action-based interventions (White & Epston, 1990).

Metaphorical or dramatic methods allow family members greater freedom to experiment by virtue of the "pretend" nature of the activity. Madanes (1981) uses numerous "pretend" directives in her work, and Andolfi, Angelo, Menghi, and Nicolo-Corigliano (1983) play with the concept of the metaphorical object in the family. In addition, creative arts therapists have applied art (Landgarten, 1987), dance (Bell, 1984), psychodrama (Leveton, 1977), multimodal play (Harvey, 2000), and music (Decuir, 1991) in family therapy.

The cases featured in this section demonstrate the powerful therapeutic factors associated with the use of action methods in family therapy. Much of families' history, dynamics, and concerns remain hidden from observers and over time their communication processes become embedded and unexamined. Action methods externalize these elements and dynamics through concretizations that are more readily observable and alterable. Action methods also provide family members opportunities to serve as witnesses to one another's experiences, enhancing cognitive distance and accompanying opportunities for reflection and insight (Andersen, 1991).

Through action methods, family members can experiment with alternative behaviors, roles, and interaction patterns in low threat situations (Minuchin, 1974). Rather than merely discussing proposed changes in interactions and relationships, family members experience them directly—bypassing defense mechanisms, evoking increased empathy and cognitive/affective shifts, and creating new relationship possibilities (Haley, 1976; Minuchin, 1974).

REFERENCES

Andersen, T. (1991). *The reflecting team: Dialogues and dialogues about the dialogues.* New York: Norton.

Andolfi, M., Angelo, C., Menghi, P., & Nicolo-Corigliano, A. (1983). *Behind the family mask: Therapeutic change in rigid family systems.* New York: Brunner/Mazel.

Bell, J. (1984). Family therapy in motion: Observing, assisting and changing the family dance. In P. Bernstein (Ed.), *Theoretical approaches in dance-movement therapy* (pp. 23–41). Dubuque, IA: Kendall-Hunt.

Decuir, A. (1991). Trends in music and family therapy. *Arts in Psychotherapy, 18,* 195–199.

Duhl, F., Kantor, D., & Duhl, B. (1973). Learning, space, and action in family therapy: A primer of sculpture. In D. A. Bloch (Ed.), *Techniques of family psychotherapy.* New York: Grune & Stratton.

Haley, J. (1976). *Problem-solving therapy.* San Francisco: Jossey-Bass.

Harvey, S. A. (2000). Family dynamic play. In P. Lewis & D. Johnson, (Eds.), *Current approaches in drama therapy* (pp. 379–409). Springfield, IL: Charles C. Thomas.

Imber-Black, E., Roberts, J., & Whiting, R. (Eds.). (1988). *Rituals in families and family therapy.* New York: Norton.

Landgarten, H. B. (1987). *Family art psychotherapy.* New York: Brunner/Mazel.

Leveton, E. (1977). *Adolescent crisis: Approaches in family therapy.* New York: Springer.

Madanes, C. (1981). *Strategic family therapy.* San Francisco: Jossey-Bass.

Minuchin, S. (1974). *Families and family therapy.* Cambridge, MA: Harvard University Press.

Palazzoli, M., Cecchin, G., Prata, G., & Boscolo, L. (1978). *Paradox and counterparadox.* New York: Jason Aronson.

Papp, P. (Ed.). (1977). *Family therapy: Full length case studies.* New York: Gardner.

Satir, V. (1967). *Conjoint family therapy.* Palo Alto, CA: Science & Behavior Books.

Whitaker, C., & Napier, Y. (1978). *The family crucible.* New York: Harper & Row.

White, M., & Epston, D. (1990). *Narrative means to therapeutic ends.* New York: Norton.

1

DYNAMIC FAMILY PLAY WITH AN ADOPTIVE FAMILY STRUGGLING WITH ISSUES OF GRIEF, LOSS, AND ADJUSTMENT

STEVE HARVEY

Editors' Introduction: Steve Harvey's approach draws from a variety of action methods, including collaborative art, dance and movement, drama, story-telling, and interactive games to create an integrative approach to therapeutic family play. Traditional methods of play therapy with children are here extended and adapted to involve the entire family in this multidimensional treatment process. The therapist, assuming the role of improvisational play coach, counters the family's loss of creativity and spontaneity in response to existing anxiety-provoking themes as opportunities to incorporate these themes into therapeutic family play activity, thereby transforming them.

In this chapter I discuss dynamic family play, my own expansion and interpretation of traditional play therapy, to facilitate successful problem resolution and adjustment in an adoptive family struggling with trauma, grief, loss, and disrupted attachment. Dynamic family play is an action method particularly useful in helping families with young children address emotionally charged issues through integration of play episodes with verbal discussion of their experiences. The development of and theoretical rationale for this method are rooted in observations of the use of natural spontaneous play in families to creatively generate improved coping, adjustment, and problem-solving.

Dynamic family play, designed to address both presenting problems and core family conflicts, consists of activities such as collaborative art, movement, drama, story-telling, and video-making. Verbal discussion of interaction patterns and emotional events that have affected family life is alternated with play episodes. Although all family members participate in treatment, individuals or dyads are often seen separately to address issues specific to that subsystem.

A central premise of dynamic family play is that creativity occurs spontaneously and naturally in any family. This creative ability contributes to the family's skills in coping, adaptation to change and adversity, motivation for problem-solving, and general emotional climate. Therefore, the primary goal of this approach is to help family members use their natural creativity in daily activities and develop, through play, metaphors that are meaningful, emotionally significant, and contribute to conflict resolution. Unresolved emotional events negatively affect a family's spontaneity and creativity. Much of this process is unconscious, especially among children.

In dynamic family play, family interactive patterns, themes, and metaphors are identified in expressive play activities. Through coaching, families learn to elaborate and extend the meaning of their metaphors, change problematic interactions and behaviors, and improve their motivation and shared emotional climate. Homework augments in-session activities. Verbal processing of these activities highlights and helps members consciously integrate new learning and behaviors into family functioning.

Action methods in dynamic family play consist of a specific progression of play activities, strategic coaching, use of verbalization, and therapist participation. The play setting and the therapist's use of self also are major elements of dynamic play therapy.

RATIONALE FOR EXPERIENTIAL INTERACTIVE PLAY

In general, the expressive methods of dynamic family play are best suited to families with children younger than teenagers, in situations involving basic emotional issues (e.g., attachment, separation, loss, trauma), and when either the parents or the therapist more fully engage children in the treatment process. However, some teenagers may engage in play methods with their family quite productively.

Dynamic family play is most effective in addressing family issues that resist more traditional behavioral and verbal approaches, such as cases (a) involving strong emotional turmoil, particularly emotion related to disrupted attachment, separation, and loss or trauma; (b) in which active and motivated engagement of children is considered important; and (c) where helping families develop more flexible, creative, and positive interactions is a goal. Dynamic family play provides even very young children a way to participate on an equal footing with their more verbally adept parents or older siblings. Play in which everyone's participation and contributions are valued helps engage young children in the therapy process. Dynamic family play is useful for families who need positive emotional experiences with one another to change. Mutually expressive play can help such families experience intimacy, perhaps for the first time. These moments can be quite powerful in facilitating change.

BENEFITS OF NATURAL INTERACTIVE PLAY

Spontaneous interactive play between parents and children is one concrete way natural creativity is both expressed and generated in families. Such play can emerge at any time and introduces a shared positive feeling among the players. Family members usually discuss their play easily in encouraging and organizing ways. In families experiencing significant stress, such play and conversation are difficult to generate.

Interactive play can generate attachment or, at least, the motivation to engage in positive mutual experiences. Researchers and clinicians (Harvey, 1994a; Stern, 1985; Tortora, 1994) interested in infant–parent play have observed how playful exchanges develop into a natural dance or choreography involving eye contact, smiling, and responsiveness in mutual nonverbal communication. As a child grows, such games become more elaborate—involving sound and face-making, verbal exchanges, and larger sensorimotor play such as running, jumping, and tumbling—and often include the active participation of parents. In children's preschool years, parents and children engage in dramatic role-playing in addition to a wider variety of physical games.

A visit to any playground or park where young children and their parents are playing reveals a wide variety of family play activities. Play contributes to developing humor and story-telling as families mature. In observing family play, one is struck by the spontaneity and naturalness of the participants and the spirited and emotional joining that is generated. This bonding is evident in the players' mutual improvisation, enjoyment of each other, and flexible conflict resolution. The family freely discusses such episodes—describing what is occurring, giving verbal meaning to the play activity, and planning play activities.

Images and themes related to emotionally charged events and conflicts are repeated in these play episodes. When families can continue their play interactions, these themes can resolve and transform emotional tensions that threaten their relationships. Such adjustments easily occur when the players are enthusiastic and discuss play themes in positive and meaningful ways. In this way, these episodes become an antidote to highly charged emotional events associated with conflict, trauma, and loss.

Examples of common themes include an injured toddler casting a willing parent in the role of doctor to "cure" him, an infant frightened by separation initiating nonverbal "face games" to cue her parent's visual attention and secure embrace, a preschooler's "magical" transformation of himself into a superhero as his mother applauds, or a teenager's use of humor during conflict with a parent to reduce tension and restore harmony. In these examples, the play partners freely acknowledge to each other the meaning and positive outcomes of their play actions. Ideally, families' mutual play produces a healing process in which their mutual creativity, imagination, and attribution of meaning to their play transforms emotionally laden themes in a way that the players experience affiliation, intimacy, attachment, and affirmation.

An example of family play involved a toddler rejecting his father, preferring his mother's attentions instead. The boy invited his father to play a familiar game in which his father would throw him into a pile of pillows. The boy added to the game by wiggling away into the pillows. His father added the response of reaching under the pillows to "find" his son, grabbing him while they both laughed with delight. The game clearly helped relieve tension created as the family developed new relationship and role alliances. Through his participation in this play, the father reaffirmed his attachment to his son. The mother, who had been watching, offered verbal encouragement. The parents used this play scene as a metaphor to discuss changes in their relationship with their son.

Positive experience with play clearly contributes to a family's emotional growth. However, for families with children who have experienced abuse or trauma or that are in the midst of loss or divorce, such mutual play can be very difficult and painful. When a 10-year-old girl was asked to complete a drawing with her adoptive father, she drew a picture of a person seriously injured in a car wreck while, on the far side of the paper, her father drew a park. As the drawing continued, the girl illustrated how the person in her story died. Meanwhile, the father continued drawing the park, seemingly unaware of the serious emotional theme his daughter was portraying. The activity ended quickly, with very little mutual engagement or shared creative development. The two exchanged virtually no positive feeling, and neither acknowledged the content of the other's picture.

The girl reported that she had been trying to hurt herself by hitting her body with her toys. The father stated he was increasingly frustrated with his daughter's oppositional behavior and negative mood and had become more withdrawn from her. The parent–child alienation and daughter's thoughts of self-harm were clearly expressed in the brief drawing and story-telling activity. The verbal interview afterward produced no positive change and did little to help father and daughter resolve their emotional conflict. The conversation was dominated by the father's description of the problems his daughter was having, while the girl became more withdrawn.

These two examples show how the differences in a family's coping resources can affect the quality and style of interactive family play. An important task for the play therapist is to help families enlist their own natural resources of play and creativity to resolve emotional conflict, rebuild intimacy, and produce more successful coping. In the case of the father and adopted daughter, the therapist helped parent and child extend and develop their story to include a hospital with doctors helping the car wreck victim. Both father and daughter then discussed the meaning of these pictures for them.

Building on the foundation of natural interactive family play, dynamic family play encourages family members to actively play together, identify when play "breaks down," and then use these breaks to develop new play interactions with motivation and spontaneity. Insight-oriented discussions encourage replacement of negative associations or interpretations with more constructive meaning. Inherent to this practice is the idea that a family will develop solutions and meaning through their play process that will generate new content in the emerging themes and images and produce positive feelings among the family players.

DYNAMIC FAMILY PLAY

The progressive stages of play activities used to develop interventions follow from a family's initial orientation to the use of play activity through their ability to make use of independently generated play. This progression proceeds from (a) a basic evaluation in which presenting problems are identified verbally and in play; (b) directive therapy focused on specific issues, during which the therapist coaches the family in more flexible play interactions; (c) the crystallization of a "core scene" that defines and addresses a family's specific emotional issue and characteristic interaction patterns; and (d) finally, the family's successful generation of their own play and conscious addressing of their problems with more spontaneity, creativity, and motivation.

Play Setting

The appropriate setting in which to conduct dynamic play therapy is a large room that can accommodate a variety of expressive and imaginative activities and allows family members to freely use whole body movements. There should be opportunity for activity such as chase games, tug-of-war, and hide-and-seek. Stuffed animals of various sizes help suggest dramatic play scenarios about family. Large pillows can help make physical play safe and be used to construct houses and walls. Colorful scarves and elastic ropes are useful props for physical games and dramatic activity. Large newsprint paper and markers, crayons, pencils, and clay should also be available.

In general, the play material is relatively nonspecific and designed to help family members use their physical, dramatic, and artistic imagination to transform these materials into what their play demands in the moment. It is helpful to have a video camera and monitor in the room so that action episodes can be taped and reviewed.

Therapist's Use of Self

In dynamic family play the therapist assumes many roles. As interviewer, the therapist leads a variety of assessment and problem-solving activities that help family members relate their history, describe their current problems, report their emotional states, and gain understanding of their family themes and interaction patterns. The therapist's roles when leading play episodes are quite varied and call for a "master player" who can create a playful atmosphere in which expression is both motivated and meaningful.

An aspect of being this master player is active coaching of the play and the players by the therapist. The central goal of this coaching is to help the family develop their own natural play and, when it breaks down, to discuss how this play related to their problems and then regenerate collaborative family play. The coach takes several roles, including director of new play activity, actor in the play, or therapist facilitating change from play to discussion and back to play again. As a coach, the therapist should provide developmentally appropriate, challenging, semistructured activities using drama, art, movement, story-telling, and video. The coach must recognize when play begins losing its organization and mutual interest and help family members change their interactions to develop new play activity that has more emotional relevance. In addition, the therapist at times acts as a participant/ observer within the play to ensure that the cues of the players are incorporated as play continues. The therapist observes and verbalizes emotional states and themes as families improvise play more independently.

The therapist must flexibly move between all these activities and roles to ensure that the family's play process allows them to address their problems and emotional conflicts with honesty and develop play improvisation that is relevant to their conflicts.

Initial Evaluation

During the initial evaluation the therapist observes or videotapes the family in varied play situations using predetermined evaluation activities. Through verbal interview, the therapist reviews presenting problems and obtains a clinical history of attachment, loss, separation, ongoing conflict, and emotional trauma. Evaluation activities include such things as asking the family to play a game of "Follow the Leader," with everyone taking a turn as leader; to complete a drawing together; or to use large stuffed animals to improvise a story about a family.

The main task during these initial sessions is to help family members make connections between the content and style of their play and the emotional–behavioral themes they verbalize. Therapy goals are then defined in both play and verbal terms. The therapist is primarily an observer in these initial sessions, reflecting and summarizing information and asking questions to better define problems and relevant history.

Evaluation activities typically consist of play tasks in which most families will participate without much preparation. These play tasks stimulate interactions that provide examples of family intimacy, conflict negotiation, and emotional metaphors. When most families are asked to take turns playing Follow the Leader, for example, the resulting play usually includes enthusiastic sharing of ideas generated by each family member. Parents can easily accommodate and encourage younger children to lead when they can follow the example of older family members. One family member's leadership is often picked up and extended by another. The exchange of leadership is encouraged and cooperative. However, when families experience power struggles or are unable to resolve conflicts, the change of leadership in the game often produces interpersonal difficulties. The game then stops generating creative "fun" and breaks down.

Other tasks that assess possible problems include (a) evaluating the attunement of parent and child by having the parent calm the child after swinging the child into a pile of pillows, (b) assessing physical intimacy by asking parent and child to make faces at each other from a close distance, and (c) evaluating members' understanding of family interaction by having each draw a house and take turns drawing themselves coming out of the houses to meet one another.

Following the initial evaluation activities, the therapist asks the parents for a thorough verbal description of their presenting problems and history, noting significant emotional events. Parents (and children, if old enough) are asked to give concrete behavioral examples of their problems. Parents, without younger children present, are asked about major losses, separations, deaths, and experiences with psychological trauma that they or their children may have had. Prompting the family to recognize the metaphorical value of their play interaction, the therapist then helps the family make connections between their play episodes and the emotional themes and issues presented verbally. Therapy goals are developed through both verbalization and use of play.

For example, a single mother brought her 8-year-old son to therapy because he was very oppositional at home. When she and the boy were asked to draw houses on a large piece of paper and then take turns drawing themselves coming into the common area, the boy drew slash marks over his mother's drawing of herself. She then reported that her son's best friend was stabbed and killed a year earlier. When the therapist noted the similarities among the drawing, the murder, and the boy's recent behavior problems, the boy and mother easily made these connections. Mother and son then were able to address both the oppositional behavior and the death of the friend in interactive play.

A more complete listing of evaluation activities and more thorough presentation of how such play material is integrated into verbal clinical material is presented in other writings (Harvey, 1991, 1995, 2000a).

Initial Games

Following the evaluation period, the therapist introduces organized "initial games" to help families improvise play around specific problematic themes. These games have simple rules, initially set by the therapist, that help families focus on developing successful play. It is expected that their play will break down and that such breaks reflect basic emotional conflicts.

For example, a child who has become withdrawn and secretive as a result of his parents' reluctance to discuss painful issues could be asked to play a game in which he tries to avoid being touched by a ball or scarf tossed by the parent. As this game begins, the prop thrown by the parent is labeled as a "telling ball" (or scarf). The parent is instructed to ask the child personal questions as the parent attempts to throw the prop so that it touches the child. The child is informed that he must answer the question if the prop touches him. Withdrawn children typically do not want to verbalize their thoughts or feelings and become quite adept at avoiding the parent's tosses of the play prop. As the game progresses, the therapist helps the parent and child recognize the game as a metaphor for their mutual reluctance to express their feelings and use their game performance as a way to both understand and alter their emotional constrictions.

Play flow refers to the interactions in which family players generate mutual play, while *play breaks* are those behaviors that stop such mutual play activity. When coaching an initial game, the therapist recognizes and uses naturally occurring play breaks in the development of later more successful scenes. Breaks can be introduced by any player and may take several forms but typically are outside of the implicit or explicit rules of the play activity (e.g., a player's cessation of play, small injuries, opposition).

In this phase of treatment, a main aim of coaching is to help parents and children begin to enjoy more organized improvisation together and generate "expressive momentum" when play breaks occur. *Expressive momentum* refers to shared mutual creativity and interest in continuing a shared play state. It is during this play state that players generate new metaphors together that often solve interactive difficulties. During this process, parents and children become more intimate, flexible, and responsive to each other, enjoying what is normally seen and described as the fun of play. Therapeutic activity during this stage includes helping families explore the metaphor-making possibilities of the various play modalities. Coaching facilitates family members' success with "natural play" in relatively short play scenes by finding a play form adequate to the expression of the more difficult feelings they experience.

This coaching is often quite directive, as family members in conflict often do not know how to play together. The therapist becomes a participant/observer of the play—sometimes modeling or leading positive play expression, sometimes suggesting variations, and always observing mutual expression and the emotional states generated. Verbal strategies here consist of labeling emotional states and connecting them to play activities. Connections between play and home behavior also are made during this time.

A father reported that his 7-year-old son had become increasingly angry and sullen after his parents' divorce, which they had not discussed with him for several years. In the session, father and son could not express to each other their feelings about their family life. They were instructed to play telling scarf, during which the boy tried to avoid being hit by scarves his father threw at him. Soon the boy began using pillows to protect himself from the scarves. He was totally hidden, giving his father no target. Play flow was interrupted, and the game stopped. Neither could generate any further play activity.

The therapist noticed this breakdown of expressive momentum and suggested that the father change the game by crawling into the boy's hiding place to find him. A game of chase spontaneously developed, ending when the father finally caught the boy. They both began laughing and showing emotional relief. Afterward, father and son were able to respond verbally to the therapist's questions and to each other, describing how much they missed each other and affirming the positive feelings each had for the other.

Additional lists of initial games are presented in Harvey (1990, 1991, 1993, 1997a, 1997b, 2000b, 2001). Several case studies in Harvey (1990, 1993, 1994b, 1994c, 1995, 2000b) described how the therapist coaches clients in moving from play breaks into more meaningful metaphors.

Core Scene, Individual and Dyadic Play, and Ritual

In the next phase of treatment, the therapist helps the family identify their core play scene and verbalize their central emotional issues. This is accomplished as the therapist helps identify repetitive themes in a family's improvised play and the family verbally reports their emotional experiences during play. Often, during this stage of treatment, children are seen individually or with one or the other parent. The therapist becomes more of an observer and therapeutic verbalizations are more reflective of emotional content emerging from the play.

During these play episodes the therapist encourages more play theme development and elaboration of emerging images. These play images and themes often reflect highly stressful emotional issues associated with loss and trauma. The therapist attempts to discuss such themes with families to help clarify their meaning.

During the spontaneous play between the father and son described earlier, the therapist noticed that their expressive activity continued to stop after a relatively short time. This stopping was identified as a play theme. The therapist asked to see the boy alone for a few sessions. When questioned about his difficulty playing with his father, he talked about feeling unsure of his father's feelings for him since the family breakup. He then discussed his emotional response to the realization that his parents were going to separate, describing this feeling as his "heart cracking." The therapist helped the boy produce a drawing of this experience and then use this drawing to tell his father of his feelings. Father and son took the drawing home as a reminder that they needed to make special time together to "mend the heart." The therapist coached them in how to extend their play metaphor to improve their interactions at home in a deeply significant way.

Free Play and Termination

Finally, the family is helped to improvise their own play together and discuss how this play is meaningful and relevant to them. Such play, freely generated among all family members, uses the curative forces inherent in naturally occurring play. The therapist helps families verbally reflect on their play metaphors and gain insight into their meaning and application. Treatment termination issues are then addressed.

In their final sessions, the father and son described above related how the telling scarf game developed into a game of chase, how the boy drew his cracked heart and, finally, how they were able to make special time together and mend the heart. Use of play activities and images made their progress and success in therapy very concrete.

Integration of Verbalization and Play Activity

In a successful dynamic family play, the therapist discusses the family's play interaction with them to connect play activity with verbally reported problems and emotional issues. Verbal connections are made between episodes of interactive play and family problems. Similarly, verbal identifications of old and new interactions are made. Although verbal processing of play experiences is necessary to the treatment process, spontaneous and creative family play has its own pace and timing, and families should not be interrupted with verbal comments during active generation of play.

The goals of insight and change are integrated through verbal interviews in which the family describes both immediate and past problems. Questions are directed to both adults and children during the initial parts of sessions. Interactive play then proceeds for a portion of the session, followed by verbal processing of the play experience. Verbal connections between play and family life help players together make meaning of the play.

CASE PRESENTATION

Presenting Problem

Mrs. Grey requested help for her newly adopted 5-year-old daughter Brandy. During an intake interview, she reported that the girl had been in the home for only 4 months but had significantly disrupted their family life. When asked to describe Brandy's behavior, she stated that the girl was very aggressive toward her and her 8-year-old biological son Brian. Brandy had threatened to hurt herself with a kitchen knife and had used the knife to cut the family's pet cat. Brandy slept only a few hours a night and seemed agitated and restless all the time. Brian, who previously had a calm behavioral style, had become upset and angry and constantly wanted to fight with Brandy. His academic work had deteriorated from his usual exceptional performance, and he had become extremely moody and spent a great deal of time crying.

Mrs. Grey, her husband, and the two children participated in an initial evaluation. During the session each member of the family, beginning with the children, was asked to describe problems the family was having. Brian reported that he just couldn't stand his new sister and "wanted to kill and bury her." He described Brandy's aggressiveness toward him and the cat, her yelling, and her theft of things from his room. Brandy then reported that "no one liked her" and began to cry. The parents stated that both children refused to listen and fought continually. The whole family reported that there was too much disagreement and too little cooperation. Family life had become unbearable.

The children were asked to go into another room and make drawings of themselves and their family. The parents then were asked about their own family histories. They disclosed that their family life had been very satisfying until two years ago, when their younger biological child, Sandy, had died following a year-long medical problem. Sandy was 5 years old when she died; Brandy was the same age when she came to live with the Greys. The Greys did not consider the similarities between Sandy and Brandy significant.

Both parents reported that they had been physically abused as children and did not want that for their children. Mrs. Grey's mother had died when Mrs. Grey was young, and Mr. Grey had come from a large family. They both wanted several children and considered adoption the only viable option for a large family. The first step toward having more children was bringing Brandy into their family. They wanted to keep her, but things were becoming unbearable. They were considering returning Brandy to the child protective services agency and stopping the adoption process. They had never considered how past events might be influencing their family's current situation but were willing to explore how these factors might be contributing to their current problems.

The Greys were told very little about Brandy before they adopted her. She was the youngest of three girls taken from their biological parents' home due to extensive physical and sexual abuse and family violence. Investigators were not able to determine the extent of abuse Brandy had experienced, although her older sisters had been the targets of significant physical and sexual abuse for much of their lives.

The children returned and showed their pictures. Brian had drawn a picture of himself near his home. He included several ghosts flying above the house. Brandy's pictures were remarkable for their immaturity. She had difficulty making a shape for her body and covered her self-drawing and the lines she identified as representing the house with hard scribbles. Brian stated that the child in the picture was scared of the ghosts but that he never thought about things like that. Brandy refused to comment on her picture. Both children said that they had enjoyed the drawing far more than the talking. They were shown the playroom before they left and were excited about coming back to play again. The parents also agreed to come back to play together and see if they could learn anything as a family about how they might change their behavior. It was important that the children wanted to attend the next session and that both they and their parents knew that they would be expected to play together.

Evaluation Play

The Greys were led into the playroom and asked to play a game of Follow the Leader, with everyone taking turns at being the leader. Mrs. Grey explained the game to both Brandy and Brian and asked which child would like to go first. Brian nominated himself and began by bouncing a ball he found. He passed it to his mother, who did the same. Brandy then grasped the ball, threw it to the other side of the room, and laughed quite loudly. Mr. Grey verbally attempted to redirect his adoptive daughter, while Brian became quite angry. Mrs. Grey then began to skip and asked the other family members to follow her. Mr. Grey took Brandy's hand to help her skip after Mrs. Grey. Brian protested. Brandy stated she wanted to be the leader and began to run away from the others, asking them to chase her. Brian continued his protest to his father. Mrs. Grey looked up and said this was the kind of confusion she experienced each day. Both she and Mr. Grey asked to stop. The game was finished in less than 5 minutes.

The Greys were next asked to sit around a large piece of paper and were given a box full of crayons. They were asked to each draw a house and then take turns drawing themselves coming out of their houses to meet each other. Mrs. Grey sat down next to Brandy to help her make a house, while Brian and Mr. Grey sat apart talking about what they could do together when they came out of their houses. Father and son drew themselves riding bikes toward a park. Mrs. Grey helped Brandy draw herself going to the park to swing with her mother and talked about how the two of them could join Brian and Mr. Grey. Brian then drew a ball and offered to play catch with Brandy. Once all were at the park, Brandy began drawing over the other figures, disrupting the activity. After about 10 minutes, the parents decided to stop the activity, saying they didn't want another argument to develop.

The family was then shown the large pillows and stuffed animals and asked to make a story about a family. Brandy immediately went under the pillows, saying she had found her "home," while her adoptive mother, her adoptive father, and Brian began using the other materials to make a house and table and to cast several large animals in family roles. While the parents were making their story, Brian began burying several smaller puppets that he said represented a brother. After some consideration, Brian would bury each puppet until he found the "right one" with which to play.

Brandy was then invited to join the rest of the family for a dinner. She, meanwhile, had covered herself with a large scarf and looked through a gap between her pillows. Mrs. Grey then handed her a smaller stuffed animal and invited her to come to a "dinner all the animals were having." Brandy brought her animal to the table, saying that there were several monsters in her "home." The family of animals and puppets then began to have a meal. Brandy began to laugh loudly, and her silliness disrupted the activity. The parents stopped the drama after about 15 minutes. The family stated that Brandy's disruption of the session was very similar to what often happens in their home life.

After the evaluation activities the therapist helped the family make connections between their reported problems and the problems in the play. The therapist pointed out how many times family members had attempted to involve one another in mutual activity but how something had always oc-curred to prevent them from sustaining enjoyable play.

The family developed a list of examples of breaks in their play action. The therapist pointed out many ways the family had stopped the flow of ideas from developing into more enjoyable play activity. The therapist pro-posed that improved play interactions might serve as a model to improve relationships at home.

Brian said he would play with Brandy more often if she would "listen to him." Brandy said she just wanted her adoptive brother to be "nicer." The therapist pointed out that both Brian and Brandy had introduced monsters, ghosts, and other figures that perhaps the whole family could help "tame" at some point in their play sessions.

It was important to point out the children's repeated introduction of fearful images that the family had not incorporated into their play. The therapist should provide concrete examples from the play and use terms that can be related to play action.

The therapist next reflected the children's difficulty in playing together without disruptions. He suggested that perhaps their play could be more fun if they learned to take turns when they played together and also how to play alone. The parents agreed that this might be something they could help the children do. The whole family agreed that an initial goal was to help Brian and Brandy find a way to play both separately and together. The parents agreed that this achievement might generate solutions that could be used to begin improving home activities as well.

These activities were selected for structured observation of the Greys' interactions to sample a range of interactions. Each activity requires a different style of participation and allows the family's interactive style to emerge in several types of play episodes. Families typically display more physical interaction in the Follow the Leader game. Such action requires bodily self-control, awareness of other moving bodies, and regulation of physical expression of emotions. Emotions that emerge in this context most often are related to basic attachment. Difficulties in negotiating the physicality and leadership aspects of Follow the Leader often reflect underlying problems with trust, basic attunement, or physical empathy. The Greys' problems with this game were likely associated with the attachment-related problems reported verbally.

Successful family drawing and story-telling often involve reflection and consideration of expression and reveal inner models of relationships. Difficulties in these activities may indicate problems in conceptualization, planning, and expectations of family relationships. The Greys' problems in completing these activities revealed difficulties in their internal conceptualization of a family and positive family interaction.

Family dramatic play requires some development of positive family roles. In addition, dramatic themes, metaphors, and images that emerge often illuminate the emotional conflicts a family is experiencing. Especially important are repetitive themes, intrusive images that have no relevance to the immediate story, and metaphors that relate to strong emotion. The Greys' dramatic performance suggested several family problems. Brandy's behavior revealed conflict in accepting Mr. and Mrs. Grey in parenting roles and her ambivalence about joining the family. Brandy's inclusion of monsters and Brian's burying of several rejected puppets introduced dramatic action that was ignored by the parents while they were preparing for the dinner activity. Such separation of images suggests a metaphor for the unresolved loss of Sandy and intrusive fear of the abusive trauma Brandy may have experienced in her birth family's home.

The Greys' focus on the more "normal" activity of preparing dinner and unconscious dismissal of the more fearful images further suggested that the parents were not yet ready to address these more difficult concerns. By failing to acknowledge Brandy's monsters and Brian's burying of toys and drawing of ghosts, the parents were unwittingly excluding the children's very strong emotional expression, which likely contributed to the disruptions in the play. The therapist suggested that these themes actively be addressed in future family play. While the parents admitted that avoidance of threatening themes might be occurring in their family, they and the therapist agreed that more verbal exploration of these themes would wait until both they and the children could engage more easily in play together.

Initial Games

After the evaluation sessions, the family agreed to use play to first address the relational difficulties between Brian and Brandy. It was decided that Mrs. Grey and the two children would participate together in play. The parents and the therapist decided that Mr. Grey's attendance in these initial sessions was not necessary because he was less involved in the children's day-to-day activities. The therapist decided to introduce more directed play activities for the children and put the mother in the role of the children's play coach. The therapist took the role of the "coach's coach."

This intervention was designed to introduce more structure and form into the children's play by adding turn-taking. The therapist addressed a deficiency in the mother's role by making her a more active leader and organizer of the children's interactions. These play directions were developed from observations of how the family's play had broken down in the original evaluation play.

In the next session, the therapist again addressed the children's problematic interaction. After obtaining a report of their behavior since the last visit, the therapist structured physical activities in which both children took turns running under a parachute while the mother, therapist, and other child raised it up and down. Once the children could accomplish taking turns, they were asked to show different feelings with their bodies as the parachute went up and down. These activities were highly structured to help both children have an enjoyable play experience together. The addition of rules helped Brandy and Brian establish a focus and organization to their physical expressions. This intervention was important given the nature of the children's problems at home and the difficulties observed in their play during the evaluation session. Mrs. Grey was able to use this play structure to be an effective leader of the children's activity. At the end of the session, all three reported that they had enjoyed their play together and seemed hopeful that progress could continue at home. The therapist helped them design an activity in which they could plan and implement some turn taking at home.

At the beginning of the next session, the mother reported that although the children had participated in some turn taking, their fighting had become much worse. Brandy had continued to take things from Brian's room, and he had become quite angry. The two had spent a great deal of time crying or yelling at each other.

This increase in conflict was unexpected, because the previous intervention had been designed to help decrease negative interactions by adding more structure and limits.

The therapist decided to help the mother and the children design a game representing the home problem and learn to control the game with in-office coaching.

The therapist set up an initial structure in which each one of the children could begin play improvisation and their mother serve as the coach to design solutions to potential problems.

The children were asked to make a wall across the play space using pillows and then divide the rest of the play props so they could each play in their "own room." Each child could go into the other child's "room" only with permission. The game produced much arguing about the division of playthings and where to place the wall. The mother was able to help facilitate negotiation through several disagreements. However, the children's tension continued to rise, and neither was able to accept the mother's solutions for long. Both children resorted to taking each other's chosen materials and pushing over each other's pillows. The session ended with both children crying on separate sides of the room. Mrs. Grey became overwhelmed with choosing which child to help. When she chose to hold Brandy, Brian continued to take all of Brandy's play material. He then used all the props to bury himself and began yelling that he wanted Brandy to leave the family for good. He also asked if his dead sister could come back and replace Brandy.

This total breakdown of the play state into such strong emotional expression shows how a family's experience with basic conflict such as loss intrudes into play. This kind of break must be addressed by the therapist to keep expressive activities within a range of safe experience. Clearly the children's underlying conflicts had introduced a significant break in their play flow. The emotional intensity was too high and destructive to produce positive outcomes in interactive play without some change. Continuing further play interaction threatened the emotional safety of the playroom for the children and was contraindicated at this time. The therapist and mother together explored how best to structure the expressive activities for the next series of sessions. This discussion helped reinforce her role as a competent parent.

The therapist and Mrs. Grey agreed that each child should come individually and have some time with her during the next series of sessions. These sessions would continue until each child could develop play that addressed basic conflict and then communicate that conflict with the parents. The parents could then take a more supportive role.

Individual and Dyadic Play

Brian wanted to come to sessions alone and had plenty of ideas to sustain his play without outside structure. He was encouraged to engage in improvisation with the play material. The therapist's main intervention was to encourage him to extend his ideas, help him use other media, and verbally reflect his feeling states and repetitive themes. Brian's main activity for his first few sessions was to make a room, then destroy it, showing a high degree of physical and emotional intensity. He would next bury himself under all the play props. During one session, he buried several puppets in a large parachute and became very distressed when he couldn't find them again. The therapist waited until this moment to bring up the possibility that Brian's play might be an expression of his feelings about the sickness and death of his sister.

The timing of this discussion was cued by Brian's clear repetition of the burying theme and great distress he spontaneously developed during this activity. These repetitions indicated that this boy could be ready to verbally acknowledge his response to Sandy's death, confiding first in the therapist and later seeking security and acceptance from his parents. The therapist judged that bringing up this subject without this combination of play theme and openly displayed distress would be premature, and Brian's reaction would be primarily defensive.

When the therapist asked Brian who was lost, he stated that he had been thinking of his sister's funeral that had occurred a year earlier. He had not discussed this event since that day and described how overcome with sadness he had been. Mrs. Grey was asked to join her son, and the two talked about Sandy's death. Both expressed significant grief. In a later session, Brian and his mother were asked to review Sandy's life using picture albums and include Mr. Grey in this activity. In a final session, the Greys and Brian talked about what actually happened and how they felt during Sandy's final year, recounting how they watched her become sicker, the day she died, and the funeral. Brandy was not included in this session.

The family reported feeling significant sadness in this session and relief at finally being able to discuss their fear as Sandy deteriorated and their overwhelming grief at her death. Brian reported that he felt abandoned by his parents because of their emotional withdrawal from him after the funeral and their unresponsiveness to him over the following year. He told of how he had been having real conversations with Sandy's spirit at night for quite some time, talking to her about how lonely he was without her. The Greys were quite moved by their son's disclosures, stating that they were unaware of his distress and experiences. During the next session, the Greys and Brian reported that they had experienced significant catharsis. The parents established a "special time" for Brian in which they spent time only with him. Brian reported that he no longer needed to listen to Sandy, as he now had his parents back again. He stated that he was ready to begin to accept Brandy.

Brandy and Mrs. Grey also had several sessions together during this time. Both reported that Brandy had been having difficulty sleeping due to nightmares and that she was continuing to show aggression toward herself during the day. Brandy was also becoming concerned about monsters.

The therapist introduced the game structure of "Monster" (Harvey, 2001). In this game, the parent and child together chase away a monster while the therapist approaches them with a stuffed animal or other play prop. The therapist then coaches the parent and child on chasing away the monster using their own spontaneous ideas, especially if breaks occur and the child is unable to take action. This game introduces the parent and child to a way of more productively and creatively coping with overwhelming fear or posttraumatic reactions. The parent is cast in a protective role, and the child is helped to successfully generate play that "chases" the monster away as a parent provides safety, assistance, and encouragement. The therapist ensures that this play produces positive outcomes and has expressive momentum.

Mrs. Grey and Brandy played several versions of this game over many sessions. At first, Brandy could do nothing when the therapist slowly brought a large stuffed animal toward her and her adoptive mother. Mrs. Grey was also at a loss as to what to do as Brandy's "protector." As the stuffed animal came closer, both Brandy and Mrs. Grey stopped moving. However, the therapist noticed that Brandy was looking away. He suggested that Brandy's eyes had the power to send the large bear away and that Mrs. Grey could help by pointing out good places to send the bear. In a short time, the mother and daughter had coordinated ways to stop and vanquish the monster.

The therapist noticed the child's physical reactions to the game as it was initially being played. He then helped Brandy and Mrs. Grey use this idiosyncratic action to individualize the game. This change encouraged Brandy to engage in more creative and successful physical action.

Using the therapist's idea to generate success, Brandy and her mother were able to spontaneously improvise several other ways to get the monster to leave, including throwing all the large stuffed animals out of the window, kicking them away, and even building a safe house of pillows that no stuffed animals cast as monsters could enter. This play was extended to include constructing a large monster from several pieces of paper and putting it in "jail." Mrs. Grey and Brandy began to thoroughly enjoy their play together.

The therapist noted how much fun the two were having as a cue that they were developing expressive momentum and could together creatively address Brandy's more fearful emotional states.

Brandy was asked to draw monsters at home and have Mrs. Grey get rid of them according to Brandy's directions. Brandy told her adoptive mother to tear them up, which Mrs. Grey did with enthusiasm.

In a following session, after Brandy and her adoptive mother made a safe house with pillows, Brandy left to chase away a monster by herself. At this time, she stopped moving and began breathing in a very quiet and constricted manner. Brandy had stopped playing and was truly overcome by fear.

This physical reaction indicated that Brandy was experiencing a very strong emotion that was intruding into her play. This break was a cue to develop play action in which the mother could respond in a sensitive and supportive manner to help Brandy recover a sense of safety. This action would facilitate more secure attachment and offer a metaphor to discuss such attachment feelings with both Mrs. Grey and Brandy.

The therapist noticed this break in the play and asked Mrs. Grey to come out of the house and sit next to the "dead" body of Brandy. In a few minutes, Brandy began to move her fingers. The therapist encouraged Mrs. Grey to touch the moving fingers to "bring them back to life." Soon Brandy began to move her whole body in an "alive" dance. This sequence was repeated several times, much to the delight of both Mrs. Grey and Brandy. In this way, the therapist coached the mother to extend the play state to incorporate Brandy's moment of becoming overwhelmed by fear into a play flow that creatively resolved the emotional tension.

Brandy's dance of delight at the monster's departure was developed from her expressive momentum and the attunement offered by Mrs. Grey. This play episode offered an important concrete metaphor for both parent and child about their development of attachment. The therapist developed an intervention in which Mrs. Grey and Brandy switched media, developed drawings, and made a book about their story of improvised dance and drama. This technique of switching media to other expressive forms was introduced to help the family expand their internalized meaning of this very successful event.

Brandy and Mrs. Grey made several drawings about her dancing away the monsters, which the therapist helped them make into a book. Mrs. Grey was asked to read this book to Brandy at bedtime. Mrs. Grey and Brandy were able to make up several stories in which the monsters were always sent away and Brandy was kept safe by her adoptive mother. Mrs. Grey and Brandy reported that the stories were successful in producing feelings of intimacy and closeness between them. Brandy's sleep improved significantly, and she stopped having nightmares.

During these sessions, Brandy disclosed that she had experienced many frightening things in her first home. She was unwilling or unable to elaborate, however. The therapist chose not to continue questioning about the earlier abuse Brandy may have experienced. Such questioning while Brandy was involved in play action might have created confusion about what events had actually occurred. Such confusion can lead children into making false statements about their abusive past. The therapist chose to encourage Mrs. Grey and Brandy to use their play to express their strong emotions of fear, the need for safety, and the development of intimacy through their play metaphors.

Soon after these sessions, the child protective services agency told the Greys that Brandy's older siblings had made credible reports that Brandy had experienced significant sexual and physical abuse. Both parents attended a more typical verbal session to discuss this revelation and review the play expressions by both Brian and Brandy in the previous sessions. The children were told that the therapist would be meeting with their parents and what was to be discussed. In this session, the Greys were helped to make sense of Brandy's behavioral conflicts and use her play metaphors to understand how difficult it had been for her to trust them. The Greys also developed insight into how strongly the death of their daughter had affected their family. They identified how emotionally difficult it had been to develop attachments between Brandy and themselves while they were still grieving their loss. For the first time they could discuss how their family history of loss had contributed to their reluctance to address the strong emotional issues they were confronting. Mr. Grey decided that it was time he become actively involved in the expressive portion of therapy. This decision was welcomed by Mrs. Grey and supported by the therapist.

Core Scene, Ritual, and Termination of Treatment

The therapist then introduced the idea of developing a ritual to resolve Sandy's death and then to welcome Brandy into their family. In this discussion, the family identified these two themes as being central to their difficulties. The Greys understood how this action could help them address the loss of Sandy in a concrete way that the children could understand and leave them freer to form attachment with Brandy. The family decided to create separate rituals for a farewell to Sandy and the "adoption" of Brandy. The Greys, including Brian, decided that it was important for Brandy to attend the farewell ritual. The benefit of having Brandy attend the farewell ritual was to help her learn the family's history in a direct and open way by witnessing the event. The goal of the welcoming ritual was to accept Brandy, with all her emotional baggage, into the family.

The Greys reviewed family albums with pictures of Sandy to introduce her to Brandy. They chose pictures to bring to the ritual that best represented their experience of Sandy. During the ritual itself, the family told stories about these pictures and then produced a drawing of these and other stories about Sandy. The ritual ended with the family leaving the drawing at the therapist's office. The ritual was very cathartic and actively included Brandy.

A few weeks later, Brandy's welcoming ritual took place. Prior to this event, the family made a photo album of pictures of Brandy's life before and since she came to live with them. The family helped her write descriptions of what happened during the events depicted by the pictures. During the session, the Greys all produced a large drawing of Brandy involved in family activities, including imagined future events. Each member included drawings of the positive interaction they most enjoyed having with Brandy. The family decided to destroy one of the paper monsters Brandy and her mother had constructed in earlier sessions. Brandy had requested that this art piece be torn up as a way the family could keep her safe. Each family member then promised to accept Brandy even if she had problematic behavior. The event was videotaped, and the tape was given to the family to take home and watch.

Some play sessions attended by the whole family followed the rituals. The play was improvisationally generated by the family, was positive in nature, and was remarkable for the shared cooperation between all the members. The themes the family generated were fanciful and lacked repeating fearful images. The parents and the children reported that behavior had improved significantly at home and that they talked about their feelings more often. They also reported they played together more often and found it enjoyable. Plans were made to end the therapy. A termination session was held in which the family produced a collage of the important events they remembered. Therapy was concluded after approximately 1 year. The family was advised that, because of the significant trauma Brandy had experienced, she might need further treatment as she faced new developmental challenges.

CASE DISCUSSION

Engagement and Resistance

Not all families participate in expressive play activities as readily as the family in this case study. The Greys were highly motivated because of their desire to adopt Brandy and the extreme trouble she was causing in their day-to-day life. However, some families' expressive style or experience of the problem does not lend itself easily to play. Some presenting problems can better be addressed in briefer forms of intervention (e.g., behavioral). The therapist should consider the ages of the children, the kind of problem presented, and whether the children can be engaged in treatment in a motivated manner.

Once the therapist and the family agree to use expressive methods, it is important that the therapist present the interactive play as one element of treatment used in combination with verbal interview and other behavior techniques. Play episodes are presented as experiments or improvisations that can be useful in understanding and dealing with emotional material that is difficult to address verbally due to the intensity of the experience or the younger age of the family members involved. If play becomes more disorganized and is not helpful to the family, the therapist can stop the activity and explore how play activity can be better structured to achieve desired outcomes. In such situations, the therapist can point out to the parents that successfully extending play episodes requires sensitivity to children's initiatives and active parental participation. At this point, the therapist can lead discussion about the metaphorical possibilities of interactive play to help families gain an understanding of the purpose for continuing play activity. The therapist helps the family use metaphors from their ongoing mutual play to identify emotional conflicts that may contribute to the breakdown of their play process.

Such joint problem-solving usually helps families maintain ongoing engagement in the play therapy process. This situation occurred in the case study when the joint play between Brian and Brandy produced an aggressive situation that the therapist and the mother believed to be destructive. As the therapist and parent discussed this situation and explored ways to solve this problem, they agreed that each child should have more individual time to express his or her personal conflicts. The mother became an active designer of the interventions and kept her investment in treatment.

To engage the family more completely, the therapist should address the family's presenting problems in designing or discussing play activity. Even though dynamic family play is designed to address underlying emotional issues, expressive activity should be clearly related to the problems of a family's day-to-day life. A basic assumption of this approach is that powerful emotional conflict, such as is involved with trauma and loss, will emerge in play metaphors as play improvisations become more organized by the players. If the therapist is sensitive to what families report about their home life and what is occurring in their play, relevant connections can be made between play metaphors and daily behavior.

In the case study, the monster game was introduced when Brandy was having fears and nightmares about monsters in her daily life. When she stopped moving during her play, her mother was directed to sit next to her. Mrs. Grey then developed a "dance" with her moving fingers that invited Brandy's response and led to Brandy's full-body dancing. This spontaneous action was related to Brandy's actual fears at home and had meaning for both mother and daughter. By designing and relating play to immediate stress, most families can begin to see the meaning and usefulness of such activity. This connection between in-office play and behavior at home is also made through the use of therapist-assigned home activities. Several examples of such connection were described in the case presentation.

Successive Uses of Similar Methods

Dynamic family play is designed around the idea that each family's interactive play will have a unique style, content, and story about the important emotional events that make up family history. This story is expressed in the idiosyncratic episodes of playful interaction in daily life. When these emotions are overwhelming to family members, this story becomes harder to see and interactive expression becomes more disorganized or defensive. The dynamic family play therapist addresses strong emotion by introducing gamelike activity to help family members organize their play around certain themes. As the therapist notices breaks of family play flow, he or she uses these deviations to coach members to develop more creative versions of the initial play structures. Each time the structures are repeated they are creatively extended. In this way, the therapist can help families develop the therapeutic power of their play episodes by using repetition and expansion of themes.

Use of repeated initial game activity and expansion of players' repeated themes occurred in the case study presented here. The therapist introduced the game of Monster to help organize Brandy's fearfulness and her adoptive mother's ability to provide safety. As Mrs. Grey and Brandy spontaneously introduced deviations into their play expression, the therapist helped them change the play drama to incorporate their "mistakes" using more creative and unique expression. This process of repetition and elaboration helped the play develop more personal relevance. For example, as the therapist noticed Brian's repeating theme of burying, he encouraged him to elaborate on this theme until it became a fully developed metaphor for his strong feelings of loss.

Empirical Support

At present there is very little research on dynamic family play. While case study evidence is quite positive from several sources, no organized or controlled research efforts have been conducted on the outcomes. Harvey and Kelly (1993) did look at the number of attunements and play breaks of attuned play in a single case over time. A young boy was observed in interactive play with his birth mother and with his foster/adoptive parents when the child was 18 months and later when he was 3 years old. The child had been removed from his mother's care because of extensive physical abuse and later adopted. He was seen at age 4 in a family play situation with his adoptive mother. Sessions were videotaped and later reviewed. Categories of attunement of parent–child interactive play and breaks were operationalized and reliably counted. Observations of play episodes or parent–child and child-only play revealed the boy to have avoidant attachment with his birth mother and secure attachment with both of his adoptive parents. At both ages 18 and 36 months the boy showed a significant number of breaks and a low number of attunements in interactive play with his birth mother. However, in play with his foster/adoptive parents, the same boy showed almost continual attunement. Few play breaks were noted. Later this boy's family play showed behaviors and themes that could be related to his earlier ratio of play flow to play breaks. Such images related to intrusive fearfulness. This study suggested that the process and themes of parent–child interactive play are related to attachment history.

Harvey and Soderquist (1995), in a yet unpublished study, observed videos of the structured interactive play of 12 families in which at least one child had been sexually abused at least 2 years earlier and of 13 families with children who had no reported abuse experiences. The families with the abused children had received verbally oriented treatment at the time of the reported incidents. Family play was operationalized and reliably rated for attunement or nonattunement. Families with children who had been abused showed less attuned play than their nonabused counterparts. This finding was significant in that the children who had experienced abuse continued to show disruptions in their play interactions even when their families had been supportive and they had received therapeutic attention to address the issue.

Clearly more controlled outcome studies that compare families with whom interactive play is used in therapy with other forms of treatment need to be carried out to better understand how such play interventions affect family functioning. Additional research needs to be conducted to develop an understanding of which families are best able to use more playful action methods and for which families more verbally oriented approaches will yield better outcomes.

REFERENCES

Harvey, S. A. (1990). Dynamic play therapy: An integrated expressive arts approach to the family therapy of young children. *Arts in Psychotherapy, 17*, 239–246.

Harvey, S. A. (1991). Creating a family: An integrated expressive arts approach to adoption. *Arts in Psychotherapy, 18*, 213–222.

Harvey, S. A. (1993). Ann: Dynamic play therapy with ritual abuse. In T. Kottman & C. Schaefer (Eds.), *Play therapy in action: A case book for practitioners* (pp. 371–417). Northvale, NJ: Jason Aronson.

Harvey, S. A. (1994a). Dynamic play therapy: An integrated expressive arts approach to family treatment of infants and toddlers. *Zero to Three, 15*, 11–17.

Harvey, S. A. (1994b). Dynamic play therapy: Creating attachments. In B. James (Ed.), *Handbook for treatment of attachment–trauma problems in children* (pp. 122–233). New York: Lexington Books.

Harvey, S. A. (1994c). Dynamic play therapy: Expressive play intervention with families. In K. O'Connor & C. Schaefer (Eds.), *Handbook of play therapy: Vol. 2. Advances and Innovations* (pp. 85–110). New York: Wiley.

Harvey, S. A. (1995). Sandra: The case of an adopted sexually abused child. In F. Levy (Ed.), *Dance and other expressive arts therapies: When words are not enough* (pp. 167–180). New York: Routledge.

Harvey, S. A. (1997a). The scarf story. In H. Kaduson & C. Schaefer (Eds.), *101 favorite play therapy techniques* (pp. 45–50). Northvale, NJ: Jason Aronson.

Harvey, S. A. (1997b). The stealing game. In H. Kaduson & C. Schaefer (Eds.), *101 favorite play therapy techniques* (pp. 150–155). Northvale, NJ: Jason Aronson.

Harvey, S. A. (2000a). Dynamic play approaches in the observation of family relationships. In K. Gitlin-Weiner, A. Sandgrund, & C. Schaefer (Eds.), *Play diagnosis and assessment* (pp. 457–473). New York: Wiley.

Harvey, S. A. (2000b). Family dynamic play. In P. Lewis & D. Johnson (Eds.), *Current approaches in drama therapy* (pp. 379–409). Springfield, IL: Charles C. Thomas.

Harvey, S. A. (2001). Volcano, monster. In H. Kaduson & C. Schaefer (Eds.), *More favorite play therapy techniques* (pp. 183–192). Northvale, NJ: Jason Aronson.

Harvey, S. A., & Kelly, E. C. (1993). The influence of the quality of early interactions on a three year old's play narratives. *Arts in Psychotherapy, 20,* 387–395.

Harvey, S., & Soderquist, M. (1995, October). *Results of the Malmo project.* Presentation at the 28th Annual Conference of the American Dance Therapy Association, Rye, New York.

Stern, D. (1985). *The interpersonal world of the infant: A view from psychoanalysis and developmental psychology.* New York: Basic Books.

Tortora, S. (1994). Join my dance: The unique movement style of each infant and toddler can invite communication, expression, and intervention. *Zero to Three, 15,* 1–10.

2

RESCRIPTING FAMILY DRAMAS USING PSYCHODRAMATIC METHODS

LINDA K. OXFORD AND DANIEL J. WIENER

Editors' Introduction: Linda K. Oxford and Daniel J. Wiener present "family narrative therapy in action" with a personal and unique method of using psychodramatic techniques to invite and sustain a high level of engagement with all members in collaborative defeat of the common family problem. Unlike the highly linguistic, sometimes formulaic, traditional applications of narrative therapy, this action approach is highly improvisational and driven by the clients' experience in the moment. Through psychodramatic enactments, family members are engaged at multiple levels of experience, enabled not only to externalize but also to concretize and interact with the family problem, experientially assess its influence on their family, and alter their relationships with it and with one another.

The case featured in this chapter illustrates the application of psychodrama and narrative therapy, specifically John Byng-Hall's (1995) approach to revising family stories and scripts, to treatment of a family reeling from the death of the family matriarch. Because of the difficulties inherent in working with multiple protagonists, psychodrama is not typically conducted with a family system, rather with an individual, as the client. However, as this case convincingly illustrates, a modified psychodramatic approach to treatment of family systems can be both efficient and effective. The strengths-based, solution-focused theoretical orientation of the therapist also contributes to the success of her approach to addressing this family's grief, loss, and disorganization.

PSYCHODRAMA AND FAMILY THERAPY

J. L. Moreno's application of his psychodramatic methods to treatment of couples and families in the 1930s introduced a long tradition of action methods in family therapy and offered a clear theoretical rationale for moving beyond the verbal description of family interactions and relationships to physical enactment of family dynamics in the therapy session (Compernolle, 1981; J. L. Moreno, 1969; Z. T. Moreno, 1991). Virginia Satir (1964, 1972) drew from psychodrama, gestalt, the encounter movement, and communications theory to develop her unique and dynamic methods of family therapy. Salvador Minuchin (Minuchin & Fishman, 1981), Walter Kempler (1973, 1981), Fred and Bunny Duhl (Duhl, Kantor, & Duhl, 1973), Peggy Papp (1980, 1990), and Richard Chasin and Sallyann Roth (Chasin & Roth, 1994; Chasin, Roth, & Bograd, 1989) were also influenced by psychodrama. Psychodramatic enactment is particularly suited to the narrative therapy approach developed by David Epston (White & Epston, 1990) and Michael White (1995) of exploring a family's cocreated roles and stories, externalizing the problem, promoting collaboration in challenging and defeating the problem, and cocreating new family scripts (Williams, 1989, 1994).

THEORETICAL FOUNDATIONS

The presenting problem that the family brings to therapy may be less problematic than the family's story about the problem, which may itself be maintaining or escalating the problem. The problematic story then becomes the therapist's primary target for systemic change.

According to John Byng-Hall (1995), family scripts develop when a family resolves a predicament in a way that is remembered. The family creates a story that makes meaning of the solution and establishes it as a model for solving similar problems that arise. This story, after being reenacted on several occasions and incorporated into the family's repertoire of roles and behaviors, evolves into a script.

As explained by Byng-Hall (1995), "Scripts prescribe the action to be taken now and in the future, whereas the stories give an account of the action that was taken in the past" (p. 25). That is, *stories* support and perpetuate the family's beliefs about the problem and its solution, while *scripts* define what the family is to do in response to their beliefs about a particular problem. Conflicts arise when family scripts are dysfunctional, prescribing a course of action and sequence of interactions that fail to resolve the problem. Presenting problems, or symptoms, result when the price for adhering to familiar patterns of interaction is too high, either in emotional pain or failure to achieve desired outcomes.

As does Byng-Hall, we view family problems as arising from the family script and help families explore ways to revise dysfunctional scripts. In problematic family stories, one or more family members typically are blamed for creating or maintaining the problem. The family's rigid adherence to an inadequate family script supported by this story has become the primary problem. Fundamental change in the problem-solving script is necessary for the family to become more resourceful and adaptive.

When scripts are "rewritten" through dramatic enactment, family stories also change as new stories, or narratives, are cocreated to support these revised scripts. While most family therapy approaches attempt to alter stories and relationships through verbal discourse, dramatic enactment enables families to revise scripts and stories by altering their here-and-now interactions.

Narrative therapy begins with separating the identified patient from the problem by naming and externalizing the problem, explores the family's cocreated stories, and challenges the ineffective roles and scripts adopted by family members (White & Epston, 1990). Psychodramatic methods take this process a step further by separating the problem experientially, rather than simply linguistically, from the person, thereby creating immediate opportunities for altering family members' relationships with the problem and with one another. Integrating these two approaches allows the therapist and family to explore in action the family's relationship with the problem and how it has disrupted their lives and relationships.

When the family confronts the externalized problem and exposes its "hidden agenda," family members are quickly motivated to develop cooperative strategies to challenge and defeat the problem. Attribution of malicious intent to the problem rather than to family members increases their cohesion, empathy, and mutual support and encourages them to view themselves and one another in new ways. New roles and behaviors that prove effective are validated and retained. The family's successful solution is then confirmed through the cocreation of new stories, which in turn give rise to new family scripts.

Combining psychodramatic and narrative techniques can rapidly move family members from antagonistic to collaborative positions and encourages the family to experience themselves as allies and victors in their struggles against a common adversary. The technique of *mirroring* reflects back to family members their problematic interactions and the script that sustains their self-defeating roles by allowing them to observe their enactment of present stories and scripts and obtain new perspectives on their relationships with the problem and one another. The technique of *role reversal* lets family members literally step into one another's shoes and experience the effects of the problem from another's perspective. Finally, through the technique of *future projection*, the family can discover what their lives might be like without the problem, exploring through dramatic enactment their expectations, goals, and ways to develop and nurture new behaviors, roles, and stories.

In the assessment phase of therapy, we seek to identify the patterns and themes of the family story revealed in the presenting problem and to understand the dynamics of existing family scripts. We then prepare ("warm up") the family for enactment by establishing a context of play and experimentation, fostering a willing suspension of reality testing, and providing an environment of psychological and physical safety and security. The voluntary nature of participation is emphasized, and family members are encouraged to think of dramatic enactments as "rehearsals" rather than as "performances," allowing them to try out new roles and behaviors with minimal risks. This climate of exploration and experimentation facilitates improvisation by family members when their previously scripted actions prove unsuccessful in resolving the problem. As Byng-Hall (1995) put it, the family begins with what is "too much familiar" and is then compelled to search "for something outside and beyond the known" (p. 54).

Family interaction patterns can be viewed as simply the enactment of established family roles. A *role*, defined as a set of related behaviors designed to carry out a specific act or function, is by nature relational and interactional, dependent on reciprocal role enactment by others to achieve its goals. Antony Williams (1998) noted that "roles, and then the self, are continuously being created in interaction" (p. 143). Role relationships in families may become scripted so that everyone knows what will happen next in the interaction sequence. "The concept of family scripts posits that everyone has the whole family drama encoded in their minds but identifies more with certain roles, and, in turn, is identified by others as playing particular roles" (Byng-Hall, 1995, p. 24).

Adaptive functioning of an individual or family results both from having a sufficiently large repertoire of available roles and the ability to move from one role into another as the need arises (Moreno, 1946). Healthy individuals and families exercise flexibility, creativity, and spontaneity in the roles they assume in interactions and can successfully meet a wide range of challenges and demands.

Roles that have proven to be socially effective and have been fine-tuned through practice tend to be retained and with continued use become "conserved" (Moreno, 1965). *Conserved roles*, characterized by automatic, predictable behaviors, are supported by role consensus, the general agreement among members of a group or family regarding their perceptions, expectations, and enactments of these roles. This agreement implies coordination with other conserved roles and is another way of describing a family script.

Psychodrama provides *role-training* techniques that encourage individuals to create and expand their roles. Role-training involves exploration in action of alternative role interpretations, perceptions and interactions, including behavioral rehearsal of roles in actual and simulated scenarios. Byng-Hall (1995) achieved role-training through improvising, editing, or rewriting family scripts; generating strategies to increase family security; and increasing family collaboration by altering their problem-solving methods (p. 75).

External circumstances or developmental changes may precipitate a role crisis, in which the role of one or more family members no longer fits a particular need or goal of the family. In a role crisis, family members, acting within familiar roles and established scripts, cannot respond adequately to the new situation. They must (a) expand their role repertoire, developing and manifesting alternative roles more appropriate to the specific need or goal, or (b) change the family script, altering habitual interaction sequences.

RATIONALE FOR ACTION METHODS OF FAMILY THERAPY

J. L. Moreno, widely credited with being the first to use action methods of psychotherapy, conceived psychodrama in the early 1920s. He posited two distinct aspects of healing, one of which is role expansion through role-training. Moreno believed that achieving role expansion required dramatic enactment of the problem in settings evocative of those in which the original limitations arose (*locus nascendi*) yet which provided a safe and supportive environment in which the dilemma can be resolved.

Moreno understood that verbal description of an experience is not synonymous with that experience. The client's most painstaking description of behaviors and roles that he or she enacts in life is usually an inaccurate reflection of how he or she actually manifests these behaviors and roles in situ. Similarly, verbal descriptions of other people that interact with the client are incomplete and often distorted in the client's report to the therapist. In dramatic enactment of the client's life experiences in the here-and-now therapy session, a fuller story emerges. Therefore, Moreno considered physical action within the therapy session not only acceptable but also necessary to the therapeutic process. We share his belief in the superiority of dramatic enactment to verbal communication in illuminating the client's situation and rapidly fostering change at behavioral, cognitive, and affective levels, transcending the inherent limitations of "talk therapy" through the here-and-now co-creation of new roles, stories, and scripts.

The following clinical case presentation demonstrates the effective application of psychodramatic methods of conjoint therapy to Byng-Hall's narrative approach to revising family stories and scripts.

CASE OF THE HUDSON FAMILY

The Hudson family, comprised of Sarah, age 36; Les, age 37; Marla, age 15; and Nicholas, age 7, presented for therapy five months after the death of Sarah's 74-year-old mother, Elaine. Five weeks after the death of her alcoholic husband, for whom she had served as primary caretaker for several years, Elaine came into the family home to assist her daughter following the difficult birth of Nicholas. She had remained there with her daughter's family until her death.

Nicholas had been extremely close to his grandmother and, according to his parents, had been having great difficulty coping with her death. He had resumed soiling himself at school, a problem he had previously experienced for 2 years but that had been resolved for 18 months before the death of his grandmother. Nicholas's teachers reported that recently he had become increasingly oppositional, had refused to do assignments, and was aggressive toward other students. At home, he was withdrawn from his parents, aggressive and impatient with the family's pets (2 cats, 3 kittens, 1 dog, and 3 rabbits), and unwilling to talk about his grandmother or to enter her room.

Sarah admitted that she had become very depressed since the death of her mother, with whom she had a very conflicted relationship. Sarah experienced periods of withdrawal and occasional "crying spells." Les had recently left his job of 8 years as a food service deliveryman and had begun selling insurance. The family income was seriously reduced by this job change, but Les insisted that in the long run this job would be more lucrative than was his previous one. At the time the family sought treatment, however, he was largely unoccupied during the day and usually engaged in sales calls during the evening.

Marla reportedly showed no change in functioning following her grandmother's death and appeared to be adjusting well to this loss. She was popular with teachers and peers, was active in the school band and on the volleyball and basketball teams, and maintained above-average grades. At home, she was generally quiet, good-natured, and responsible. However, she and her father often argued over household chores, with each complaining of having to do the other's work.

During the first session, the family was asked to identify the problem and describe how each of them had been affected by it. Their initial responses labeled Nicholas's behaviors as the problem and characterized Nicholas as stubborn, demanding, and oppositional. As the discussion continued, the family admitted that Nicholas was simply reacting to the grief that each of them was feeling in response to Elaine's death and to the effects of this grief on each family member. The Hudsons then agreed that their main problem was their inability to deal successfully with their feelings of grief and loss.

The family was informed that often the goal of therapy is not to get rid of the problem but rather to find new and better ways to manage it. The therapist asserted that any family would have difficulty adjusting to the loss of a family member and that often problems develop as the family struggles to find a way to deal with this loss. The family then was asked to unanimously decide on a name for the problem with which they were currently struggling. "Sadness" was described by the family as "a black hole that sucks you in" (Sarah); "a thick, dark fog" (Les); "a heavy weight" (Marla); and "like a big, mad monster" (Nicholas).

Noting that "one picture can be worth a thousand words," the therapist suggested that, rather than family members telling how the problem had been affecting them, they show how the problem was affecting each of them by *concretizing* and enacting their experiences with the problem. The family, who had successfully worked with the therapist 18 months to 2 years earlier to address Nicholas's encopresis and adjustment difficulties at school, was largely unfamiliar with psychodramatic techniques but comfortable with the therapist's sometimes unorthodox approach to problem resolution, and so they agreed to this suggestion.

Proposing that the family "try something different" that "may seem a bit strange or unusual but could prove helpful" is a generally successful means of engaging clients in action methods by piquing their curiosity and appealing to their sense of adventure. Externalization and concretization of the problem serve to separate the person from the problem not only linguistically but physically. Introducing the problem into the family's space as a physical entity breaks the identification of any individual with the problem and permits the relationship between the family and the problem to be explored and altered. Directing encounters between the family and the problem lets family members "see" how the problem manipulates and maintains power over them.

The character and intentions of Sadness began to emerge through the family's descriptions of this entity as large, dark, heavy, and threatening. Each family member's description of Sadness suggests that this entity was somehow antagonistic toward the family. The relationship of Sadness with each member of the family was explored in a scene in which Nicholas was asked to take the role of Sadness (reversing roles with Sadness) and show in action how Sadness was affecting the family. The family agreed to cooperate in the production, and Nicholas was invited to use available props such as pieces of cloth, pillows, toys, and so forth in the scene.

The technique of role reversal involves an exchange of roles and positions between the major participants in an interaction and is a means of transcending the habitual limitations of egocentricity through identification with the other. Role reversal is used to demonstrate how another character in a scene behaves, to increase empathy or insight into another's perspective, or to challenge the client's assumptions and beliefs. It is generally easier to move the family beyond talk and into action by inviting the child closest to "play age" to assume a role other than that of self and allowing other family members to remain in their own roles and respond to the child's new role during the initial enactment. Most children become quickly bored with "talk therapy" and readily accept invitations to "show" rather than "tell." The family's witnessing of the dramatic enactment fosters a heightened sense of projective identification with the protagonist and facilitates greater cohesion and empathy than does simply hearing a verbal description.

Nicholas quickly selected a large black cloth square and tied it around his neck like a cape, announcing that he, as Sadness, "is bigger and stronger than anyone." He then energetically began to push his mother under a table, where he had her curl into a ball with her face in her hands. He commanded her to "Stay there and don't come out!" He next placed his father in a corner of the room and built an enclosure around him with chairs, stating "You can't come home!" He growled, scowled, roared, and made faces at his sister as he danced around her in the middle of the room, and then, when the therapist asked him what Sadness did to Nicholas, he grabbed and began aggressively pounding a stuffed animal (which he identified as Nicholas), shouting, "Take that! And take that!" In response to the therapist's question about why Sadness would treat family members in such a cruel way, Nicholas responded in the role of Sadness, "Because I'm big and strong and important, and everybody needs to respect me!"

The action was stopped. Nicholas was asked to again reverse roles and take the role of himself having been pummeled by Sadness. The therapist then asked each family member what it was like to be in the position in which each had been placed and whether this scene was anything like how they experienced their own relationship with Sadness. Each one reported feeling very alone, controlled by Sadness, and unable to help anyone else. Marla added, "So I just do what I can to help me and not be any trouble." Nicholas declared, "Nobody cares about me but Nana, and now she's gone." Sarah, Les, and Marla each in turn then were asked to reverse roles with Sadness and in that role describe what purpose and goals Sadness had in trying to control each family member.

Michael White described the technique of "externalization" (White & Epston, 1990) as a linguistic separation of the problem from the person, endowing the problem with motivation and purpose. The psychodramatic technique of concretization carries the intervention one step further by offering family members a means both of conceptually severing the identity of the individual from the problem and of visually and actively experiencing the externalized problem as a separate entity. The problem itself becomes a character in the family drama, invested with a particular role and scripted part rather than being defined as an action undertaken by one or more family members. Concretizing the problem enables families to take this distinction between the person and the problem beyond intellectual awareness and into the behavioral and emotional realms of their experience, creating new opportunities for altering their relationships with the problem and with one another.

Taking the role of Sadness and tying the black cloth over her head like a veil, Sarah (as Sadness) explained that Sarah must honor her mother and that it was Sadness's job to make sure that Sarah adequately demonstrated through her grief the depth of her love and respect for her mother and her great importance in Sarah's life. When asked to describe exactly what Sarah must do to show the depth of her love and respect for her mother to Sadness's satisfaction, Sadness declared that Sarah "could never do enough" to show her mother's true importance in her life. Sadness was then asked, "Is what you want Sarah to do with her grief different from what Elaine would want her to do with her grief?" Sarah, in the role of Sadness, appeared somewhat taken aback, then rather sheepishly acknowledged that Elaine would be quite upset at the extent of Sarah's demonstration of grief over her death and would insist that Sarah "get over it and on with her own life." Sarah was then asked to reverse roles with Sadness, become herself and tell Sadness, now represented by an empty chair draped with the black cloth that Sarah had removed as she resumed her own role, what she must do to appropriately honor her mother. In her own role, Sarah stated that she must find a way to honor her mother's memory that satisfied her need to grieve but allowed her to get on with her own life, as her mother would have wanted her to do.

Next Les, rather self-consciously taking the role of Sadness, stated that he (Sadness) wanted the family to believe that it could not go on without Elaine and added that Elaine had said many times that "if it were not for her, the family would fall apart." When asked, "How do you affect Les?" Les, in the role of Sadness, replied, "I keep him discouraged and separated from everyone he cares about." In response to the question, "How do you do that?" Les (as Sadness) replied, "I tell him he is a real loser, that he is a big disappointment to his wife and kids, and that they don't really want him around." "What is it Les has lost that makes him a loser?" asked the therapist. "Self-respect—and the respect of his wife and kids," he replied.

Sarah, Marla, and Nicholas were then encouraged to tell Sadness whether Sadness was accurately describing how they felt about Les and to correct anything said by Sadness that was not true. All three adamantly denied that they considered Les a "loser" or a "big disappointment" and confronted Sadness with lying to Les about how they viewed him.

The therapist kept Les in the role of Sadness at this point rather than returning him to his own role so that the family was able to speak openly about their feelings toward Les as if they were outside of Les's hearing, without his presence influencing them to edit their comments. This technique is a variation of the "behind the back" technique described by Kipper and by Starr (Kipper, 1986, pp. 271–272; Starr, 1977, pp. 129–130). Furthermore, by leaving Les in the role of Sadness, the therapist increased the likelihood that the family would move to defend Les against a common antagonist. Even family members who are habitually hostile toward each other rarely are willing to permit an "outsider" to denigrate a family member. Once the therapist was satisfied that the family supported and affirmed Les, he could safely take back his own role.

Les was then asked to reverse roles with Sadness and resume his own role. After he did so, Sarah and the children were directed to tell Les how they really felt about him.

These enactments permitted the family to see themselves as performers of roles following a script that had to be altered if Sadness was to be prevented from disrupting family members' relationships. When the externalized problem's "hidden agenda" is exposed and malicious intent attributed to it rather than to family members, the family is motivated to develop cooperative strategies to challenge and defeat the problem. In the previous enactments, Sadness became an unwelcome intruder rather than the central dominant figure. This new perception of Sadness as an adversary allowed the family to begin altering their family script as Sarah and the children challenged Sadness's attempt to disempower Les and exclude him from the family system. Their defense of Les marked the beginning of the family's collaboration in "de-throning" both Elaine and Sadness and restoring Les to his rightful place in the family system as a competent provider, parent, and spouse.

Sarah admitted that she had been frustrated by Les's decreased income and absence in the evenings and went on to tell him that she missed his presence in the home and needed his help and support. Les immediately started to justify his job choices but was interrupted by the therapist, who instructed him to "just listen." Sarah emphasized her desire for togetherness as a family and for Les to be more of a partner to her. She stated that he had been very unavailable to both her and their children since his job change and that she had felt overwhelmed by the demands of juggling parenting, homemaking, and doing her own job as a day care teacher. Sarah also noted that as she and Les became more distant from each other, Sadness had become a larger and larger presence in her life.

Marla and Nicholas expressed their impatience with their father's long work hours and their desire for him to be more available to them. Marla complained to Les that he was always too tired to do his usual household chores, which were then left to her. She went on to say that he "never really talks to" her but instead teased her to the point that she became upset and embarrassed and "just wants to get away from [him]." Nicholas, who had become increasingly agitated as his mother and sister spoke to his father, generally ignored his father and attempted to distract his mother and sister. When asked to tell his father what Sadness left out about how Nicholas feels about him, Nicholas said that he got mad when his father "acts like he doesn't have time for [him] or want [him] around." In response to the therapist's encouragement to tell his father what he would like to have happen, Nicholas stated that he would like to do something with his father "just by ourselves, without Mom or Marla or anybody else."

Les was then asked to think about what his family had said and to address Sadness, again represented by the black cloth draped over an empty chair. Les declared to Sadness, "My family is the most important thing in my life, and you have no right to keep me away from them. I won't let you go on keeping us apart."

Finally Marla assumed the role of Sadness and in the role declared that she (Sadness) was punishing the family for criticizing and arguing with Nana (the children's name for Elaine) and "saying mean things to her." In response to the question of how Sadness affected Marla, she (as Sadness) observed, "I make it hard for Marla to stay at home, and I make it hard for her to leave. She thinks that something bad is going to happen at home and that she needs to be able to find a way to stop it." When asked how Marla could keep something bad from happening at home, Marla, still in the role of Sadness, replied, "She can't." When asked if there was anybody else who could keep something bad from happening at home, Marla (as Sadness) said, "Maybe if the whole family worked together the way they're supposed to, they could do it."

Following these enactments, family members were invited to come together as a group and share their experiences in these scenes. Sarah expressed hope that, because they have seen what Sadness has been doing to each of them, they can find ways to change things for the better. When asked who she thought would be most likely to initiate those changes, she ruefully responded, "Probably me—that's who it's usually left to to do things around here." Marla reported that she was very uncomfortable during the enactments and was fearful of what might happen to her family. In answer to the therapist's question about what it would take for her to feel more comfortable and less fearful, Marla replied, "For all of us to get along better and do what we're supposed to do." Asked to explain what she meant by "do what we're supposed to do," she said, "You know—everybody do their part."

In these initial vignettes, information about family relationships, roles, and scripts emerged. Each family member's enactment portrayed family members as isolated from one another in their grief, feeling very alone and unsupported, and unable to help themselves or one another. Dissatisfaction with this script and desire for change is evident on the part of at least one family member, Sarah, who acknowledged frustration with Les's unavailability and passivity. She identified the disconnectedness between herself and her husband as a major factor in the overwhelming power of Sadness. A subtle shift in both Les's role and the family script occurs with Les's declaration to Sadness, "My family is the most important thing in my life, and you have no right to keep me away from them. I won't let you go on keeping us apart." With this statement Les directly challenged Elaine's prediction that "if it were not for her, the family would fall apart." Marla echoed this shift toward greater collaboration and connectedness in her tentatively offered but solution-focused comment, "Maybe if the whole family worked together the way they're supposed to, they could [keep something bad from happening]." Enactments in this initial session serve both diagnostic and interventive functions. Psychodramatic techniques can very quickly "make the covert overt," allowing both the therapist and the family to "see" the situation at hand. This opportunity to share one another's experiences often results in increased empathy, support, and understanding ("action insight") among family members, even in the initial session.

In the next session, family members, in their own roles, were asked to imagine a straight line running from one end of the room to the other. They were instructed to imagine that this line represented a continuum, with Sadness having 100% control at one end and the family member having 100% control at the opposite end. Each family member was instructed to place himself or herself on the line in the spot that best represented "the degree of control Sadness has over your life at the present moment." Once they had done so, each family member was then asked to identify one thing that had him or her in this position at present.

Sadness_____(S)__(N)___(L)_____(M)_____Family
in Control   in Control

Use of this *spectrogram*, a psychodramatic/sociometric technique, allows family members to "see" where they stand on critical issues both for themselves and in relation to others.

The spectrogram is a powerful and versatile tool for concretizing scaling questions and helping clients experientially validate changes that have occurred from some point in the past to the present time. The spectrogram can be used to demonstrate that change happens all the time and so instill hope and expectation that positive movement can occur. By comparing their present positions on the scale to their positions in the past, the possibility of further change is introduced. The spectrogram puts narrative therapy's concept of "news of difference" (Sanders, 1985) in action rather than simply describing it cognitively.

Sarah, standing closest to the end representing Sadness having total control, disclosed that her guilt over not being more appreciative of her mother and "doing more for her" during her lifetime kept her in this position. Les, standing at a somewhat greater distance from this pole, stated that he was kept in this position by his feelings of failure as a provider for his family and his resentment of the family's dependence on Elaine and view of her as the head of the household. Nicholas, standing between his mother and father on this imaginary line, declared that his life was controlled by Sadness because "no one else can do what Nana did." Asked to describe what Nana did that was not happening now, Nicholas replied that "nobody else likes me or has any time for me." Marla, standing midway between the two poles, stated that she was kept stuck in the middle by her family's grief and admitted her fear that the family would "come apart" if she did not help hold everything to-gether.

Next, family members were asked to place themselves in the position on this same continuum that best represented the greatest degree of control each of them had had over Sadness at any point over the five months that had passed since Elaine's death. In response to this direction, each family member then moved to a point on the line that was indicative of Sadness having a lesser degree of control over him or her.

Sadness_____(S)___(L)_____(N)_____(M)____Family
in Control   in Control

In turn, family members were asked to identify at least one thing that was different at that time that would account for Sadness having less control of their lives. Sarah stated that she was less under Sadness's control when working at her job tending preschoolers. Les noted that he was less controlled by Sadness when driving around in his car and smoking cigarettes. Marla said that she was less influenced by Sadness when she was playing basketball or volleyball or was with her friends. Nicholas reported that Sadness had less control over him when he was doing something fun with Mom or Dad.

The exercise contained the embedded suggestion that family members had some agency over Sadness and so encouraged them to recover hope and optimism about their future as they came to view themselves as capable of prevailing over Sadness. Byng-Hall (1995) noted the importance of developing "a hopeful script in which the expectation is of reasonable success and not of failure or tragedy" (p. 75).

Finally, family members were asked to place themselves on the line in the position representing the degree of control they wanted Sadness to have over their lives in the future. Each was then asked to say why he or she chose that spot and to identify one thing that would need to change for each of them to be in their desired positions.

Sadness_____(M) __(L)__(S)__(N) Family
in Control   in Control

Sarah, taking a position at the end of the spectrogram opposite her original position, admitted that she would have to let go of her guilt over not having done more for her mother to take her desired position. Les, standing very near her, stated that he would have to be able to support the family financially and have the respect of his wife and children. Marla, standing a very short distance from her parents, declared that the family "would have to work together more" to control Sadness. Nicholas, who initially tried to take his mother's position on the spectrogram by pushing her off it, at length insinuated himself into the spot at the very end of the spectrum representing his having complete control over Sadness. When asked what it would take for him to have such great control over Sadness, he replied that he would need help from the Power Rangers (small action figures he has been collecting for several years). In response to a question about how the Power Rangers could help him, he asserted that they could "beat up Sadness." When asked what people in his life had more power than he did and could help him beat Sadness, he identified his parents.

During this session with the Hudson family, which took place one week after their first appointment, the therapist explored ways the family had begun changing its relationship with Sadness. To investigate ways the family has successfully managed Sadness in the past, family members were asked to identify which of them has successfully confronted Sadness at times over the past five months and to describe how they have stood up to or defeated it on those occasions. Several of these scenes illustrating victory over Sadness were briefly enacted, allowing each family member to demonstrate how on at least one occasion he or she was successful in challenging, escaping, or overcoming Sadness.

Other than for the enactment of such scenes, this approach is similar to a narrative therapy approach in which the identity and life story of the individual begin to be "rescripted" through the process of uncovering historical evidence to support that person's competence and heroism (White & Epston, 1990). As in solution-focused therapy, it is important to look for moments when the person or the family has successfully challenged the problem and to help clients notice what they are doing differently at those times that the problem is not present or has been successfully overcome (de Shazer, 1985). Improvisational enactments may be staged which dramatize ways in which the family or client has "outwitted" the problem (Wiener, 1994). Some clients may have difficulty identifying times when the problem has been less of a problem. Such clients can be asked to rate themselves in relation to a particular quality, behavior, or desired change by means of a scaling question or spectrogram and to then describe what has produced movement in a positive direction.

As these dramatic vignettes proceeded, there was an accompanying rise in the spontaneity, playfulness, humor, and energy level of family members. The family was next asked to consider who among them Elaine would consider most likely to be the one to lead the family in successfully challenging and defeating Sadness. The family initially seemed at a loss for a response to this question, then Marla rather hesitantly suggested that her grandmother would consider Nicholas most likely to find a way to defeat Sadness. Sarah and Les readily agreed, with Les wryly observing that Nicholas was the only one in the family that Elaine believed could do anything right. Nicholas brightened and grinned at these comments, agreeing that Nana would think him the most likely one to find a way to beat Sadness.

The therapist asked Nicholas to tell what Nana was like and about his relationship with her. He characterized her as "always on [his] side," "treating [him] special," "able to keep secrets," and "fun to be around." Next, the family was asked if one of them could "be Nana" and show how she fit into this family. Marla volunteered to take the role of her grandmother and proceeded to go to Nicholas, take him into her arms, and assure him that she was now here and that everything would be all right. She went on to say that he was very special to her and she had confidence he could do anything he chose to do.

The therapist then asked Nicholas to become Nana and Marla to become herself. Nicholas in the role of Nana was directed to tell Marla what she had seen in Nicholas that made her believe he could outwit and defeat Sadness. In Nana's role, Nicholas informed Marla that Nicholas is smarter than everybody thinks he is and is certainly smarter than Sadness. He went on to say that "Nicholas knows a whole lot about fighting and winning because he watches Power Rangers (a cartoon television series) and plays with them (his extensive action figure collection) all the time."

Having Marla assume the role of Nana (because she had first advanced Nana's opinion about who could best solve the problem) allowed Nicholas to receive the validation he had lost with Nana's death. Putting Nicholas in the role of Nana allowed him to identify and claim for himself the qualities he possessed that would help him overcome Sadness.

Nicholas was returned to his own role and asked to face the therapist. With their arms extended and hands touching palm to palm, Nicholas was instructed to push against the therapist's hands with all the energy he had available to lead the family in fighting Sadness. He vigorously pressed with all his might, backing the therapist up a few steps as he roared enthusiastically.

In this final activity, Nicholas demonstrated not only willingness but also enthusiasm for "pushing Sadness out of the picture" to obtain his parents' attention and approval.

Nicholas was asked to consider over the next week how he might lead the family in overcoming Sadness so that it no longer controlled their lives, and the family was encouraged to take note of anything they observed Nicholas doing that seemed a successful strategy for defeating Sadness. Nicholas stated that he liked it when he was more powerful than anyone else in the family. Guiding the family in empowering Nicholas to lead their fight against Sadness not only altered his position as identified patient but also began to alter the family script that had cast males as incompetent.

In the beginning of the third session, Sarah and Les reported that, over the past week, Nicholas had no episodes of encopresis and that his interactions with teachers and classmates were much improved. At home, he was more animated and sociable, more cooperative with family members, and gentler with family pets. He had casually and seemingly comfortably talked about his grandmother on a couple of occasions but continued to avoid going into her bedroom.

Sarah noted feeling more energetic and less depressed, being more involved in activities with the children, and having no crying spells for more than a week. She expressed relief that Les has been more available in the evenings and more actively involved with both her and the children. She described him as more accommodating in his interactions with Marla and said that antagonism between father and daughter had largely dissipated.

Les agreed that he has made an effort to spend more time with the family over the past week and stated that Sarah has been much more cheerful and pleasant. He and Sarah praised Nicholas for his cooperative attitude at home and at school and observed that Sadness seemed to have much less control in their home.

The therapist then asked each family member to show with their hands and bodies what amount of Sadness seemed to be in the home when they first presented for therapy three weeks ago and how much of Sadness's weight each of them was carrying at that time. Everyone in the family stretched their arms out wide to demonstrate how large a load of Sadness they had been carrying at that time, and Les pretended to stagger under the weight of the burden. Sarah spontaneously moved closer to him and reached out as if to help him balance the load. Both children immediately moved in to form a circle with their parents, all with hands upraised as if all were carrying the same large burden.

The therapist asked them to hold their positions and remarked that the family seemed to be bound together by the common task of carrying the weight of Sadness. Family members were then each asked to describe what it is like to be in the position they adopted in this sculpture, and they unanimously expressed feelings of weariness and anxiety. Sarah stated that she feared that if she did not maintain her position the rest of the family would be crushed under the weight of Sadness. Les said that he felt frustrated and trapped and was tired of being unable to do anything about it. Nicholas said that he felt big and important in helping his parents but that he would rather be doing something fun with them. Marla echoed Nicholas's wish to be doing something more fun and admitted that she felt "worn out" by the situation and wanted "to find a way to just get away."

The family was then asked to show with their hands and bodies what amount of Sadness has been in their home and how much of Sadness's weight each of them has been carrying this week. Sarah cupped her hands into a small ball and said she has felt very little burden of Sadness this week. Nicholas placed his thumbs and forefingers together in an "eensy-weensy spider" gesture and squinted his eyes as if looking at a very tiny object. He stated that he had felt Sadness "shrinking" this week and had not been bothered at all by it. Marla agreed that Sadness seemed to be much smaller and that she had felt "lighter" that week.

Les acknowledged that Sadness had been less of a burden but went on to say that some of the Sadness he carried was related to his feelings of failure to provide for his family as he believed he should and his unwillingness to face his wife and children as a result. When asked what it had been like to spend more time with his family this week, Les said that he felt "more needed and appreciated" and less self-critical. The rest of the family was then asked what it had been like to have Les around more that week. Sarah expressed gratitude that Les had been more of a partner to her rather than leaving it to her "to deal with everything" and also her desire for him to continue his greater support and involvement with her and the children. Nicholas stated that he wanted to spend more time with his dad and "hated it" when he was too busy for him. Marla acknowledged that having her dad around more had "been okay," smiling at him as she spoke.

The family's sculpture of jointly carrying Sadness represented a shift from the previous story in which each struggled with Sadness in isolation. The shift in each family member's subjective experience of Sadness and the resulting change in their perceptions of their relationship and interactions with Sadness strongly suggested that a change in the family problem-solving script had occurred. The therapist's next intervention was designed to further explore this shift and reinforce the development of more functional and adaptive family scripts.

The therapist asked the family what ideas they had about what had happened to cause Sadness to diminish and where it had gone. Nicholas replied that Sadness was in Nana's room and left the family alone as long as they stayed out of the room. Sarah agreed that Sadness lessened when the family wasn't focused on Nana's illness and death but instead focused on going on with their lives together in the here and now. Marla said that she felt less sadness when she was involved in doing something with others, and Les stated that he felt less sad when he felt valued and appreciated by his family and had confidence in himself as a husband and father.

The therapist invited the family to imagine what their life together might be like if Sadness were no longer in the picture. Family members were asked to choose a scene where they believed Sadness would be least likely to show up and threaten the family. Nicholas quickly suggested a family camping trip, and the other members of the family enthusiastically agreed that Sadness was unlikely to appear there. The family was instructed to set the scene for enactment of this camping trip and was encouraged to experiment in the drama with how they might be as a family without Sadness present.

Family members used furniture and props to set up a camping scene, and in their roles as campers soon decided to go fishing. Arranging chairs to replicate the close seating in a small "bass boat," they animatedly went through the motions of baiting a hook and "trolling" for bass. The family enacted the fishing scene with a great deal of cooperation, positive interactions, affectionate joking and touching, and humor. Each family member seemed engaged with the others and displayed much spontaneity and laughter. When they were asked where Sadness is in the picture, all insisted Sadness was nowhere around them, and Sarah laughingly suggested that it had been "left behind."

A variety of techniques can be used to explore what clients' futures might be like without the problem. What will they be doing with the time and energy they previously spent on the problem? How will their lives be different? Future projection techniques (Chasin et al., 1989) allow clients to enact specific scenes in the future and explore their expectations, desired outcomes, and ways to develop, nurture, and rehearse new behaviors and roles. Enacting future projection scenes, what

Byng-Hall (1995) termed "previewing" (p. 73), such as living "happily ever after," can be used to validate ambivalence about change. Psychodramatic techniques such as "The Magic Shop" (Kipper, 1986, pp. 247–251) can be used to help the family or client identify what would have to be relinquished to obtain the desired change.

Family members were next asked to try to "catch" one another over the next week at moments when one of them saw another successfully escape or evade Sadness and to each notice when they themselves were more successful in standing up to Sadness's attempts to manipulate them. They were congratulated on their success in collecting evidence that they had all been winners over Sadness in the past, praised for their progress in cooperatively using their resources to lessen the grip of Sadness on the family, and assured that they possessed the skills and ability to find a way to go on together as a family without being bound together by Sadness.

Such "news of difference" can be illustrated through psychodramatic enactment of a scene or scenes in which the problem is absent or is less of a problem. This scene can be contrasted with a scene in which the problem occurs. Identifying what happens differently at those times when the problem is less of a problem helps clients recognize what they are already doing that is working, magnify or expand these behaviors, and develop optimism and hope that they have the knowledge and ability to overcome the problem (de Shazer, 1985). Shifting the focus from the initial problem script to the exceptions to the problem helps clients to identify attitudes and behaviors that further the change process.

In the fourth session, family members were questioned about their success in catching one another in standing up to Sadness and in noticing their own successes in overcoming Sadness. Each was asked to describe in as great detail as possible the moment he or she considered each family member's greatest triumph over Sadness during the past week. The tone and demeanor of each member of the family, recounting one by one the "moments of heroism" displayed by the other family members, conveyed great respect, affection, and pride toward the individual whose behavior was being described.

Les remarked that it felt good to hear that on more than one occasion his wife and children saw him as powerful and successful. He confessed that he and other family members were quick to criticize one another and often neglected to offer one another praise or compliments. He went on to say that he was proud of the way the family was working together and giving one another support and encouragement.

The therapist cautioned the family that Sadness would likely resurface at some point and that they must be alert to any indications that Sadness was regaining control in the family. The therapist further suggested that the family rehearse a response to any reappearance of Sadness that posed a threat to any family member.

Family members were asked how they imagined Sadness might try to regain control over the family and what things could happen to make them more vulnerable to Sadness. Marla said she was most likely to be overpowered by Sadness when lonely and bored. Sarah added that she was susceptible to Sadness when feeling frustrated and tired. Les stated that when disappointed, he was vulnerable to Sadness. Nicholas replied that he was most likely to be attacked by Sadness when nobody would pay attention to him. All agreed that Sadness was most likely to try to regain power over each of them when they were alone with no one else readily available to provide support and assistance.

The family was asked to enact a scene in which Sadness was making an attempt to take greater control of the family and to try out different ways they might thwart Sadness. Les offered to take the role of Sadness in response to the therapist's request that one member of the family volunteer for the role. Other members of the family were instructed to each set a scene in which Sadness would be likely to return. Les, as Sadness, was asked to choose the family member whom he believed could be most easily manipulated by Sadness and engage that person in an interaction.

Sarah chose to set a scene in which she was alone in the kitchen at night after everyone else had gone to bed, facing a mountain of dirty dishes and laundry. Marla constructed a scene showing herself alone in her room on a weekend afternoon, alternately wandering aimlessly about the room and sitting on her bed with a sigh. Nicholas set a scene in which he placed himself on the back steps outside the kitchen door, waiting for his father to return home from work on a weekday evening.

Les, in the role of Sadness, initially approached Marla. Marla was asked to reverse roles with Sadness and show how Sadness sought to control Marla. Les then assumed the role of Marla in the interaction. Marla, as Sadness, began to attack "Marla's" self-confidence and self-esteem. Sadness went on to challenge "Marla's" ability to maintain the interest and support of her friends, predicting that she could not depend on anyone to remain in her life.

"Marla" and Sadness were then once again asked to reverse roles and repeat the exchange, with Les now back in the role of Sadness and Marla in her own role. Following the therapist's direction to match Marla's presentation of the role, Sadness repeated the monologue while Marla listened. When she did not respond to Sadness, the therapist inquired whether or not she believed what Sadness had just said to her. Marla replied that she was unsure. She was asked to come out of the scene and watch the interaction between Marla and Sadness in the role of observing ego, a psychodramatic technique called *mirroring*.

Mirroring, or having family members witness the action from outside the scene, allows the family or individuals to observe their present stories and obtain new perspectives on their relationship with the problem and with one another.

Nicholas and Sarah were invited to enter the action one at a time in Marla's role and demonstrate one way Marla could choose to handle Sadness. Les again repeated Sadness's speech. Sarah, now in the role of Marla, listened briefly and then announced, "I don't have to stay here and listen to this; I can go find someone more positive to be around or something more enjoyable to do." She then began to walk out of the scene. When Sadness asked her "Where are you going?" she retorted, "Somewhere I don't have to be around you!"

Nicholas then entered the scene in the role of Marla, and Sadness began the same speech. Nicholas, as Marla, put his hands over his ears, closed his eyes, and began loudly singing "La, la, la, la, la," increasing the volume and dancing around when Sadness persisted in his monologue. Marla was then asked to take the role of Sadness, and Les was asked to assume Marla's role. Marla had begun to speak as Sadness when Les suddenly leaped toward her and began tickling her. The enactment dissolved amid Marla's shrieks, her father's shouts of laughter, Nicholas's cheers, and Sarah's flustered reproof of Les.

When everyone had caught their breath, Marla was asked to describe what she had seen members of her family do when confronted by Sadness in these enactments that she thought would be effective. She replied that she was surprised to see her mother walk out on Sadness and after witnessing this action had realized that she, too, could choose to stop listening to Sadness. She said that she had tried Nicholas's tactic of ignoring Sadness or simply drowning it out and distracting herself but had found this strategy less successful because it allowed Sadness to remain nearby.

Nicholas was reminded that the family had earlier identified him as the one most likely to lead the family in a campaign against Sadness and asked if he would be willing to take responsibility for being on the lookout for any attempt by Sadness to threaten the family. He eagerly accepted this assignment, and the therapist warned Nicholas that he must be especially alert to any "sneak attacks" on himself by Sadness.

The therapist went on to express concern about what Sadness might be doing unobserved in Elaine's room and asked if the family was comfortable with Sadness occupying an entire room in their home. The family quickly expressed the desire for Sadness to leave the home. Sarah added that Sadness could "maybe visit occasionally—but only for a little while!"

The therapist then asked the family which of them would be best able to help the family take back their home from Sadness. Les pointed to Sarah, and the two children followed his lead. The therapist asked Sarah if she believed that it is possible to honor Elaine's memory in the family without giving the whole room to Sadness. When she firmly answered "Yes," she was instructed to "show in action one way it might be done" and was asked to set a scene in which she stood outside the closed door to her mother's room.

In response to Sarah's physical agitation and change in respiration as she constructed this scene, the therapist asked her, "What are you feeling at this moment?" Sarah answered that she was "very nervous" and anxious. The therapist asked her to take a step back from the door and notice whether her feelings changed. Sarah replied that after moving back a step she felt less anxious and could "breathe easier."

The therapist asked Sarah what she would like to do to both honor her mother and begin to move Sadness out of the room. She immediately responded that she would like to "open the door, open the curtain, and put flowers or a plant in the room."

As the therapist, I had a brief moment of panic as I contemplated the symbolism and psychological consequences of the family watching an arrangement of cut flowers slowly wither and die and so suggested an ever-blooming plant such as an African violet. However, I was also aware that this concern was my own rather than a part of the family's story or script and may have had an entirely different meaning for them. It is important that therapists conducting experiential therapy be able to clearly distinguish between their own personal issues and those of the client or family, lest they find themselves conducting their own drama rather than their client's.

Sarah was then asked to face the door and describe what she would see in the room when she opened the door. She stared as if looking through the door and described Elaine's bed and nightstand, her dressing table and chair, and her curtained window. At this point, she was instructed to "reverse roles" with the room and describe herself and her experience as Elaine's room. Sarah closed her eyes and sighed, then she spoke.

"It would be so good to have air again! I miss the warmth and light of the sun, and the air in here is so still and close with the door always shut. It feels dark and heavy and oppressive in here, and I wish someone would come and bring light and life back into me." Sarah was returned to her own role and directed to pick up something to represent a plant and, when she was ready, to open the door and walk in.

Sarah took a deep breath and stepped into the room. She went straight to the area where she had indicated there was a window, drew back the curtains, and made the motion of opening the window. She stated that she could hear birds singing outside the window and feel a slight breeze. She was directed to walk around the room and choose the spot where the plant should be placed. After she did so, the therapist asked Sarah to look around the room and say anything to the room that she wanted to say. The rest of the family were invited to enter the room if they wished, "since the door is still open"; to look around; and to "maybe even bring something into the room or take something from the room with you."

During the fifth and final session, the Hudsons reported that they had experienced no real problems over the past week. Sarah had "aired out" Elaine's room and placed a potted plant in the window. Marla had looked through her grandmother's costume jewelry box and worn a string of her beads to school; Nicholas had looked through his grandmother's photograph albums and the book of Bible stories she used to read to him. He later took the Bible book to his father one evening and asked him to read him a story from it, which Les did. Afterward, Nicholas took the Bible story book to his room, where he has kept it from that time on.

During this session the family was asked to consider how they would live in the future without Sadness—what they would be doing, how things would be different, and so forth. Les stated that he would be spending more time with his family and added that last week he had offered to help coach his son's soccer team. He also had attended one of Marla's volleyball games and praised her athletic performance, although Marla insisted (while attempting to stifle a smile) that he had thoroughly embarrassed her with his cheering and shouts of encouragement.

The technique of dramatizing ideal futures involves creating a scene that illustrates the hopes or wishes of one or more family members for the family relationship. Each family member participates in portraying what could take place if that family member's goals for these relationships were realized (Chasin et al., 1989). An ideal future is thus a solution that through enactment may become a new script.

The family was asked to imagine their lives six months from now and to enact a scene that both illustrated what they would like their lives to be like and that allowed them to explore together what living that life would require. The therapist emphasized that family members should each choose a scene that could take place if the future turned out exactly as they wanted it to be. Each family member chose a scene to briefly enact.

Sarah selected a "family clean-up day" in which everyone cheerfully pitched in to get the household chores done. In her enactment, she portrayed her husband and children (in role reversals) as working cooperatively and enthusiastically to clean the house as she worked alongside them. Les and the children were directed to take their own roles and portray them exactly as Sarah had demonstrated. The scene progressed with Les, Marla, and Nicholas playing their roles just as Sarah had. The therapist interrupted the action to have Sarah step outside the scene and watch as her children and husband cleaned the house. In response to the therapist's question about whether this scene accurately captured her desire for the future, Sarah laughed and replied, "This would be my wildest dream come true!"

Les chose a scene in which the family was enjoying a cookout together, and he was "grill master." In his scene, Marla and Nicholas were helpful and cooperative as they responded to their father's directives to "hand me the water bottle," "bring me a glass of lemonade," "set the table," and so forth. Sarah was attentive and amicable, asking him how his day had been and offering words of encouragement and support in regard to his new job. In her own role in this scene, Sarah dutifully asked Les how his day had been but then interrupted his description of his difficulty making this month's sales quota to say, "Maybe it's time you give this up and look for a job with a more dependable income."

The therapist immediately called for a role reversal between Sarah and Les, then asked Sarah (in the role of Les) to repeat to "Sarah" (the role now held by Les) "his" concern about making the monthly sales quota and to then tell "Sarah" what "he" needs or wants from her. Sarah (as Les) spoke to "Sarah," acknowledging anxiety about making the sales quota and then asking "Sarah" if she "would just stand by me and let me try to make this work out." Les (as Sarah) was told to respond to this request the way he would most like Sarah to respond. He then responded in Sarah's role, "I want this job to work out for you, too. I believe that you can be really successful with this company. I'm sorry for being critical; I'm just tired of having to struggle to make ends meet and want us to have a dependable income. I'm scared that we won't be able to pay for things we need. But I love you, and I'm on your side." Sarah nodded in assent as Les spoke in her role.

The therapist then reversed them back into their own roles, and Sarah was instructed to play herself in this scene "just as Les portrayed [her]." She repeated the lines almost verbatim with great feeling and energy but then became somewhat hesitant and subdued as she softly said, "But I love you, and I'm on your side." She was asked by the therapist to repeat that line with greater volume and intensity, which she did, and then she was asked to again repeat it with still greater volume and intensity. This third time, she looked directly at Les and declared in a strong voice, "I love you, and I'm on your side." When the therapist asked Les what it was like to hear that from Sarah, tears came to his eyes as he replied, "I can't remember ever hearing her say that before. It felt really good. I wish she would say it more often."

Les's "ideal future" scene represented a shift from his role of absent or incompetent provider to the role of an involved provider who nurtures his family emotionally as well as providing for them materially. A further shift was evident in this scene as Sarah and Les began to adopt cooperative rather than antagonistic roles. Conducting role reversals between spouses and other family members requires a high level of theoretical and technical sophistication on the part of the therapist. Traditional role reversal methods may escalate antagonistic positions and rapidly heighten affect, with the result that the couple adopts increasingly polarized and adversarial rather than cooperative stances. The clinician must bear this risk in mind when directing role reversals between family members and modify the technique accordingly. For a more general discussion of the problems inherent in integrating psychodrama with family therapy, see Seeman and Wiener (1985).

Marla chose a scene in which she could have a gathering of "friends over without the family doing anything embarrassing" or Nicholas "bothering us." In Marla's enactment, Sarah briefly appeared to offer snacks to the group, which was gathered in the family room, then retired to the kitchen to help Nicholas do his homework at the kitchen table. In Marla's portrayal of Les, Les briefly and cheerily greeted the group as he passed through the family room on returning home from work. He continued on to the kitchen and offered to take over helping Nicholas with his homework while Sarah fixed dinner. The scene ended with the family rather nonchalantly bidding Marla good-bye and telling her to "have a good time" as she left with her friends "to go out for pizza or something."

In his own role in the scene, Les entered the kitchen, sat down, and watched as Sarah and Nicholas worked together on Nicholas's homework. Once prompted, however, he quickly offered to take over the job of helping Nicholas and soon was engaged with his son while Sarah busily began dinner preparations. Marla was invited to view the scene from outside the action using the mirroring technique and was asked if the scene was exactly as she wanted it to be. In response to the question, Marla shook her head and stated, "It would be better if Dad helped Nicholas with his schoolwork and Mom took a break, maybe went for a bike ride or something. She's always saying she never has time to exercise." She re-entered the scene, took the role of her father, and said to her mother, "Why don't you take a break for a while and let me take care of things here?"

Marla's previous role in the family script involved an injunction that she stay home and be available to her family "in case something bad happens" and a belief that bad things happen as punishment when one or more members of the family engage in mistreatment of others ("doing mean things"). This belief was reflected in her earlier declaration that Sadness was "punishing the family for criticizing and arguing with Nana" and "saying mean things to her." Marla's directing in the enactment involved the structural shift of having her father take charge to give her mother a break, thereby moving her father into the role of involved husband and father and providing herself and her mother with "role relief." The cooperation of her parents and the consideration of family members for one another's needs in her ideal futures scene allowed Marla to take the developmentally appropriate step of decreasing her executive function in the family system while increasing her involvement with her peer group. She was thus able to retire her role of family caretaker and allow her parents to assume that function.

Nicholas initially decided to construct a scene in which the family went swimming, then switched to a scenario in which he and his father went fishing together while his mother and sister sunbathed. In Nicholas's portrayal, his mother and sister were both rather passively uninvolved in the action while he and his father were animatedly engaged with each other. During the enactment Nicholas, in the role of his father, sat very close to his father (who was in Nicholas's role) and demonstrated patience in his instruction to "Nicholas" about proper fishing technique, frequently praised "Nicholas's" efforts and accomplishments, and displayed genuine pleasure in his company.

When Les took the role and interacted with Nicholas in the same manner, the boy appeared absolutely delighted and was very affectionate and responsive toward his father. Both father and son seemed to enjoy this scene very much. At its conclusion, Les admitted that he has spent little one-on-one time with his son and resolved to schedule regular father–son activities with him. When asked by the therapist what things he and his father would both enjoy that the two of them could do together, Nicholas flashed a big grin and yelled "Go fishing!" Asked if there was anything else he would like for "just the two of them" to do together, Nicholas shrugged, lifted his hands with palms up, and said, "I would just like to have him come home and talk to me sometimes."

At this comment from his son, Les spontaneously disclosed that as a child, he had always been afraid of his father—a critical, stern, and emotionally distant man. He had tried desperately and unsuccessfully throughout his childhood to win his father's affection and approval and had been mortified by his father's obvious disappointment in and frequent public humiliation of him. Les acknowledged that he had adopted some of his father's style in his own interactions with Nicholas and said to his son, "Even though I get frustrated when you don't mind your mother and me and when your teachers send home bad reports, I still love you and am glad you're my son." He pulled Nicholas to him and gave him a somewhat clumsy "bear hug." The therapist quickly cued him to continue holding Nicholas until the boy moved away. Les complied but seemed somewhat anxious about doing so. When Nicholas at length pulled away, the therapist said softly to Les, "It's still hard to risk being pushed away by someone you love, huh?" Les nodded in agreement.

The therapist then asked the family to share with one another what they had learned during these enactments about what would have to happen for their lives to be the way they would like them to be. Each member of the family was able to identify a personal choice or change that would have to be made for these ideal futures to become a reality.

Sharing *traditionally follows the action phase of a psychodrama and promotes cognitive integration of any changes experienced during the enactment. Unless such cognitive integration occurs, the action experiences are less likely to result in lasting change. The power of action techniques lies in their ability to promote learning at behavioral, affective, and cognitive levels and to foster rapid integration of insight and experience.*

A RETROSPECTIVE OVERVIEW OF RESCRIPTING IN THE HUDSON FAMILY

The Hudson family script involved replication of a household headed by Elaine, an overfunctioning mother who, along with an emotionally and often physically absent spouse, reared their daughter (Sarah) to become an overresponsible adult who herself married an underfunctioning spouse (Les). Replication of the family script continued as Sarah and Les also reared an overfunctioning daughter (Marla) and underfunctioning son (Nicholas).

When her husband died, Elaine lost her primary relationship and role, both of which had served as sources of her self-identity. Serving as primary caretaker for her daughter and infant grandson afforded Elaine an opportunity to continue a familiar and valued role. However, her "theft" of this role from her son-in-law and daughter created tension and conflict in the family system.

Elaine's assumption of the role of head of the household was passively accepted but deeply resented by both Sarah and Les, although neither challenged Elaine for this position in the ensuing seven years. Their resignation to Elaine's dominance of the family reflected a family script ascribing ultimate authority to the "senior" family member. This hierarchical structure and role assignment was linked to a religious injunction that children must "honor their parents" and a belief that "honor" required obedience. Thus, Sarah and Les were unable to both honor Elaine and challenge her authority. Although Sarah, in particular, often protested Elaine's dictates and even argued with her, her dissent was limited to efforts to persuade Elaine to change her mind. Nicholas's appeals to Elaine when either of his parents made a decision he considered unfair or unacceptable were followed by Elaine's chastising the offending parent, usually in full view and hearing of the entire family. With Elaine's exclusive claim on the role of parent, Sarah and Les were reduced to the status of children.

Elaine's death left the family without a head of the household, precipitating a crisis in the family of her daughter and son-in-law. Sarah resisted assumption of the role and became increasingly resentful of Les's failure to take it up. Nicholas's regression and presenting symptoms of encopresis and aggression may be viewed as an escalating communication of his need for someone to claim the role of parent and head of the family. In the resulting crisis, Sadness took charge of the family in much the same way that Elaine earlier had done. However, the family was able to cooperatively challenge Sadness in a way that they had been unable to challenge Elaine and successfully place Sarah and Les in their rightful roles as parents and family leaders.

Early in therapy Les had stated that Sadness wanted the family to believe that it could not go on without Elaine and added that Elaine had said many times that "if it were not for her, the family would fall apart." He characterized Sadness as keeping him discouraged and defeated in his efforts to succeed in his role as provider to the family. Les's belief that his family was disappointed in him and did not really want him around (his story) influenced the role he assumed in family interactions (passive avoidance) and became incorporated into the family script. A primary component of this family script was illustrated by Nicholas's presentation of Sadness as keeping his father unavailable to the family when, in the initial enactment, he placed his father in a corner of the room and enclosed him with chairs, stating, "You can't come home!"

Sarah's frustration with Les's decreased income and absence in the evenings; her confrontation of Les with her desire that he "be more of a partner to her"; and her complaint of being overwhelmed by the demands of juggling parenting, homemaking, and her job were additional elements in the dysfunctional family script. Their marriage seemed to replicate the experiences and script of Sarah's parents' marriage and likely reflected the dominant script in both partners' families of origin. Both Sarah and Les found themselves being drawn into roles, interaction patterns, and stories they neither valued nor desired. Although both their stories were from similar scripts, their interpretation and experience of their respective roles were quite different.

Sarah noted that as she and her husband became more distant from each other, Sadness had become a larger and larger presence in her life. While Elaine's death left unfilled roles in the family, Les's unavailability to the family created role conflicts. Marla complained that her father "was always too tired" to do his chores, which were then left to her, and that he "never really talked" to her. Nicholas attributed his anger to his father's "acting like he doesn't have time for me or want me around." Nicholas's statement may be an indication that he was already being role-trained to take on his father's role in the family script. Likewise, Nicholas's closeness to Elaine (Nana) can be seen as an effort to obtain the attention and approval of the head of the household.

The first indication that Les was unhappy with his role in the family script and was open to role-training and role expansion appeared with his declaration to Sadness that "My family is the most important thing in my life, and you have no right to keep me away from them. I won't let you go on keeping us apart." Marla echoed this shift as she hesitantly suggested that solving the problem was dependent on family cooperation or collaboration. Once the family displayed motivation to cooperatively resolve the problem, therapeutic interventions were directed toward fostering increased empathy, support, and collaboration as family members rehearsed and reinforced script changes.

In follow-up contact with the family six months after treatment, the therapist spoke with both Sarah and Marla. Sarah reported that Les had quit his job in insurance sales shortly after the family completed treatment and was working in a delivery job that allowed him to be home evenings and weekends. Sarah continued her job in the day care center and had become active in a parent support group and a 12-step group (Adult Children of Alcoholics; ACOA). She stated that she and Les were continuing to share parenting and home maintenance responsibilities and that it "finally feels like there are two parents in the house." She went on to say that Nicholas was "a handful" but was better accepted by peers and functioning satisfactorily at school. Marla proudly announced that she had obtained her driver's license, and her mother laughingly added that, after considerable struggle, she had finally begun to accept the idea of her "little girl growing up."

EMPIRICAL SUPPORT

The method featured in this chapter is an action approach developed through the integration of psychodramatic techniques with narrative and solution-focused therapy methods. As in the case of many integrated treatment approaches, there is no body of empirical research that substantiates the effectiveness of this method. However, this fact should in no way be construed to mean that the method is unsupported by a well-developed and sound theoretical foundation or at odds with well-established theories of how people change. Clearly, the responsible use of this method with any clinical population requires that the therapist be attentive to therapeutic outcome and guided by the differential effectiveness of treatment.

CONCLUSION

The linguistic interventions of methods such as narrative therapy may change clients' stories. However, dramatic enactment permits individuals and families to challenge and alter the scripts underlying these stories and so may effect a more pervasive and substantive change in perception, behavior, relationships, and interactions. While language may be used to alter the meaning of an experience, dramatic enactment has the power to alter the experience itself.

A clinical dilemma evident from the first session with the Hudson family was how the therapist could offer guidance, structure, and solutions to this family without the family ascribing to this therapist the vacant role of parent. In dramatic enactment transference to the therapist is minimized as the family's projections are incorporated into the action, from which the therapist/director is removed, rather than focused on the therapist. The family takes ownership of the production and so quickly claims credit for solutions that are discovered and created as the enactment unfolds. In this way, dependence on the therapist is minimized, and the family is encouraged to look within itself for solutions. Psychodramatic techniques such as mirroring, role reversal, and future projection encourage rapid shifts in experience and perspective that allow clients to become aware of expanded options, explore new possibilities, and experiment with new ways of relating to one another. Once played out in dramatic enactment, interaction and relationship patterns, or scripts, are no longer abstract and unconscious but are overtly visible and subject to conscious change. Family members thus experience themselves and one another in new roles and identities, becoming the heroes and heroines of new dramas which, if successful, become the foundation of new stories and scripts that support and sustain these new and more functional roles, relationships, and competencies.

REFERENCES

Byng-Hall, J. (1995). *Rewriting family scripts: Improvisation and systems change*. New York: Guilford.

Chasin, R., & Roth, S. (1994). Entering one another's worlds of meaning and imagination: Dramatic enactment and narrative couple therapy. In M. F. Hoyt (Ed.), *Constructive therapies* (pp. 189–216). New York: Guilford.

Chasin, R., Roth, S., & Bograd, M. (1989). Action methods in systemic therapy: Dramatizing ideal futures and reformed pasts with couples. *Family Process, 28,* 121–135.

Compernolle, T. (1981). J. L. Moreno: An unrecognized pioneer of family therapy. *Family Process, 20,* 331–335.

de Shazer, S. (1985). *Keys to solution in brief therapy*. New York: Norton.

Duhl, F. J., Kantor, D., & Duhl, B. S. (1973). Learning, space, and action in family therapy: A primer of sculpture. In D. A. Bloch (Ed.), *Techniques of family therapy: A primer* (pp. 47–63). New York: Grune & Stratton.

Kempler, W. (1973). *Principles of gestalt family therapy*. Salt Lake City, UT: Deseret.

Kempler, W. (1981). *Experiential psychotherapy with families*. New York: Brunner/Mazel.

Kipper, D. A. (1986). *Psychotherapy through clinical role playing*. New York: Brunner-Mazel.

Minuchin, S., & Fishman, H. C. (1981). *Family therapy techniques*. Cambridge, MA: Harvard University Press.

Moreno, J. L. (1946). *Psychodrama* (Vol. 1). Beacon, NY: Beacon Press.

Moreno, J. L. (1965). *Who shall survive?* (Rev. ed.). Beacon, NY: Beacon Press.

Moreno, J. L. (1969). *Psychodrama* (Vol. 3). Beacon, NY: Beacon Press.

Moreno, Z. T. (1991). Time, space, reality, and the family: Psychodrama with a blended (reconstituted) family. In P. Holmes & M. Karp (Eds.), *Psychodrama: Inspiration and technique* (pp. 53–74). London: Routledge.

Papp, P. (1990). Future perfect, The use of structured fantasy in couple therapy. In R. Chasin, H. Grunebaum. & M. Herzig (Eds.), *One couple, four realities: Multiple perspectives on couple therapy* (pp. 25–48). New York: Guilford.

Papp, P. (1980). The use of fantasy in a couples' group. In M. Andolfi & I. Zwerling (Eds.), *Dimensions of family therapy* (pp. 73–90). New York: Guilford.

Sanders, C. (1985). "Now I see the difference"—The use of visual news of difference in clinical practice. *Australian and New Zealand Journal of Family Therapy, 6,* 23–29.

Satir, V. (1964). *Conjoint family therapy*. Palo Alto, CA: Science & Behavior Books.

Satir, V. (1972). *Peoplemaking*. Palo Alto, CA: Science & Behavior Books.

Seeman, H., & Wiener, D. J. (1985). Comparing and using psychodrama with family therapy: Some cautions. *Journal of Group Psychotherapy, Psychodrama, and Sociometry, 37,* 143–156.

Starr, A. (1977). *Psychodrama: Rehearsal for living.* Chicago: Nelson-Hall.

White, M. (1995). *Re-authoring lives: Interviews and essays.* Adelaide, South Australia: Dulwich Centre Publications.

White, M., & Epston, D. (1990). *Narrative means to therapeutic ends.* New York: Norton.

Wiener, D. (1994). *Rehearsals for growth: Theater improvisation for psychotherapists.* New York: Norton.

Williams, A. (1989). *The passionate technique: Strategic psychodrama with individuals, families and groups.* London: Routledge.

Williams, A. (1994). Clinical sociometry to define space in family systems. *Journal of Group Psychotherapy, Psychodrama, and Sociometry, 47,* 126–144.

Williams, A. (1998). Psychodrama and family therapy—What's in a name? *International Journal of Action Methods, 50,* 139–165.

RECOMMENDED READING

Blatner, A. (1994). Psychodramatic methods in family therapy. In C. E. Schaefer & L. J. Carey (Eds.), *Family play therapy* (pp. 235–246). Northvale, NJ: Jason Aronson.

Holmes, P. (1993). The roots of enactment—The process in psychodrama, family therapy, and psychoanalysis. *Journal of Group Psychotherapy, Psychodrama, and Sociometry, 45,* 149–162.

Remer, R. (1986). Use of psychodramatic interventions with families: Change on multiple levels. *Journal of Group Psychotherapy, Psychodrama, and Sociometry, 39,* 13–29.

3

USE OF CEREMONY IN MULTIPLE FAMILY THERAPY FOR PSYCHOLOGICAL TRAUMA

HADAR LUBIN AND DAVID READ JOHNSON

Editors' Introduction: At first glance, the therapeutic uses of rituals and ceremonies, which rely on orchestrating scripted performances, may appear antithetical to both the spirit and practice of improvisation. In Hadar Lubin and David Read Johnson's practice, however, stressed and traumatized clients benefit from the structure of these methods while the therapists improvise within the structure they have created to attend to the specific and individual needs of their clients. Were they not to improvise thus, the ceremonies could readily be experienced as impersonal, authoritarian, and antitherapeutic. The effective use of these ceremonies requires public performance skills additional to those ordinarily provided in the training of therapists.

This chapter describes the therapeutic use of organized ceremonies in multiple family groups whose members experience the effects of psychological trauma. We show how the ceremony emerges from a long tradition of action methods in family therapy and offer several theoretical rationales for its use, particularly in the multiple-family context, in which large-group dynamics mirror the societal context within which many traumatized families have struggled. The particular challenges posed by the traumatized family are reviewed, and then four ceremony formats are presented in detail using case material of several trauma populations. We hope that readers will note both the unique contributions of ceremonial interventions as well as their continuities with other family therapy practices.

ACTION METHODS IN FAMILY THERAPY

The use of ceremony emerges from a long tradition of action methods in family therapy, beginning with Virginia Satir (1967) and other experien-

The authors acknowledge the contributions of Susan Feldman, MSW, and Alice Forrester, PhD, to this work and also the support of the National Center for PTSD, VA Medical Center, West Haven, CT.

tial family therapists; progressing through the prescribed family rituals of the Milan group (Palazzoli, Cecchin, Prata, & Boscolo, 1978) and the therapeutic rituals of Imber-Black, Roberts, and Whiting (1988); and culminating in the work of the narrative (White & Epston, 1990; Williams, 1989) and creative arts therapists including art (Landgarten, 1987), dance (Bell, 1984), psychodrama (Leveton, 1977), multimodal play (Harvey, 2000), and music (Decuir, 1991).

Most authors who have used action methods with families have described similar theoretical rationales. The first therapeutic factor is externalization. Family systems are often highly charged, multilayered complexes of rapidly interacting communications. Much of a family's history, control functions, and concerns remain hidden from outside viewers and often from the family members themselves. The intensity and frequency of interaction among a small group of people leads to much of the process becoming embedded and unexamined. Action methods, by translating the family dynamics into physicalized forms, concretize these elements and dynamics. They then become more readily observed by family members and less easily controlled or manipulated by the family's automatic control subsystems. The focus of attention is shifted away from the rapid back-and-forth of verbal dialogue that has no "outside" onto an external "tableau" that each member can more easily apprehend. Problems are now expressed as obstacles within these action tasks, providing a powerful means of achieving externalizing conversations, as narrative therapists have advocated (White & Epston, 1990). Through the ritual, task, or ceremony, each family member is offered the role of witness. Cognitive distancing among members is therefore enhanced, allowing greater opportunity for reflection and insight. The therapeutic effect of such witnessing has been developed further by Andersen (1991) and his use of the reflecting team.

Behavioral engagement is another therapeutic factor. Action methods encourage family members to actually demonstrate within the session aspects of the behaviors they desire at home (Minuchin, 1974). Rather than merely discussing proposed changes in relationships, action methods allow members to experience how they feel when confronted with the actual behavior, either when accomplished as an "exercise" within the session or in between sessions at home (Haley, 1976). Holding hands, sitting next to each other, reading a letter together, being held—simple actions though they be— can evoke a tremendous amount of understanding and shift in feeling and can cut through otherwise very rigid defenses. Minuchin (1974), who referred to this process as "restructuring," wrote, "In restructuring, the therapist creates scenarios, choreographs, highlights themes, and leads family members to improvise within the constraints of the family drama . . . . Restructuring operations are the dramatic interventions that create movement toward the therapeutic goals" (pp. 138–139).

An extension of restructuring has led several family therapists into metaphorical territory, using methods that heighten the significance of the family's struggle. Metaphorical or dramatic methods may also allow greater freedom for family members to experiment due to the pretend nature of the activity. Thus, Madanes (1981) used numerous "pretend" directives in her work, and Andolfi, Angelo, Menghi, and Nicolo-Corigliano (1983) played with the concept of the metaphorical object in the family. As an example of this principle, Harvey (2000) used a simple game with foster families, in which the child is asked to hide in a large cardboard box, which is described as a present for the foster parent, who opens it up to receive the child. Inevitably the child jumps out into the foster parent's arms. Such exercises dramatically illustrate to all parties the underlying desired relationships, which have often become distorted or forgotten in the maze of problems that have distracted them.

> The family ritual, especially in that it presents itself on the level of action, is closer to the analogic code than to the digital. This preponderant analogic component is, by its nature, more apt than words to unite the participants in a powerful collective experience, to introduce some basic idea to be shared by everyone. (Palazzoli et al., 1978, p. 96)

THE NATURE OF CEREMONY

Ceremonies are rituals used to contain disturbances within a social order, particularly disruptions of established relationships (Goffman, 1971). Changes in social status, birth, puberty, marriage, promotion, retirement, aging, and death involve the rearrangement of existing relationships, requiring adaptation by the individual and the community. Ritual serves to acknowledge a change without threatening the overall social order. The ceremony gives sanction to a transformation and is often led by the representative of the established order. Disturbed families presumably have made poorer adaptations to changing circumstances and, in particular, many families have tremendous difficulty integrating or adapting to traumatic experiences of their members. Therapeutic ceremonies designed to facilitate the integration of such traumas by the family therefore may be of significant value.

Ceremonies are symbolic events, and thus they have much in common with theater (Scheff, 1979). Ceremonies usually involve an entrance (e.g., a procession accompanied by music or singing) into a specially demarcated area, which serves the function of separating the ritual space from normal reality. The authority (e.g., priest, mayor, general) is then introduced, followed by some type of evocation of the distressing or challenging situation (e.g., death, marriage, adulthood). The next stage involves the symbolic enactment of the transformation of relationship required by the situation. This may involve a test or a sacrifice (i.e., in the Bar Mitzvah when the child has to read from the Torah and give a talk or in Communion when the participants receive a wafer from the priest). This is followed by formal recognition by the authority of this transformation, marked by an award, certificate, hat, ring, or other concrete symbol of the new status that is bestowed on the participants. Often there is recognition by the assembled community through unison vocal response or applause. An exit processional often ends the ceremony.

The ceremony thereby contains the disturbance in relationships through a restatement of the pledge to the group and its authority. When the established authority is particularly threatened or vulnerable, ceremonies are highly proscribed and involve little if any spontaneous contribution from the participants. Whether the threat to the existence of the community is a relationship, an idea, or intense emotion, the ceremony will attempt to ward off its emergence. Any departure or error raises intense anxiety and is seen as a sign of bad luck, because the containing function of the ritual has been compromised. When the intent of the ceremony is to help individuals in the community adapt to a crisis, then the ceremony may be less suppressive of emotion and reveal more clearly the disturbances in relationships.

Thomas Scheff, in his book *Catharsis in Healing, Ritual, and Drama* (1979), articulated a theory of ritual that focuses on the management of emotional distress. He introduced the concept of *aesthetic distance* to indicate an intermediate level of arousal that is optimal for adaptation, catharsis, and integration. A person may be underdistanced when he or she is overwhelmed by the emotion and overdistanced when he or she is not at all aroused. A good example of aesthetic distance is when one experiences a painting of a nude as a work of art rather than as sexually arousing. Likewise, it is essential in ritual that the danger be represented but not experienced as real. The value of a ceremony thus is enhanced if the participants are at aesthetic distance, being both emotionally engaged and yet aware of its symbolic nature.

Generally, the need for distancing increases according to the strength or threat of the distress. Among primitive cultures, in which emotional arousal tended to be high, ceremony was needed to contain these emotions and thus served a distancing function by being very stylized and formal. In the modern day, when audiences are far more overdistanced and not overwhelmed with emotion, generally ceremonies need to serve underdistancing functions.

THERAPEUTIC CEREMONIES

Most ceremonies have the therapeutic properties of strengthening the bonds of individuals to their community and in giving reassurance against the anxieties and fears of life. However, for ceremonies to be therapeutic they must help individuals process their distressing emotions. Thus, therapeutic ceremonies function less as methods of supporting the existing social order, of warding off unconscious or disturbing emotion, and of suppressing individual expression. Because therapeutic ceremonies are intentionally designed to enhance the self-esteem of the participants, they must give more room for the expression of feelings by the individual members. Therapeutic ceremonies provide specific times for spontaneous, individual actions or comments by members. Therapeutic ceremonies also allow for greater arousal of the disturbing situation and therefore for greater emotional catharsis. The content of the threatening situation is less suppressed or cloaked.

Healing ceremonies, through their use of formalization and dramatization, also confer on the participants the feeling that what is occurring has broader significance to the society at large (Johnson, 1987; Lubin & Johnson, 1998). The symbolic transformation of relationship that occurs at the heart of the therapeutic ceremony must therefore synthesize personal and social meanings of the "illness," such as overcoming posttraumatic stress disorder (PTSD) and acting to stop violence. Framed within the ceremonial space, such transformations are afforded the implicit or explicit approval of the "congregation," representing the larger society.

FAMILY TREATMENT OF PSYCHOLOGICAL TRAUMA

Our work has focused on the use of ceremonies with families experiencing the effects of psychological trauma in one or more of their members. In trauma, the victim has often been sucked into the hole of his or her traumatic schema, altering his or her relationships with the family and the world in dysfunctional ways (Figley, 1989). Often the victim pulls other members of the family into this vortex, and the family's mode of coping with the traumatized member leads to cognitive distortions, secondary traumatization, and dysfunctional relationships throughout the family (Johnson, Feldman, & Lubin, 1995). Once the specific traumatic event has passed into history, often family members no longer attribute their problems to the event, and cause and effect are displaced onto current stressors, successfully hiding the root of the problem from the family's view. The family becomes increasingly polarized and consumed by unsolvable conflicts. These conflicts evoke the traumatic memory in the victim without any overt recognition of the parallels between the two worlds. The resulting overlap of relationships prevents the original conflict from being resolved. The family members become triangulated with a shadow. Over time, typical conflict patterns within the family become shaped by the traumatic material of the victim, as the family system unknowingly assimilates the traumatic experience. We believe this process may be the mechanism by which secondary traumatization occurs, in which trauma is passed on to the next generation (Johnson, Feldman, & Lubin, 1995).

Thus, the resulting conflicts within the family are efforts both to symbolize and avoid the traumatic experience. The rigid pattern of interaction maintained in the family does not allow for a working through or mourning of the past as it interferes with the present. As a result, the memory remains unmourned and unacknowledged; family members feel misunderstood, shamed, and enraged; and communication ends because no one can listen without reacting defensively. Family cohesion often deteriorates dramatically during these states of polarization.

Treatment

Family treatment for trauma victims should focus on repairing the shattered relationships that have resulted from the original traumas, through detriangulating the family from the traumatic scenario and identifying more adequate coping behaviors among members (Figley, 1989). The combined effect of the trauma and the shame experienced afterward has usually disrupted the entire family's connections to each other and society. These families therefore present with formidable problems that are often difficult to address solely within an individual family therapy context. Most traumatic experiences (e.g., rape, abuse, combat) have important societal dimensions, and much of the family's shame, denial, and stress can be traced to their inadequate posttrauma adaptation to society. We have found that the multiple-family group format, whenever possible to convene it, is a tremendously powerful and helpful arena for trauma survivors to heal and that the use of ceremony substantially enhances its impact.

The role of multiple-family therapy with such families offers unique advantages in the overall treatment; in this environment, each family member finds support in members of other families who are in the same position or role. Thus, isolated individuals within the family system may find a voice through a member of another family. Second, each family is able to witness similar dynamics in other families who are struggling with similar issues; many members will find themselves offering advice to another family that would best be followed in their own. Third, the gathering of multiple families demonstrates the universality of these problems, decreasing the feelings of shame and fear that the family is alone in its dysfunction. Especially in trauma treatment, this process facilitates the sense that the "enemy" is "out there," depersonalizing the problem.

Ceremony is a natural intervention in the multiple-family therapy context, given the typically large number of individuals present. The ceremony serves as a focusing device that organizes and concentrates the attention of the group members on specific conflicts, issues, or challenges. Ceremonies allow for the evocation of distressing emotions within a safely contained structure, that is, the achievement of aesthetic distance (Obenchain & Silver,

1992). Finally, ceremonies help to recontextualize the experience of trauma victims, thereby giving meaning to their alienation (Silver & Wilson, 1988).

Ceremony can be used both as a one-time intervention and as a component of an ongoing therapy process. It can be used at the beginning, middle, or end of the treatment. It can be used for its immediate effects or for facilitating the therapeutic processes in other settings, such as individual or family therapy sessions.

The Therapist's Role

Usually the therapist convenes or leads the ceremony and in this role represents the authority invested by the larger society (e.g., like the mayor, president, priest). In this role, the therapist must communicate to the participants that society condones the ceremony. In addition, it is critical that the therapist acknowledge society's own participation in creating the conditions for the trauma (e.g., supporting sexist representations of women) or in letting down the clients after they were victimized (e.g., blaming veterans for the war). The purpose of the ceremony is not to express sympathy for poor, traumatized people, nor should it be a self-created protest by and for survivors. Rather, to be maximally therapeutic, the ceremony must represent a transformation of society's attitudes as well as those of the clients and their families. This interaction is played out in the call-and-response framework between the traumatized members and the collective.

Therapists serve as managers and coordinators of these interactions, as well as emotional containers for the collective experience. Thus, therapists must be able to feel and express deep empathy with these families and to be aware of their own personal connection to these issues, although rarely will they be called on to reveal these to the families. Last, therapists should have knowledge about using the physical space to dramatize the ceremony effectively, elements that contribute to the therapists' role as presiding witness of a very powerful and intense event.

CASE EXAMPLE 1: FOSTER CHILDREN

The first two ceremonies that we describe were used in a specially funded program for foster families who were struggling with difficult children with a poor history of attachment in previous placements. This program, Hands Around the Home, involved the collaboration of a community foster care agency, a private clinic specializing in PTSD, and the foster families. Foster children, most of whom have experienced numerous psychological traumas, often develop attachment and behavior disorders that make successful placement in foster families extremely difficult. The foster parents at first show tremendous tolerance and care for these difficult children, but as their rejecting behavior continues and even intensifies, many foster parents give up and return the children to the state, solidifying in a child's mind that he or she is unlovable, defective, and alone. Hands Around the Home was designed to use several interventions, including therapeutic ceremonies, to directly address the attachment challenges within these families.

Eight foster families were selected for the 20-week program, which consisted of a large group meeting for 15 minutes, simultaneous play therapy for the children and psychoeducational meetings for the parents for 1 hour, followed by a social time with dinner for a half hour. Therapeutic ceremonies were included at the beginning and end of the program and two times during the program. The children ranged in age from 9 to 14 years, and half were White and half were African American or Hispanic. Five staff worked with the groups. The evaluation of this experience by the participants and agency staff was extremely positive, and as of two years after the group, nearly all of the children were still successfully placed with their foster parents.

The Entry Ceremony

We have constructed several ceremonies that mark either the beginning of the program or an individual family's entrance into an ongoing program. For traumatized families, entrance into such a program is of great significance, for they anticipate and fear that their horrible story will have to be retold and that they will re-experience the pain and shame associated with having been victimized. Delaying or avoiding the identification of the reason for their participation will often increase their fear and lead to dropping out. On the other hand, too rapid or intense revelation may also overwhelm them. The entry ceremony is an excellent means both to facilitate the revelation and acknowledgment of the horror and to encapsulate it with cognitive distance to reduce the possibility of flooding.

The important principles in designing such a ceremony include (a) strong and clear leadership from the program director or therapist, (b) representation of the anxiety-provoking situation, (c) representation of the desired transformation, (d) support from the audience acting as societal witnesses, and (e) a structured closing. Departures from the script or other unexpected events are not uncommon and are not interfered with by the leader, other than to calmly return the group to the script and maintain the overall structure of the ceremony.

The following ceremony was conducted at the first session of Hands Around the Home, which included 8 families (14 foster parents and siblings, 10 foster children, and 5 staff). Note that words spoken by Everyone are spoken in unison, after the leader speaks the line; this is the call-and-response method.

The room is set up with a large square of chairs. All the parents are lined up on one side, the children and one staff member on the opposite side. The therapy staff are lined up at the head of the room between them. Everyone is given the script of the ceremony.

Leader: Welcome. We have gathered here today to help these young people in their journey to make a home. Their birth parents were not able to take care of them and have placed them in our care. Some birth parents were too young; some did not know how; some had their own problems to deal with; some were not good parents. All of them shed tears when their children left them. Are we willing to listen to these children's stories?

The anxiety-provoking situation—the giving up of the child by the birth parents—is immediately mentioned, as are the reasons both good and bad for their decision. The shedding of tears is also mentioned to acknowledge the emotional tone underlying this situation.

Everyone: Yes, we are willing to listen.

The entire group acts as a witnessing chorus and is given lines that denote the desired behaviors.

Leader: Do we realize that only through the effort of many people will these children find their way to a home?
Everyone: Yes, only with the help of many people will we succeed.

The staff member brings each child to the front and introduces him or her by name.

Staff: This is Natasha [a girl, age 9].
Leader: Natasha, were your birth parents unable to take care of you?
Natasha: Yes.
Leader: Do you realize that this was not your fault?
Natasha: I guess so.
Everyone: This was not your fault.

The resounding volume of the entire group reciting this phrase always has a strong effect on the participants.

Leader: Do you know that you are a good person who deserves to be cared for?
Natasha: (pauses) Uh-huh.
Everyone: You are a good person.
Leader: Do you realize that, even though you had bad luck in the past, good things can happen to you in the future?
Natasha: Yes, I hope so.
Everyone: May good things happen to you.

Natasha's foster parent is brought up to the front and introduced.

Staff:	This is Evelyn.
Leader:	The State of Connecticut is asking you to care for this child. Are you, Evelyn, willing to take care of Natasha?
Evelyn:	(pauses) Yes I am.
Leader:	Are you willing to try even though the situation will not be perfect?
Evelyn:	Yes.
Leader:	Are you willing to try even though you are not this child's mother or father?
Evelyn:	I will try even though I am not your mother (her eyes tear up).
Leader:	Do you realize that this child may not be able to show you her love at times because she needs to protect herself from feeling any more pain?
Evelyn:	Yes, I will try to remember this.
Everyone:	We know how hard this can be.
Leader:	Yet this is your choice?
Evelyn:	Yes, this is my choice.
Everyone:	We appreciate your choice.

The parent is being challenged by painful truths which, if accepted, establish the significance of the parent's role. The symbolic statement of choice almost always evokes emotion, and when followed by the affirmation of the collective, offers the foster parent a type of public support he or she rarely receives.

Leader:	(to the parent) Now, turn to your child and join hands and say after me, "I want to take good care of you."
Evelyn:	(taking Natasha's hands and beginning to cry) Natasha, I want to take good care of you.
Leader:	(to the child) Now tell your foster parent, "I want you to take care of me."
Natasha:	I want you to take care of me. (They embrace spontaneously.)
Everyone:	You have our blessings.
Leader:	Evelyn, you may take Natasha back to your seat. (They return together to the seats.)

This is the representation of a transformation, from separate individuals to a new foster family, bonded by a mutual pledge based on desire. The physical action, a simple holding of hands, embracing, and returning together to their seats, serves as the concretization of this transformation. The final collective blessing serves as the approval of this transformation from society.

After each child has completed the ceremony, everyone stands in a large circle and holds hands.

Leader:	These are the hands around the home, hands of the children, hands of the foster parents, hands of the social workers, and hands of the state. Let us work together. (The group spontaneously applauds.)

The Interactive Lecture

In many trauma populations and their families, interaction with health care providers has been unsuccessful and has resulted in guardedness or generalized hopelessness, based on a feeling that no one can help them unless they have gone through the same experience. The interactive lecture is one way of altering the usual psychoeducational format to address these concerns. In many of our groups with trauma survivors, we use a special psychoeducational lecture format not to impart information as much as to symbolize a transformation; thus, it is ceremonial in structure. This method is embedded within our model of interactive psychoeducational group therapy for PTSD (Johnson & Lubin, 2000; Lubin & Johnson, 1997, 2000; Lubin, Loris, Burt, & Johnson, 1998).

The lecture-as-ceremony is particularly relevant in larger groups and multiple-family groups. Essentially, the therapist stands up and uses a marker board to present a schematic lecture on a relevant but anxiety-provoking topic for the group members. In multiple-family groups, the therapist acts within the role of "expert" who is imparting information to the group. The aim of the lecture material is to engage the audience in the core problematic issues troubling them, although the presentational style is formal. This formality provides the container and authority necessary for the ceremony. Examples of content include PTSD and the Family, Discovering Forgiveness, Trauma and Its Aftermath, and Effects of Trauma on Relationships.

Inevitably, the material evokes the traumatic schemas within group members, who then reveal these feelings in their questions to the therapist. Typically the essence of their challenge consists of the ideas "therefore the situation is hopeless," "you are wrong because you don't know what we went through," or "so the world is a dangerous place, and it makes sense for me to remain in fear." These challenges to the flow of the lecture allow the therapist to then shift his or her focus onto engaging with the clients in a symbolic enactment of the desired transformation. Although there is a measure of improvisation here, the therapist follows several basic principles: (a) the therapist generally moves physically closer to the group members, breaking the previous spatial configuration and symbolizing an "approach"; (b) the therapist attempts to dramatize the possibility of the desired outcome in the here-and-now interaction with a group member; and (c) the therapist is prepared to deal with a successful or failed demonstration of this behavior by the group member. The main aim is to confront the members with information that is discrepant from the traumatic schema, to introduce uncertainty into their notions of what is possible. The movement from the board symbolizes the therapist's entry into the traumatic schema, although modeling a stance of courage and respect. Later, the therapist will move back to the board, representing a return to a stance of educator and container.

In a lecture on hope, for example, one child said in response to a question, "There's no point to ask for help, I just want to stay out of the way." The therapist paused and then moved toward the child, "so you feel there is no point in asking for help, even if it is offered to you?" The child nodded. The therapist moved to him and offered his hand. Everyone in the room was very attentive during this awkward moment. The therapist said, "I am offering you my help, even though I'm not sure that our work will succeed." After a brief, excruciating moment, the child smiled and reached out and held the therapist's hand. They held this moment for awhile. If the child had not reached out, the therapist would have nevertheless demonstrated the impact of the trauma on children's ability to ask for help, which would have evoked much comment and encouragement from others in the group. After all, it would be apparent that the client could have reached out but chose not to, just as they do daily with their foster parents.

The therapist then asked each foster parent to turn to his or her child and hold out his or her hand to them. Most, but not all, of the children responded by grabbing their parent's hand. Many were crying with deep emotion, evoked by a simple, symbolic act in response to a challenging statement by one of the children. The fact that not all of the children reached out only underscored the tremendous importance of this act and the difficulties facing every family in their efforts to bond.

In another lecture on the subject of trust that focused on the multiple placements that these children had experienced, the therapist was talking about the effect of broken promises on the children. The interest of family members appeared to be high. As a demonstration, the therapist came toward a boy (age 14) and said, "I'd like to make you a promise." The boy immediately retorted, "Forget it." "But I would like to make just a really small promise to you." "Good luck," the child replied. The therapist then explained to the group that he assumed that the boy was refusing his promise because his previous experience of promises was that they had all been broken. "Yes!" came the response from several of the children. "So to go along with a promise is just to be. . . ." "A really big sucker!"

The therapist then asked the entire group if this meant that there was no way that any sort of promise would be appreciated by these kids, which stimulated a very heated discussion. No promises, then no trust, then no success. Finally one parent pleaded, "I know my child does not trust me, because I can still decide to send her back to the state, like has happened to her before. But I am still going to try to fulfill my promises to her now." The therapist, coming close, asked, "You mean even though she has no reason to believe you will come through for her, you are going to try?" "Yes, I am." The therapist then moved over to the first child (not of the parent who had spoken), "Even though it is unlikely she will come through, if she did, would it be a good thing?" The boy paused for a very long time, and the tension in the room was very high. "Yes, it would be good." The therapist moved back to the parent and repeated, "Yes, it would be good," and she burst into tears. Her foster child, sitting next to her, spontaneously threw herself into her foster mother's arms (the first time this had ever happened).

Performing the Leader Role

In general, the therapist, after one or more of these enactments, returns to the head of the room and the board, resuming his or her previous role as educator. However, the therapist must demonstrate that, as a result of these engagements with the clients, he or she, too, has been altered. The therapist may hold his or her gaze on the group members while being silent and thoughtful or may make a statement to the group members articulating the challenges they face together and the determination to persevere. The therapist then turns to the board and makes a few concluding or summarizing remarks. In the case of Hands Around the Home, the therapists worked with their awareness of the tremendous challenges these foster families faced in attempting to create and sustain caring attachments.

This form of ceremonial intervention has also been used successfully with families of traumatized women, adolescents, and veterans. It can be smoothly integrated into almost any psychoeducational format. By producing a transformative enactment between a family member and the therapist, it brings a sense of aliveness and immediacy to these lectures, as well as addressing the important concerns of family members regarding the therapists' ability to help them.

CASE EXAMPLE 2: VIETNAM VETERANS

We used several ceremonies in an inpatient program for Vietnam veterans with PTSD (Johnson, Feldman, Lubin, & Southwick, 1995; Johnson, Feldman, Southwick, & Charney, 1994). In addition to an entry ceremony, psychoeducational lectures, and a ceremony for the dead, the following two ceremonies were used. The program was a 4-month intensive treatment consisting of individual, group, and family therapy; medication; and vocational and rehabilitation modules (see Johnson et al., 1994, for more detailed description). The veterans were in their 40s and had had numerous difficulties (e.g., severe symptomatology, substance abuse, hospitalizations) over many years. Families of the 10–12 veteran cohort were invited to participate in a family day event several times during the program, during which the ceremonies occurred.

The Letter Ceremony

One problem in multiple-family groups is that, because of their size, many more timid or less powerful individuals are silenced, even though they hold very important perspectives, feelings, or information. The letter cer-emony is an excellent exercise to use during the middle phases of multiple-family work, when the group is sufficiently warmed up to the various issues and when direct confrontation will be beneficial. The challenge in multiple-family therapy is to allow direct confrontation to occur without a feeling of "ganging up" on someone. The letter ceremony circumvents this problem by two distancing maneuvers: (a) the confrontation occurs in a "letter" form and (b) is from a group to a group.

This ceremony was useful in breaking through a particular obstacle in trauma treatment with veterans; the general tone of the program was to place the veteran in the "victim" position, having experienced the trauma of war and then a rejecting welcome home. However, in family sessions, spouses and children reported significant levels of emotional or physical abuse by the veteran, placing him in the "perpetrator" role. A tension therefore existed in the family between expressing sympathy for their veteran husband or father and at the same time expressing anger and sadness over their mistreatment by him (Rosenheck & Thomson, 1986).

The families were divided into subgroups according to their social role—parents of the veteran, spouses, siblings, children, and the veterans—and told to spend 45 minutes to write a collective letter to the veterans (or the veterans to their families). Each subgroup was provided a staff member who helped to facilitate this task and encourage a full reporting. One member of each group was then selected by the group to read this letter when everyone gathered in the large group room.

During these meetings, spurred on by the task of writing a letter, the group members struggled with integrating the wide range of thoughts and feelings they had about their veterans. Similarities and differences rapidly emerged, leading to engaged discussions over what should be included in the letter. Often with help from the staff therapist, the groups came to realize that almost any reaction had legitimacy and could be included, even if there were contradictions between ideas. The anonymity of the author of each line provided members some comfort in including strong feeling.

In the current case, all the subgroups then gathered in the large group room, which was set up with chairs in a large rectangle, with each subgroup sitting together. The staff were lined up at the head of the room. The 44 people included 11 veterans, 7 parents, 9 spouses, 9 children, and 8 staff. After a silence, the staff stood up, and one staff member read their "letter."

Dear Veterans and Families and Friends,
   The Vietnam War affected us all. The battle on the field is over, but unfortunately the war has continued on two fronts. There is the battle going on inside each veteran struggling with his memories; then there is the battle in finding a way to come home, to get closer to his family. Each of you faces many obstacles—for the enemy is strong: the enemies of hopelessness, of frustration, of stigma, of abuse, of grief, of apathy. Yet

we are all here tonight—despite everything that has happened. We, the staff, pledge to you that we will continue to engage in this struggle. For we believe the work is important, not just for you but for us and for the generations to come.

The staff letter is designed to heighten the significance of the event, to identify ahead of time that confrontation of problematic behaviors is acceptable, and to frame the event. The letter also acknowledges that the staff must struggle with these issues.

Then they sat down, and the parents were asked to stand. One father read the letter, his hands shaking.

> Dear Sons,
> We've experienced agony, anguish, anger, and fear for your very life as well as sanity since your return from Vietnam. We've seen you change from a happy, wonderful boy, proud to be in the service, into an angry, withdrawn man. You seem old to us. We have lived with anger at the country, at the doctors, at the President, at ourselves. We did the best we could. We'd like to have you back. We'd like to have your love. . . .
> We love you,
> Your Moms and Dads

After they sat down, the wives stood up.

The protection of anonymity of the collective letter paradoxically allows more direct expression of pain, which was deeply felt by this group of women, who huddled together holding each other as one began to read.

> My Dear Husband, (she begins to cry)
> You have made us feel hurt, overwhelmed, alone, resentful, and empty. You have hurt us with your words and sometimes with your hands. We recognize that you got the short end of the stick from the government. But we can't change that. We have to make a fresh start now and build for the future, hopefully for us and our children. The illness has consumed us also. We miss the women we used to be. We want you as our husband and father of our children. We'd like you to open up. We want you as our friend.
> Come home,
> Your wives (Nearly all the women are crying at this point, as well as some of the veterans.)

The sight of a group of wives weeping is effective in breaking through the veterans' denial because their usual means of dismissing their own particular wife's criticisms fails against women they do not know. At the same time, they are seated with their own group, which provides some support for them.

Next the children, ranging in age from 5 through 19, stood. By this time the emotion in the room and the anticipation of what the children would say were intense. In the ceremonies we have conducted with veterans, it is at this point that their defenses against acknowledging the impact of their own behaviors crumbles, whether or not they have children present.

The children stood, and a 12-year-old girl read.

> Dear Dad,
> We love you, and we're proud that you are in the hospital getting help. We think we know what your problems are, but we're nervous because we are afraid you might get mad if we tell you. There are two sides to you: Sometimes, you're mean and destructive, and sometimes, you're sweet and caring. Sometimes we want to hide the keys to protect you from drinking and driving. Sometimes we worry that you will die. Dad, we see you making some success. We like it when you're home to play with us. We care about you so much, we're proud of you, and we want you to be proud of yourself.
> Love,
> Your kids

The children have often been silenced within the family household and, even if they have spoken up, have been isolated as individuals and their opinions dismissed. Once delivered as part of a group of 9, their message is received with newfound authority, and the veterans' response nearly always indicates that they have been heard. The letters almost always include negative and positive aspects, but particularly important are those behaviors and feelings that are desired and that serve as clarifying beacons for further treatment efforts on everyone's part.

Then the veterans responded with their letter.

> Dear Family and Friends,
> We thank you for being here, for standing by us, after all that has happened. We know we haven't been the best example as a father, husband, or son. We are deeply sorry for not showing enough love, for the abuse, for not being sensitive enough to you, and not being able to trust you. Thank you for holding the family together while we have been here. You have given us courage to face our PTSD. And for all this sacrifice, perhaps you will get us back—willing to listen, with a new attitude, and able to spend time with you and our dear children. We look forward to the day when we can look in your eyes and say, I love you, with feeling. Instead of harshness, tenderness. Instead of isolation, communication.
> We love you so very much,
> The Vets

At the end of the reading, the leader indicated that people should rejoin their family units, which occurred in the midst of a great deal of weeping and hugging.

The format of this ceremony allows for disturbing and intense emotions to be shared. In individual families, communication is hampered by the defenses, explosiveness, and endless repetitions that prevent each person from listening. Every statement has its counterargument. In the group setting, the intensity of the individual relationships is mediated, so that the same message may more easily be heard. Each member has the support of others in his or her role, so the overall sense of safety is much greater.

When the children's group reads their letter, and often one of the youngest children reads it, the veterans' capacity to defend themselves against their own lack of responsibility in the home collapses. Even those who do not have their children present, seeing these children speak directly to their fathers is enough to connect them to their shame and guilt. Yet the ceremony is clothed in an atmosphere of hope, tolerance, and collaboration rather than punishment, so that their guilt is associated with a positive emotional atmosphere. The ceremony also provides a model for the kind of direct communication individual families will be taught during the program.

The Graduation Ceremony

The ending of a trauma program or the departure of a member is another excellent time to incorporate a therapeutic ceremony. Often the graduation, closing, or "crossing-over" ceremony mirrors the entry ceremony (Johnson, Feldman, Lubin, & Southwick, 1995). Usually there is a demonstration of recovery or resolve to fight on or triumph over the traumatic experience, often involving some form of personal testimony. The presence of many family members in the group provides a powerful witnessing environment. Generally, the symbolic enactment includes the "return" of the victim into the family's embrace, thereby representing the welcoming home that did not occur. In addition to the Vietnam veterans described here, we have used this graduation ceremony as part of an outpatient women's trauma program for several years with equal success (Lubin & Johnson, 1997).

Ron was a Vietnam veteran who served two tours in intense combat. He had numerous traumatic experiences, both as witness and perpetrator, and when he returned to the United States he was ridiculed and shunned by his family, particularly his father, a World War II veteran, who felt ashamed of his son. Ron spent a decade as part of a motorcycle gang, then settled down as a carpenter, got married, and had three children. He drank heavily and was emotionally distant and at times abusive to his family, although he cared greatly about them. He had been troubled by flashbacks and nightmares for many years, particularly an incident in which he witnessed the torture of a Vietnamese family. He had protested but was threatened at gunpoint by his own commanding officer. Attending the graduation ceremony were his wife, three children (ages 23, 18, and 13), and his father (his mother had died several years earlier). He had not known that his father was going to come.

The leader led the veteran cohort of 10 men into the large community room and asked Ron to step forward. His family members were then asked to stand up across the room from him.

Maintaining distance between the client and their family members is an important symbolic indicator of the chasm that separates them and over which they must pass during the ceremony and in their lives.

Leader: Are those gathered here willing to be witnesses for this Vietnam veteran?

Audience: Yes, we are.

Beginning the ceremony with a statement of commitment by the societal witnesses places the individual transformation of the clients into a larger context, as well as provides them a sense of legitimacy that many had not received.

Leader: Ron, did you serve our country in Vietnam?

Ron: Yes, I did.

Leader: When was your tour of duty?

Ron: 1968–1969 and 1970–1971.

Leader: In so doing, did you put your life at risk?

Ron: Yes, sir.

Leader: Did you see death, stupidity, fear, or cowardice?

Ron: (pauses to compose himself) Yes.

Leader: Did you see courage, love, and heroism?

Ron: That, too.

Audience: (in unison) That is war.

Leader: Did you do things that you regret?

Ron: Yes, I did.

Leader: That you were proud of?

Ron: No.

The negative answer here only underscores the pain these veterans feel, and the therapist does not indicate any disapproval of such answers.

Leader: Did you have experiences that are beyond words?

Ron: (looks at the therapist, pauses, and nods)

Audience: That is war.

Leader: When you returned home, were you properly debriefed?

Ron: No.

Leader: Were you ignored, stigmatized, or ridiculed?

Ron: (glances quickly at his father) Yes.

Audience: We let you down.

Leader: Were you ever accepted as you were, a soldier who did his duty, the best way that he could?

Ron: Most of the time I pretended I had never gone.

Audience: We let you down.

The client is in a vulnerable, sensitized state, filled with his traumatic schemas; the repetition of these basic, normative statements is designed to interfere with these traumatic voices. The acknowledgment that "society" let down the veteran often evokes a strong emotional response.

Leader:	How did this welcome affect you?
Ron:	I felt confused and ashamed. I hid. I let down my parents. I let myself go to hell.
Leader:	As a result of the war and this welcome, did you resort to cutting off the people that you love?
Ron:	Yes, very much so.
Leader:	Resort to drugs or alcohol to silence the pain?
Ron:	For years.
Leader:	Lose control of your anger and hurt people that you love?
Ron:	Too often.
Leader:	Thought about suicide as a way of ending it all?
Ron:	Many times.

Despite the obvious sympathy and support offered the client, identifying their own responsibility for their maladaptive coping behaviors is essential to provide balance as well as to establish a basis for empathy with suffering family members.

Leader:	Is there still hope?
Ron:	Yes.
Audience:	Yes, we believe there is hope.
Leader:	Even though you will live with the memories of Vietnam forever?
Ron:	Yes.
Audience:	Yes.
Leader:	Even though these things happened, and there is no way to change history?
Ron:	Yes.
Audience:	Yes.

The repetition of the "yes" provides and strengthens the ritual aspect of the ceremony, which deepens the participants' engagement with the process.

Leader:	Are you willing to accept yourself as you were, as a soldier who did his duty, the best way that you could?
Ron:	Yes, I am.
Leader:	Are you willing to try to gain better control over your anger and to try to show your love more openly?
Ron:	(looking across at his wife) Yes, I have already begun to do that.
Leader:	Are you ready to work toward forgiveness of yourself and your loved ones?
Ron:	More than ever before.
Audience:	We are ready to forgive you.
Leader:	Even though you carry this heavy burden from the past, can you still love your family and friends?
Ron:	Yes.
Leader:	Can you still search for a meaning in your life?

Ron:	Yes.
Leader:	Can you build a new future, in which you can be a contributing member of society?
Ron:	Yes.
Audience:	Yes, you can do these things.
Leader:	Despite the obstacles, do you want to return to us here in the world?
Ron:	(pauses, begins to tear up, nods)
Leader:	Say it, Ron.
Ron:	Yes, I do.
Audience:	Come home to us.

Although apparently insignificant, the smallest act of avoidance often signals an emotional conflict, in this case Ron's deep desire to be welcomed home. The simple statement by the audience, "Come home to us," addresses one of Ron's important issues, and his participation therefore is very meaningful.

Leader:	(turns to a veteran of World War II, who was specifically invited to the ceremony) Are you, veteran of World War II, willing to accept this veteran into the brotherhood of all U.S. veterans?
WWII veteran:	I am honored to welcome this veteran into the brotherhood of all U.S. veterans. (He goes to shake Ron's hand, but Ron, overwhelmed with emotion, reaches out and gives him a big hug.)

This element in the ceremony of course addresses the rift between generations of veterans that occurred during the Vietnam War and is particularly important for Ron's relationship with his own father.

Leader:	(now turns to the family members) Are you willing to help in whatever way you can in Ron's journey home?
Family:	(somewhat in unison) Yes, we are.
Leader:	Do you realize that he is suffering from a chronic condition for which he is not to blame?
Family:	Yes.
Leader:	Are you willing to accept his progress in small steps?
Family:	Yes.
Leader:	Tell him how you feel.

This is the "test" or passage that the clients and their family are asked to make in this ceremony, for addressing each other is to reveal the needed transformation in their relationship: to transcend the weight of the years dominated by the traumatic schema and to aspire to a future less burdened by blame and fear. Once through this breach, new possibilities are made available to them.

Ron's Wife:	Ron, we love you and are so proud of what you have done here in the program. I have a lot of hope that we can still put this thing together and get on with our lives. We have so much bad

	stuff to put behind us. But it seems like you are sincere in want-ing to do that.
Ron's Kids:	(They each speak briefly, saying how much they want their Dad back. As they speak, Ron, filled with shame and pride, despair and hope, cries openly. He tries to move to them, but the leader gently indicates for him to wait. This is done to maintain the emotional tension.)
Ron's Dad:	(barely able to speak) Ronny, I know now that I just didn't un-derstand, I just didn't know, and I drove you away from your mother and I . . . too long . . . . it's time . . . . I'm proud of you son. (Both he and Ron are now crying, and Ron blurts out "I'm sorry, Dad.")
Leader:	(places his hand lightly on Ron's back) Veteran, please tell your family how you feel.
Ron:	When I entered this program I thought this was my last chance before I lost you and the kids. I am amazed that you have been there for me through every thing I have done. I promise you there will be no more abuse. I promise you that I will do my best, even though I am going to need your support more than ever with my illness. I want to be with you. I am so sorry for everything. And Dad, I always loved you.
Leader:	Now, make the crossing. (The leader shakes Ron's hand, and then he walks across the room to his family, as the audience breaks into applause.)
Leader:	These few steps across the room are only symbolic ones, for it is not so easy to come home from Vietnam. The war has affected us all, and together we must work hard not to fall victim to the hopelessness and despair that besets us. I am glad to say that tonight, at least, we have not failed.

The leader reminds them that the ceremony is not reality, that hope must be fol-lowed by action, and that the enemy is strong, as a means of signaling the departure from the ritual space.

This ceremony places many demands on the veterans. They must con-front their families in a public setting. They must talk openly about their feelings. They must evaluate how much improvement they have made. They must leave the program. The ceremony dramatically enacts the acknowledg-ment by America that they have let down the veterans, that errors were made. The ceremony includes a welcome by a World War II veteran. It pro-vides space for the veteran to speak for himself about his unique experience. Finally, the ceremony underscores the importance of the family. When the veteran and his family face each other and talk to each other, the rest of the audience watches a real family interaction, and theater dissolves as an au-thentic interaction between loved ones unfolds. The audience is privileged to serve in the role of witness. Because so many in the audience share similar issues, the catharsis is powerful. In these moments, despite the realization that the illness of PTSD is strong and chronic, the sheer power of the encounter between people is enough to generate hope even among the most hopeless.

In these graduation ceremonies, the traumatized client not only symbolically demonstrates a step toward personal recovery, but the family as a whole is engaged in a reparative act. Many families who have undergone these ceremonies have told us years later that the ceremony had continued to be a guiding metaphor within the family for its continued striving for health. For Ron and his family, the program as a whole, and the ceremony in particular, remained an important foundation for continued progress over the next several years. Ron was successful in resuming his role as father and husband, and he and his father marked that night as the moment they were able to reconnect. Although he continued to experience PTSD symptoms and had difficulty resuming full-time work, Ron made significant strides in putting his traumas behind him and freeing up his resources to be more emotionally available to his family and friends.

ORGANIZATION INTO DAYLONG EVENTS

In several settings, it may be appropriate to integrate ceremonial methods within daylong family events, such as "family days" or "family weeks" in inpatient or partial hospital programs. The advantage of such a format is the opportunity for the families to be immersed in the therapeutic work, allowing greater possibilities for transformation or loosening of individual or family level defenses. We have found the following overall structure to work well in these cases:

8:30 a.m.	Gathering, refreshments
9:00	Opening session: Lecture—Trauma and Its Aftermath
9:45	Break
10:00	Multiple-family groups without identified clients meet in their own group
11:30	Break
11:45	Entry ceremony
12:15 p.m.	Lunch
1:00	Lecture—PTSD and Family Life
1:45	Break
2:00	Multiple-family groups with identified clients
3:30	Break
3:45	Letter ceremony: Groups divided into social roles
4:30	Letter ceremony: Reading of letters
5:00	Closing or individual family meetings.

In a program in which a graduation ceremony is appropriate, the graduation ceremony can replace the letter ceremony, which then can be moved to the morning session. There are, of course, many creative ways of adapting these principles to the particular clinical situation and population. For example, with smaller children, an art ceremony was used in which the children present their drawings of family life.

We have found that, in daylong events, the ceremonial structure provides a strong container for family processing, allowing the therapy staff to work more intensively. The length of time intensifies the experience and often allows for certain members to reach a crisis point and decide to collect their courage and break through old patterns, expressing deeply felt emotions or revealing long-hidden family secrets. The aesthetic form of these ceremonies seems to be a solacing influence on the emotional expression and verbal confrontation that often occurs as families address these long-standing problems.

APPLICATIONS

Multiple-family groups can be found in a wide variety of mental health settings, including inpatient, outpatient, day hospital, and residential programs. The stated aim of the sessions varies from informational to psychoeducational to psychotherapeutic. The ceremonies described here may be adapted to any of these settings and populations.

We have been able to engage families in these ceremonial activities, even though they may have not been familiar with them. For most families, the concept of a ceremony brings to mind religious services, award ceremonies, or weddings, which often have a positive or neutral connotation. In some cases, in which the clients are asked to prepare testimonies beforehand or ask their families to attend, clients will express anxiety or resistance. In these cases, it is not necessary to insist they participate. Usually the obvious significance of the event as well as group support provide enough encouragement to overcome their fears. Nevertheless, in more than one ceremony we have encountered an individual among the group of clients who chooses not to complete the ritual. Paradoxically, their presence during the ceremony heightens immeasurably the significance of the event, for it highlights the courage of the others and reminds everyone of the strength of the obstacles to recovery.

Although these ceremonies can be effective when used only once, in several clinical situations we have used multiple ceremonies over time with increased benefit; the participants usually allow themselves even deeper levels of engagement because they know what to expect and have seen the results for themselves or in other families (Johnson, Feldman, Lubin, & Southwick, 1995).

THE USE OF THE SELF OF THE THERAPIST

These therapeutic ceremonies require the therapists to feel and express deep empathy with these families and to be aware of their own personal connection to these issues. This means that the therapists must be able to use their own related history and feelings in carrying out these ceremonies. Familiarity or experience in performative modes (such as teaching, public speaking, or acting) are helpful to therapists leading therapeutic ceremonies. The ceremony, as a product or crystallization of prior therapeutic work, is an enactment and therefore calls for an active stance on the part of the therapist that goes beyond the usual listening or reflecting stance. Practice is often required under the tutelage/modeling of therapists comfortable with this model.

EMPIRICAL SUPPORT

There are no direct empirical studies of these ceremonies. However, in one study of the entire PTSD treatment program for veterans (Johnson & Lubin, 1997), the veterans from 7 cohorts rated the ceremonies among the most beneficial of the 35 treatment components in the program. Family assessments also indicated very high ratings of these ceremonies (more than 85% rated them "very or extremely effective"). In an empirical study of our treatment program for traumatized women, significant decreases in PTSD and other psychiatric symptoms occurred among 6 cohorts of women following completion of the program and at 6-month follow-up (Lubin et al., 1998). The ceremonies were of course only one component of this program and were not designed to be complete treatments in themselves. Ceremonies are best understood as enhancing or facilitating the overall therapeutic process.

CONCLUSION

We believe that the judicious use of ceremonial formats in multiple-family therapy may enhance the therapeutic process by (a) increasing cognitive distance through externalizing the family problems, (b) engaging families in new more adaptive behaviors, and (c) heightening the significance of their struggle through the aesthetic and symbolic media as well as illuminating the larger social context of trauma. The structure intrinsic to ceremony offers containment for the emotional catharsis and interpersonal confrontation that accompany therapeutic change in families.

REFERENCES

Andersen, T. (1991). *The reflecting team: Dialogues and dialogues about the dialogues*. New York: W. W. Norton.

Andolfi, M., Angelo, C., Menghi, P., & Nicolo-Corigliano, A. (1983). *Behind the family mask: Therapeutic change in rigid family systems*. New York: Brunner/Mazel.

Bell, J. (1984). Family therapy in motion: Observing, assisting, and changing the family dance. In P. Bernstein (Ed.), *Theoretical approaches in dance–movement therapy* (pp. 23–41). Dubuque, IA: Kendall-Hunt.

Decuir, A. (1991). Trends in music and family therapy. *Arts in Psychotherapy, 18,* 195–199.

Figley, C. (1989). *Helping traumatized families.* San Francisco, CA: Jossey-Bass.

Goffman, E. (1971). *Relations in public: Microstudies of the public order.* New York: Basic Books.

Haley, J. (1976). *Problem-solving therapy.* San Francisco, CA: Jossey-Bass.

Harvey, S. (2000). Family dynamic play. In P. Lewis & D. Johnson (Eds.), *Current approaches in drama therapy* (pp. 379–412). Springfield, IL: Charles C Thomas.

Imber-Black, E., Roberts, J., & Whiting, R. (Eds.). (1988). *Rituals in families and family therapy.* New York: W. W. Norton.

Johnson, D. (1987). Therapeutic rituals in the nursing home. In S. Sandel & D. Johnson (Eds.), *Waiting at the gate: Creativity and hope in the nursing home* (pp. 151–172). New York: Haworth.

Johnson, D., Feldman, S., & Lubin, H. (1995). Critical interaction therapy: Couples therapy in post-traumatic stress disorder. *Family Process, 34,* 1–13.

Johnson, D., Feldman, S., Lubin, H., & Southwick, S. (1995). The use of ritual and ceremony in the treatment of post-traumatic stress disorder. *Journal of Traumatic Stress, 8,* 283–299.

Johnson, D., Feldman, S., Southwick, S., & Charney, D. (1994). The concept of the second generation program in the treatment of post-traumatic stress disorder among Vietnam veterans. *Journal of Traumatic Stress, 7,* 217–236.

Johnson, D., & Lubin, H. (1997). Treatment preferences of Vietnam veterans with posttraumatic stress disorder. *Journal of Traumatic Stress, 10,* 391–405.

Johnson, D., & Lubin, H. (2000). Group psychotherapy for the symptoms of post-traumatic stress disorder. In R. Klein & V. Schermer (Eds.), *Group psychotherapy for psychological trauma* (pp. 141–169). New York: Guilford.

Landgarten, H. B. (1987). *Family art psychotherapy.* New York: Brunner/Mazel.

Leveton, E. (1977). *Adolescent crisis: Approaches in family therapy.* New York: Springer.

Lubin, H., & Johnson, D. (1997). Group therapy for traumatized women. *International Journal of Group Psychotherapy, 47,* 271–290.

Lubin, H., & Johnson, D. (1998). Healing ceremonies. *Family Therapy Networker, 22,* 39–42.

Lubin, H., & Johnson, D. (2000). Interactive psychoeducational group therapy in the treatment of authority problems in combat-related posttraumatic stress disorder. *International Journal of Group Psychotherapy, 50,* 277–296.

Lubin, H., Loris, M., Burt, J., & Johnson, D. (1998). Efficacy of psychoeducational group therapy in reducing symptoms of posttraumatic stress disorder among multiply traumatized women. *American Journal of Psychiatry, 155,* 1172–1177.

Madanes, C. (1981). *Strategic family therapy.* San Francisco, CA: Jossey-Bass.

Minuchin, S. (1974). *Families and family therapy*. Cambridge, MA: Harvard University Press.

Obenchain, J., & Silver, S. (1992). Symbolic recognition: Ceremony in a treatment of posttraumatic stress disorder. *Journal of Traumatic Stress, 5*, 37–44.

Palazzoli, M., Cecchin, G., Prata, G., & Boscolo, L. (1978). *Paradox and counterparadox*. New York: Jason Aronson.

Rosenheck, R., & Thomson, J. (1986). Detoxification of Vietnam war trauma: A combined family–individual approach. *Family Process, 25*, 559–569.

Satir, V. (1967). *Conjoint family therapy*. Palo Alto, CA: Science & Behavior Books.

Scheff, T. (1979). *Catharsis in healing, ritual, and drama*. Berkeley: University of California Press.

Silver, S., & Wilson, J. (1988). Native American healing and purification rituals for war stress. In J. Wilson, Z. Harel, & B. Kahana (Eds.), *Human adaptation to extreme stress* (pp. 337–356). New York: Plenum Press.

White, M., & Epston, D. (1990). *Narrative means to therapeutic ends*. New York: W. W. Norton.

Williams, A. (1989). *The passionate technique: Strategic psychodrama with individuals, families, and groups*. London: Routledge.

II

ACTION METHODS IN
GROUP THERAPY

INTRODUCTION:
ACTION METHODS
IN GROUP THERAPY

Although action methods have filtered in and out of group psychotherapy since its inception in the 1930s, various traditions and methods of
group therapy differ with respect to whether action methods are central or
peripheral to the treatment. Two group therapy pioneers, S. R. Slavson and
J. L. Moreno, each used action in a major way. Slavson invented the *activity
group* for children in which games, food, and art materials are used to achieve
the therapeutic aims of authentic and spontaneous expression (Scheidlinger,
1993, pp. 2–10). Beginning in the 1920s, Moreno developed *psychodrama*, a
complex method of group therapy involving many forms of action including
sociometric exercises (which use movement) and dramatic enactment (Nicholas, 1984).

Some of the group therapies in the humanistic psychology tradition
(Rogerian; Rogers, 1967; gestalt; Greve, 1993; transactional analysis; Berne,
1961; and sensitivity and encounter groups; Rogers, 1967), emerging and
peaking in popularity in the 1960s and 1970s, used action mostly as a warm-

---

This introduction was prepared by Mary Nicholas, PhD.

up to verbal psychotherapy. Structured action exercises, such as those involving singing, movement and dancing, touching, walking blindfolded with a sighted partner, and hitting pillows, would build interest and connection within the group which, once "warmed up," would usually move into and stay in verbal interaction. Although the warm-ups were crucial and might well be what people would remember most about the session once it was over, verbal interaction was usually considered the "real therapy."

During that same era, among a visible faction of group therapists, emotional catharsis, earlier discarded by psychoanalysis, again came to be seen as essential to effective psychotherapy. For these therapists action methods became paramount. Primal-scream groups reenacted the birth trauma with accompanying shrieks, kicks, and thrashes (Janov, 1970). Encounter group members were encouraged to stand up and really scream at each other and at people outside the group perceived to have caused them pain (Rogers, 1967). The *battaca*, a cloth or foam bat with which group members could beat a pillow stand-in for an offending person in their lives, was considered a staple in many group rooms. Hugs and physical holding were frequently used in the group to enhance the individual's ability to "let go." Bioenergetics groups, devised by Alexander Lowen out of the methods of Wilhelm Reich (Lowen, 1971), and a later offshoot, core energetics (Pierakos, 1987), relied almost solely on physical exercises designed to liberate sexual and aggressive energies considered to be trapped in neurotically based bodily tension. Also in psychodrama during this period, emotional purging through physical activities was considered valuable, whereas in periods before and after the 1960s and 1970s, the psychodramatic catharsis might be more subtle and less physical.

In contemporary cognitive–behavioral group treatment, where the emphasis is on changing clients' thinking and behavior through cognitive restructuring primarily through verbal interventions, in vivo homework assignments involving action exercises are occasionally used (Rose, 1993).

Since their inception in the 1950s, practitioners of the creative arts approaches (music, art, drama, and dance–movement therapies) have each continued to use their distinctive action methods as a central part of their group therapy work, whatever their theoretical orientations. The cases featured in this part are representative of the diversity of these creative arts therapies and well illustrate the diversity and centrality of the action methods used.

REFERENCES

Berne, E. (1961). *Transactional analysis in psychotherapy*. New York: Grove Press.

Greve, D. (1993). Gestalt group psychotherapy. In H. Kaplan & B. Sadock (Eds.), *Comprehensive group psychotherapy* (pp. 228–235). Baltimore, MD: Williams & Wilkins.

Janov, A. (1970). *The primal scream*. New York: G. P. Putnam.

Lowen, A. (1971). *The language of the body*. New York: Collier Books. (Original work published 1958)

Nicholas, M. W. (1984). *Change in the context of group therapy*. New York: Brunner/Mazel.

Pierakos, J. C. (1987). *Core energetics: Developing the capacity to love and heal*. Mendocino, CA: LifeRhythm.

Rogers, C. R. (1967). The process of the basic encounter group. In J. F. Bugenthal (Ed.), *Challenges of humanistic psychology* (pp. 261–276). New York: McGraw-Hill.

Rose, S. (1993). Cognitive–behavioral group psychotherapy. In H. Kaplan & B. Sadock (Eds.), *Comprehensive group psychotherapy* (pp. 205–214). Baltimore, MD: Williams & Wilkins.

Scheidlinger, S. (1993). History of group psychotherapy. In H. Kaplan & B. Sadock (Eds.), *Comprehensive group psychotherapy* (pp. 2–10). Baltimore, MD: Williams & Wilkins.

4

REHEARSALS FOR GROWTH APPLIED TO SUBSTANCE ABUSE GROUPS

CHARLOTTE A. RAMSEUR AND DANIEL J. WIENER

Editors' Introduction: Rehearsals for Growth (RfG) focuses on enhancing clients' spontaneity and creativity and expanding their role repertoires by means of improvisational enactments. The method is founded on the recognition that successful life performance requires adequate role and relationship development. The therapist's challenge in using RfG with substance abuse recovery groups lies in the creation of a playful, encouraging, nonjudgmental milieu that fosters the group safety, cohesion, and support necessary to promote individual engagement, motivation, and dramatic exploration of unfamiliar roles and responses. Nurturing leadership, playfulness, affirmation, and flexibility are essential components of the RfG therapist's role in working with this population.

In this chapter we discuss the benefits of Rehearsals for Growth (RfG), Daniel J. Wiener's own adaptation and application of improvisational theater techniques to relationship training, in fostering the development of skills critical to developing and maintaining a sober lifestyle. RfG games and exercises are used here to build group trust and cohesion, foster interdependence, and enhance group members' confidence in using their spontaneity and creativity to successfully and adaptively meet life demands. We draw on both traditional and revised methods of dramatic role development to equip those recovering from substance abuse problems with the roles and responses to meet the challenges of sober living, contending that few distinctions exist between life performances and theater roles.

FUNDAMENTALS OF RfG

RfG is the use in therapy of theatrical tasks, applied to social skills training and both the assessment of and intervention in relationship difficulties. These tasks take the form of staged enactments: intentional, voluntary activities in which the therapist instructs clients to perform tasks that are partly structured yet require some improvisation. The social context of RfG enactment is that of a theatrical performance, with performing clients ("players") in an area of the room designated as a stage and nonperforming clients and the therapist physically set apart as an audience. The emotional tone of RfG enactment is generally playful; the objective is revelation of habitual patterns and exploration of novel possibilities, not mastery of performance skills.

RfG *exercises* feature unusual performance rules and conditions for clients being themselves (nondramatic enactment), while RfG *games* add the dimension of pretense through clients playing characters other than themselves (dramatic enactment). Literally hundreds of distinct RfG tasks have been developed and used in therapy, and new forms and variations are devised continually. RfG exercises described in this chapter are "Mirrors," "Presents," and "Address the Telephone"; an RfG game described here is "Poet's Corner." As action methods, RfG tasks cannot as easily be manipulated as verbal discourse may be in psychotherapy; exercises require demonstrated cooperation with others to be accomplished successfully, while games elicit spontaneous responses within fictional scenarios.

More important to the effectiveness of RfG than the form of the tasks is the playful, nonjudgmental atmosphere created through group support of performances, which encourages client exploration of imagination, fantasy, and spontaneity. The fundamental rule of improvisation is "to accept all offers," meaning that all players on-stage accept the premise of whatever is cocreated by themselves and other players. Enactment of RfG games and exercises teaches cooperation with and validation of others and greater acceptance of one's spontaneous imagination and lessens performance anxiety.

Because the form of theatrical improvising used in RfG both relies on and develops relationship skills, RfG group therapy offers clients vivid experiences of affirmation, support, and prosocial playful interaction. These benefits fit well with the goals of more recently developed group approaches to substance abuse therapy, notably motivational enhancement therapy (Miller & Heather, 1986) and the stages-of-change transtheoretical model (Velasquez, Crouch, Maurer, & DiClemente, 2001). As noted by Rollnick and Miller (1995), "Readiness to change is not a current trait, but a fluctuating product of interpersonal interaction" (p. 327).

USING ACTION METHODS IN THE TREATMENT OF CLIENTS WITH SUBSTANCE ABUSE PROBLEMS

Mood disorders (notably depression and anxiety) are an endemic feature of clients who have been through detoxification (Regier et al., 1990) and are widely acknowledged as a major contributing factor in clients' recidivism. Indeed, treating substance abuse in dually diagnosed clients without attending to their accompanying affective disorders typically results in minimal lasting improvement (Grinspoon, 1991).

Evidence exists that the mood of depressed clients with substance abuse problems can be raised by physical activity (Thoren, Floras, Hoffmann, & Seals, 1990) as well as by laughter and humor (Lefcort, 1990). Action methods such as RfG are particularly well-suited to promoting activity, laughter, and humor. Encouraging indiscriminate emotional expressiveness in therapy with clients with substance abuse problems appears problematic to us, however. Because these clients have become accustomed to experiencing emotional expressiveness only when "high," they have little capacity to access this state without the use of these substances. Consequently, in recovery they lack confidence in their capacity to access emotional expressiveness and fear that to do so would risk losing self-control, leading back to relapse.

Another generalized viewpoint applied to the understanding of clients with substance abuse problems focuses on how their psychological dynamics may be counteracted by dramatic enactment. According to Moffett and Bruto (1990),

> Chronic substance abusers cope by using immature defenses (i.e., denial, projection, and acting out). These immature behaviors interfere with learning from social experience and with effective participation in conventional psychotherapies. Dramatic methods of therapy . . . offer specific advantages for the actors and the audience. Role-playing invites the immature person to project and act out in nondefensive interaction with others. The actors can tolerate exposing their problematic behaviors through roles because such behavior can be disowned (i.e., denied in oneself and projected onto the dramatic role). Similarly, the audience can engage in personal issues from a safe theatrical distance rather than completely avoiding their problems by denial or acting out. (pp. 346–347)

We believe that dramatic enactment empowers expressive behavior through which clients may create and explore healthy alternatives to their real-life roles. It should be noted that the above-mentioned advantages conferred by dramatic role-playing are not confined to clients using immature defenses.

A fundamental limitation of conventional talk psychotherapy, especially in working with clients with substance abuse problems, is that it elicits discourse that cannot be relied on as truthful. To a greater degree than with other clinical populations (except psychopaths), speech is used by these clients to deceive, persuade, and manipulate others in the service of perpetuating their abuse of drugs. Action methods call forth the use of other-than-verbal channels of communication, notably bodily posture, gestures, and movement, through which clients find it considerably harder to deceive others. As noted by Duhl (1999) when describing a client's realization after completing an action method, "The body in action did not lie" (p. 88). Furthermore, performed incongruity among the verbal content, vocal tone, and bodily movement readily reveals insincerity, defensiveness, and deception.

CASE EXAMPLE

Program Description

This chapter describes an action-based psychotherapy group (the RfG Group) in existence for two years as part of a voluntary acute treatment program for adults with substance abuse problems. The purpose of the program is to treat recently detoxed clients in an outpatient, homelike setting. The goal is to help clients maintain sobriety. The client population is approximately 75% men and 25% women; ranges in age from 18 to 60 years; and is nondiscriminatory regarding legal history, educational background, occupation, socioeconomic status, religion, and ethnicity. Their common link is an inability to control their alcohol and drug use, resulting in a lifestyle of loss, pain, and self-destruction. Many clients have been abusing multiple drugs or have a concurrent mental disorder.

Clients enter this program directly following inpatient detox programs at various facilities, entering on any day that the program is in operation and graduating on completion of 18 consecutive days of participation in treatment. Seventy-two percent complete the entire program; of those who leave, approximately two thirds do so in their first week, mainly over the first weekend. At any given time there are 6 to 20 clients active in the program. These clients typically attend 4 to 6 sessions of the RfG group and 48 to 51 sessions of the "talk therapy" groups. Individual talk therapy sessions are also scheduled with each client weekly. Some members (about 20%) are lost due to substance abuse relapse, which renders them ineligible for this outpatient program and suggests that an inpatient program may be more suitable for them. Others (about 8%) drop out or are referred elsewhere because of their more severe mental health needs.

The program offers intensive psychotherapy to clients and psychoeducation and support groups for their significant others. Clinical services to clients are provided primarily by two full-time alcohol and drug counselors who offer individual and group talk therapy. Per diem clinicians also assist when needed. One verbal therapy group provides social support for the addicted clients as well as psychoeducation concerning drug abuse, addiction, and changing behaviors and lifestyle. Another group teaches clients about their relationships with families and friends in recovery, while a separate family support group meets weekly to help the families and friends through the clients' recovery. Clients and their families are also offered couples and family therapy at their request. Following completion of the program, clients are invited to attend an aftercare group; about half use this resource.

The 1-hour RfG therapy groups featured in this chapter aim to increase the percentage of clients completing the program, to impart social skills, and to broaden affective range. RfG groups are open-ended and are typically attended 4 to 6 times by clients. The membership of any given session is likely to be about one fourth to one third first-time members and two thirds to three fourths "veterans."

RfG Group Design

Clients come to the RfG Group accustomed to the predominantly talk therapy format that characterizes the rest of the program. Their unfamiliarity with action methods initially renders some members timid and defensive when RfG enactments are introduced. Some clients flatly refuse to participate, saying that the performance aspects of these enactments remind them of oral reports in high school, during which they were required to stand up in front of the class to make presentations. Some have shared that they skipped school on those days or refused their teachers' requests to participate. However, these clients are keenly interested in how to have fun without abusing substances, so the offering of these enactments intrigues them. When reassured that no one will force them to do anything and that they are only invited to participate, they relax a little. Furthermore, when the feelings and memories of their negative experiences around performing in front of people are shown respect, clients seem to relax further and become more willing to participate. By the time clients graduate from the program, most voluntarily engage in RfG games and exercises.

The main action interventions used with the substance abuse recovery groups described in this chapter are those of RfG, supplemented by some techniques developed by Virginia Satir (Satir, Banmen, Gerber, & Gemori, 1991) and Renee Emunah (1994). Music is also used, as described later in the chapter.

Format, Rules, and Constraints

The RfG Group setting consists of a 14-by-16-foot carpeted room in which the clients are seated in a semicircle. Open space at the front of the room serves as the stage on which most performances take place. The atmosphere is kept playful and relaxed; group applause is given to show appreciation and support for each member's performance. In sharp contrast to the rigidly enforced and explicit ground rules of the verbal psychotherapy groups in the program (which are normative for much of substance abuse counseling), rules for the RfG Group are kept to a minimum to encourage freedom of expression. The primary rule is to keep yourself and others safe by using movement within your physical abilities and limitations. Group members are invited, not forced, to participate and assured that there is no preconceived right or wrong way to perform—only their way matters.

Note that the fundamental rule of improvisation, namely, to accept all offers, is deliberately omitted, as it is more important that members of these groups first experience the freeing effects of spontaneous play than that they consciously align their performances with those of others.

Instructions are given at the beginning of each game or exercise.

At times, the room size becomes a constraint (especially when the group size exceeds 12), making it difficult for members to move freely when performing some RfG enactments. The frequency of group members leaving and new members joining requires that the therapist restate some instructions frequently. It helps that veteran members often assist new members by reassuring them and sharing their positive experiences. Moreover, the willingness of veteran members to volunteer to perform enactments facilitates new member participation.

The open enrollment of the program also makes it difficult to evaluate groups as a whole from start to finish. Varying the exercises used so that the veteran members do not get bored is key to holding the clients' interest and investment in such groups that frequently change their membership. The 1-hour time frame for some of the groups limits the number of enactments that can be performed with a large group. As with any therapeutic group, it is sometimes necessary for the therapist to abandon planned interventions and accommodate responses and issues that emerge during the group.

To keep the atmosphere upbeat and to encourage play, the RfG therapist needs to remain constantly aware of his or her own affective state. Resistances activated in some group members require that the therapist be "in Self" (described further in the following section) to maintain flexibility and avoid getting caught in transference and countertransference issues. In our approach, the use of internal family systems therapy (IFS; Schwartz, 1995) language and techniques, described further below, works well in maintaining such maneuverability.

Using IFS in RfG Groups

The IFS therapy philosophy conceptualizes human personality as comprised of an internal system of parts (subpersonalities; Schwartz, 1995). These parts carry the memories, feelings, and emotional burdens taken on by individuals as a consequence of their interaction with the external world. When these parts are optimally organized under the leadership of a part called "the Self," they function in balance and harmony to take care of the individual.

When, however, parts become polarized (i.e., oppose one another), they do not trust the Self to lead; the internal system, under the leadership of these parts, then exhibits constrained organization and dysfunction. The experiential techniques of IFS therapy help the therapist not only to access and restore inner harmony of parts and Self-leadership in clients but also to stay experientially in Self and to avoid the pitfalls of countertransferences that are often encountered in groups.

IFS language is respectful and invitational, directing clients' attention to differentiate substance-abusing parts from the totality of their being. IFS technique allows clients to separate out their constrained parts, access the positive qualities of their other parts, and connect to the Self. The IFS language provides a frame for group members to connect to Self and either reassure or confront their scared parts so that these parts willingly step back and relax to allow the person's Self to play. Together with the RfG practice of inviting clients to participate in their own way, members are afforded the psychological safety needed for effective group participation.

Five Group Members

We have altered the identities of the 5 members featured in the case description that follows.

- Barbara, age 28 and a postal worker, is the only daughter and the youngest of two children. Like her father, Barbara is an addict, whose drugs of choice are alcohol and cocaine. She started using drugs as a teenager. She describes feelings of being unloved and feelings of emotional and physical abandonment while growing up. She says that her father was continually in and out of alcohol treatment. Rather than attend Al-Anon group, her mother spent much of her time at Alcoholics Anonymous meetings and inpatient couples therapy sessions with her father while her brother baby-sat her. She says that her friends, also drug users, make her feel loved and accepted. Her continued drug use threatens both her marriage and her job.
- Timothy, age 41 and a sales manager, always comes to group well-dressed yet casual in style. He is the elder of two boys who grew up living with an alcoholic mother. Like his mother, he, too, is an alcoholic who also uses Percocet. He describes himself as a perfectionist who tried to cover up for his mother's problem. Clinicians from the talk groups report that other group members there accuse Timothy of being phony. His addiction has already destroyed his marriage and now threatens his current job.
- Jarid, age 32 and a construction worker, was introduced to drugs as a teenager by older musicians whom he and his friends hung

around. His drugs of choice are marijuana and cocaine. He has also tried heroin. Jarid projects a tough-guy image, driving a motorcycle and dressing in a black leather jacket and heavy black military-style boots. Incongruously, his face is reminiscent of a young boy's. He has had difficulty with female relationships because of his substance-abusing lifestyle and entered the program when a court mandated him to do so after a conviction for driving under the influence.

- Bob, age 29 and unemployed, was diagnosed with attention deficit disorder as a child. He recalls being laughed at and called names by the other children. His parents negated his ideas and suggestions, and he grew up feeling devalued. His drugs of choice are marijuana and pain pills. He started using drugs because they helped him to forget his feelings of shame and gave him some "friends" among other clients with substance abuse problems. Bob tries to please people and says that he has difficulty saying "no." His lifestyle has also led to problems in his recent marriage.

- Ann, age 21 and a college student, is the eldest of four siblings and has a history of sexual abuse by her stepfather. She started using drugs at age 14 to numb her painful feelings. Because she knew how hard it had been for her mother to make ends meet before marrying Ann's stepfather, Ann was afraid of what would happen to the family if she revealed her secret. She recalls some unpleasant memories during childhood. Ann's drugs of choice are alcohol, marijuana and, infrequently, cocaine.

Case Presentation

The following examples illustrate the combined use of IFS verbal therapy with RfG. When offered the Mirrors exercise (described below), Barbara vowed that she would not perform in front of others. Using IFS language and techniques, the therapist thanked her for sharing the feelings of this part with the group and then asked her, "Is there more that any of your parts want us to know?" "I have never performed in front of people, even when it was required of me in 7th grade," Barbara said. The therapist then asked Barbara to let her parts know that they would not be forced to do anything that they did not want to do.

The use of IFS parts language is a verbal intervention that helps clients to distance fears by attaching these to their parts, thus reassuring them that it is not their entire being but a part or parts that carry the fear. Such language also has a reassuring effect on the rest of the group members, as they start to think about their own feelings as located in parts, simultaneously evoking group compassion, respect for individual members, and liberating all members from fears that can constrain play. Note that the therapist does not ordinarily speak directly with a part but asks the client's Self to mediate, assisting clients to come back into Self-leadership.

Barbara's Self was then invited to ask her parts, when they felt safe enough, to step back and allow her to participate in her own way. The group applauded her for her willingness to share her feelings.

Freedom of choice to participate in RfG games is important. Unlike some life experiences with harsh consequences for nonparticipatory behavior, RfG games are offered in an invitational spirit of play without coercion to participate. Hence, clients experience participation as a choice. Isomorphically, the therapist accepts the offer of the client to make his or her own choice. In doing so, emotional constraints to participation are usually lifted, which allows and encourages the client to play.

Mae, a group member who was present in a previous group session, then shared with Barbara that she, too, was apprehensive when she first performed Mirrors. Said Mae, "I actually enjoyed the experience. I will be your partner if you want."

Peer testimonial also aids in removing emotional constraints for players.

The therapist then invited any other group members who felt uncomfortable about doing any games or exercises to express themselves, adding, "There is no right or wrong way to participate as long as you are safe. No one is going to criticize your performance." Bob raised his hand and talked about a part of him that felt afraid to perform in front of people for fear of people laughing at him and calling him an idiot, like they did in elementary school. He said, "I have attention deficit disorder and have experienced a lifetime of ridicule. Even my mother laughs at me." As with Barbara, Bob was thanked for sharing the feelings of his parts and invited to stay in touch with these parts; when they felt safe he was invited to ask them to step back and allow him to participate in his own way. Another group member, Mary, said, "Me, too, I have a part like that." Again, the group applauded Bob and Mary for their courage in revealing their parts' feelings.

It was apparent to the therapist at this point that several group members had activated apprehensive parts. To soothe these parts the therapist took the group through a guided-imagery walk using recorded music of ocean sounds as background. After this exercise, the group was open to trying Mirrors and other RfG exercises.

RfG Interventions

To illustrate the action methods used in our groups, we present some examples of warm-ups and RfG techniques, followed by some examples of how they were used with the five members.

Warm-Up Exercises

Warm-up exercises play an essential part in creating a climate of safety and mutual support for participation in RfG groups. Such enactments are kept simple by using low-risk performances yet are still sufficiently powerful to help free polarized parts of those group members who may not respond to traditional talk therapy.

The developmental level of a group, which determines the optimal complexity of warm-up exercises, may be assessed through observation of group energy and cohesion (Johnson, 1991) when a task is given. As a general rule, the therapist proceeds from the simpler to the more complex, pacing the progression to the group mean. The warm-up chosen can also depend on such factors as the space available, group size, physical limitations of the group, time allotted to the group, readiness of the group to participate, and the familiarity of the group with RfG and other action activities.

Warm-up exercises can be started in any area of the group room. For example, the therapist can start by inviting members to participate while in their seats as the audience. This is especially useful when a large proportion of members are attending for the first time, when certain members of the group are actively resistant, or when some are physically challenged.

One warm-up is to pass an object around the audience and invite group members to respond to it as they handle it (a variation is to pass around multiple objects). As each member completes his response, the group-as-audience applauds. For example, when bongo drums were passed around, Bill, Timothy, and Jarid each played a solo of near-professional quality. The music from the drums really enlivened the group as they learned about the hidden talents in their midst; roaring applause greeted each person's performance.

Although the therapist was concerned that some group members who were not skilled at playing the drums might feel intimidated, the fact that all were loudly applauded by the group, regardless of their level of skill, minimized this risk. Applause shows appreciation, which raises the performer's self-esteem and also signals the end of the performance, setting the stage for the next enactment. It is likely that some members only participated in later exercises because of the positive self-esteem and improved status level generated during the warm-up exercises. Clients with substance abuse problems often talk about their lowered self-esteem and sense of powerlessness present from an early age, which may have become one of their triggers to abusing a mind- or mood-altering substance. It has been demonstrated that when people feel appreciated, even for little things, their status is raised, and they become motivated to willingly give even more of themselves.

Moving to another level of play, clients can be instructed to mime the passing around of an imaginary object, first to be received in the form it was given and then transformed to something different as it is passed on. This activity focuses the attention of other members-as-audience, whose imaginations are activated in guessing what the transformation does. Yet another variation of this warm-up has clients vary their emotional expression when receiving the imaginary object as it is passed to them.

Another warm-up exercise is to invite group members to leave their seats and greet an object (or objects) in another part of the room. For example, the therapist may invite the member to address a chair, a wall, a door, the chalk board, and so forth. Progressing further toward projection and fantasy, the therapist can also place a hat in the center of the room and invite group members to pull out whatever they wish from the hat. Members can then be asked to either explain what they pulled out or to present it in mime and have the audience guess what it is. This exercise often evokes individualized and creative expressions of self in relation to the object and activates members' performance roles of actor and audience.

Warm-up exercises may use music to help release group inhibitions and encourage members to participate. Music can be selected to set a tranquil mood or create an upbeat, energized feeling. Adding internal mental imagery or external physical movement to the music is also powerful in stimulating group participation and response. Guided mental imagery set to music is especially useful in helping group members get in touch with their internal parts and to start speaking for these parts to the group.

This exercise serves to assist the individual in focusing on the parts that do not feel safe and that need to be reassured that the individual will not be harmed. Once a member's fearful, hostile, anxious, or depressed parts feel safe enough to step back and allow the client to participate, he or she can experience self and others in new ways that lead to genuine self-expression, change, and growth.

Music used as an accompaniment to physical movement can awaken the senses. Movement may start in the member's seat and progress to moving around the room, or it may start from a standing position in the middle of the floor. Recorded music may be played and group members then invited to move like their favorite animal or to mimic the movement of a mechanical object. Members may be invited to move their bodies to the music starting with their heads and progressing down to their feet. Movement to music is more successful when the therapist selects music that is appropriate to the age, culture, and interests of the group. The therapist should also take care to select music that is appropriate to the movement exercise that will be used. For example, guided imagery requires a slow tempo, relaxation-type of music. Stretching to music may be facilitated with jazz and other upbeat music.

Music is a universal language that helps the therapist and group to develop cohesion. It serves to lift the spirit of depressed group members and to calm members experiencing anxiety. Movement helps to awaken the senses and the body to play. Music serves to add a different dimension to movement groups, although movement can also be done without music. Movement has been linked to raising endorphin levels, elevating mood (Thoren et al., 1990). Movement combined with laughter (often evoked during RfG enactments) has a potent freeing effect that promotes sharing and risk-taking.

Because of the limitation of room size, nonmovement warm-up exercises are used in the group as well. In one such verbal warm-up, used to raise both self-esteem (the regard in which a person holds himself or herself) and status level (the regard in which others hold a person), members are first invited to name one personal characteristic that they like about themselves and hope to never lose. Next, members name one characteristic that they like about the person sitting to their right that they hope never changes. This, too, is a powerful joining tool and helps to create a safe environment that promotes risk-taking. A variation of this game can involve group members identifying a trait that they do not like about themselves and want to change, followed by a statement of a trait that they do like and hope never to change. The therapist can use this information to decide which RfG exercises would be most helpful to use next.

In selecting the warm-up exercise to be used, the therapist should be listening for themes that may be beneficial to explore, using RfG or other action methods to address the issues elicited during the warm-up.

Another way used to select warm-up exercises is to consult with the clinicians who conduct the talk groups, who share the prevailing themes, moods, emotions, and issues in their work with clients. For example, in one group dealing with issues around loss, the therapist opened the RfG Group by inviting members to use the chalkboard to illustrate a personal loss. The drawings ranged from concrete representations to written words and abstract drawings. The members' drawings were processed by the entire group, which supported and applauded their willingness to share. Another group issue centered around trust. Here, group members were invited to create and enact a scene in which, as themselves, they confessed the truth to another member standing in for someone they had deceived or with whom they had not been fully honest. This exercise, "True Confession," is used both as a group warm-up and as an intervention when circumstances warrant.

This exercise has proven to be moving both for those who enact it as well as those who remain in the audience. As people share their confessions to a pretend friend or relative, their sharing often prompts others to reveal their own secrets. RfG exercises may evoke open and voluntary expressions of personal situations when the enactments address sensitive issues. This type of unburdening in a safe environment frequently brings about cathartic responses from the confessor, the actor member receiving the confession, and audience members.

As noted earlier, clients who are recovering from substance abuse problems often have difficulty being emotionally expressive because they associate such expressiveness exclusively with the "high" state. In another warm-up, "Altered States," volunteers are invited onstage to act out the same brief scene in two contrasting ways, as their "abuser selves" and as their "sober selves." Those enacting Altered States readily display expressiveness as the abuser self, despite their being substance-free when acting. This enactment leads the group to fruitful discussion centered around the question, "What does your sober self need, *besides* drugs or alcohol, to get in touch with your fun-loving, expressive self?"

The evidence of clients' ability to behave in an emotionally expressive way while substance-free counteracts their belief that drugs are necessary for the enjoyment of life. Note, too, that the progression of warm-ups from concrete to abstract representation, from realistic to fantastic enactment, and from portraying one's conventional social self to playing characters rapidly disinhibits group members and facilitates their exploration of nonhabitual actions, thoughts, and feelings.

Mirrors

Mirrors, a frequently used RfG exercise (Wiener, 1994, p. 69), provides an opportunity for players to connect and to support each other by accepting their partner's offer to play. Players in pairs stand 4 to 5 feet apart facing each other; one is designated the leader and the other, the follower. Players maintain silence while they move continuously only from the waist up (due to space constraints), with the leader initiating movement that is mirrored by the follower. After about 20 seconds, the therapist calls "Switch!" signaling that the players are to exchange roles. The players switch three more times at about 20-second intervals. Finally, the therapist calls "Mutual!" signaling players to continue simultaneous movement without a leader or follower. In variations of this game players are invited to combine mirrored or nonmirrored movement with verbal expressions of appreciation and acceptance for the partner's offer. This exercise allows each player any range of imaginative responses that they can choose to use in support of their partner's offers. Note that, as an RfG exercise, players of Mirrors are not instructed to assume dramatic (i.e., non-Self) roles, although members occasionally report doing so during postenactment verbal processing.

Even strangers can connect readily and intimately without spoken words through the shared, coordinated movement of this exercise. Mirrors has great impact because the players take the risk of being present and taking turns sharing control with one another. Participants invariably learn something about themselves and their partners as they play the game. Intimacy is both built and tested through the sustained eye contact between partners while moving. Comfort levels with reciprocal roles are also developed and tested as each player alternates turns as the leader and the follower.

In mutuality of movement without an assigned leader or follower, attentiveness and intimacy are heightened. As with RfG enactments in general, in Mirrors the willingness to enter into play leads members to experience the similarity between pretense and real life.

Contraindications for using this game would be the inability of the group members to sustain movement because of physical or visual limitations. A game of "Verbal Mirrors" (Wiener, 1994, p. 70) using simultaneous speech would then be more appropriate. Also, members who are in crisis around physical or sexual abuse issues might find it difficult to play this game due to intimacy and trust issues associated with relinquishing control to a partner.

Barbara and Mae were partners during a Mirrors exercise. They started out slowly at first, with Mae as the leader. After they switched roles and Barbara became the leader they assumed an amazing flow of synchronized and symmetrical movement. During the mutuality phase of the exercise they focused on one another so intently that they were oblivious both to their surroundings and the announcement that the exercise had ended. The rest of the group stood and watched Barbara and Mae, applauding them when they finally stopped. The partners looked somewhat embarrassed yet pleased with their performance, reporting how good it had felt. When asked if they preferred the role of leader, follower, or partner in mutuality, Barbara said, "At first, I was a little nervous. But I felt more and more comfortable as Mae and I moved together, almost without effort." Mae replied, "I remember the first time that I did this exercise. It was fine, but not as smooth. I think that I was less afraid this time, so I didn't hold back." The group applauded again.

The outcome and quality of experience when performing Mirrors varies with one's partner. Mae achieved sustained mutuality with Barbara that she had not previously experienced with three other members. Yet, in Barbara's first time of playing Mirrors, she experienced sustained mutuality.

Barbara's risk-taking overcame her fear of performing in front of others, strengthened her self-confidence, and increased both her level of trust and willingness to let go of control.

Timothy and Evelyn were present in another group that performed the Mirrors exercise. Evelyn had previously shared with the group that she has a part that is a "people-pleaser." Said Evelyn, "I try to keep everyone in my family happy by giving them what they want. I do this because I want my family to value me and to not argue. Even if I am unhappy doing something that they request, I still do it to keep peace. No one seems to care if I am happy, though." When asked what makes her happy, Evelyn said, "I am so busy pleasing others that I don't know what really makes *me* happy." When invited to play Mirrors to see how her role in her family corresponds to the role that she plays with others outside of the family, Evelyn accepted; Timothy volunteered to play her partner. Evelyn visibly struggled in leading her partner. When Timothy became the leader, Evelyn seemed more at ease. During the mutuality phase they struggled until Timothy took the leadership role. In processing the experience, Evelyn said that she was uncomfortable as the leader because she felt inadequate in pleasing Timothy. "If I knew what he liked," she continued, "I would have known how to move to make him happy. I liked being the follower because I felt that if I just moved as he did, he would be pleased. I did not worry as much about how to please him because he showed me." When asked about the mutual movement phase she said, "The mutuality was difficult for me. I still wanted him to be the leader so that I did not have to worry about not pleasing him. I guess that I try to please everyone and not myself." The therapist said, "Now that you know how pleasing others affects you, Evelyn, can you give yourself permission to please yourself?" Evelyn said, "I'll try to work on this." This led to an intense group discussion on the issues of assertiveness and cooperation in relationships.

Timothy showed how flexible he could be in leading and following, accepting a leadership role that was thrust on him by a partner who did not want to lead. He shared how this experience paralleled his life growing up with an underfunctioning alcoholic mother.

During another Mirrors exercise, Ann in the role of follower looked away frequently and had difficulty following Jarid. As the leader, Ann continued to avoid eye contact with Jarid, who struggled to follow her. During the mutuality phase, Jarid quickly took the leadership role as Ann followed with inconsistent eye contact. During the sharing, Jarid said, "I didn't like following because I like being the leader in everything." Ann, looking down at the floor, replied, "It didn't feel comfortable looking into his eyes. I've had difficulty with intimacy ever since being molested as a child by my stepfather."

The intimacy developed and shared in this game can be threatening for some clients, particularly those who have been abused. It is advisable to know some history of your participants and to make it safe for them to not participate or to even stop if it becomes too uncomfortable for them.

Mirrors offers clients an opportunity to learn about themselves and others. It not only reacquaints them with their anticipated preference for leading or following but also offers them the opportunity to develop an unfamiliar experience of mutuality in which the players, if properly aligned, can feel their movement as one person.

Poet's Corner

In the RfG game Poet's Corner, two players accept the offer to cocreate a new reality as they share in the presentation of an original poem. One player pretends to be a poet from a faraway land, reciting his poem in his native tongue by using gibberish (nonsense speech) while making broad, frequent gestures and varying vocal inflection. The other player takes the dual role of introducer of the poet to the audience and poem translator. The nonperforming members take the role of audience at a poetry reading; because audience members do not understand the poet's language, their comprehension relies both on the "translation" and the inflection and gestures of the poet.

As with other RfG games, the directions offer enough structure for the players to understand how to play the scene yet provide sufficient flexibility for them to exercise autonomy to play the way they each choose. While players of Poet's Corner may create a credible scene without attending closely to one another, far more satisfying results occur when the translator matches his translation to the gestures and inflections of the poet, and the poet, in turn, matches gestures and inflections to the content of the translation. Also in common with other RfG games and exercises, there is inherent risk in allowing one's Self to venture into the unknown. The essence of improvisation is spontaneity, the adventure undertaken when one is unable to anticipate (and hence plan for) the immediate future. One potential therapeutic benefit of improvisation is that habitual patterns of behavior are more readily put aside when encountering the unexpected. The trust developed among group members helps to create a sense of safety in this challenge. In IFS terms, this trusting, supportive climate seems to lessen the inhibitions of frightened parts while encouraging the curiosity of risk-taker parts.

Bob and Steve volunteered to play Poet's Corner in their third RfG group together. They had developed a close relationship during the time that they were in the substance abuse program. Steve was quiet and rarely spoke during talk groups.

It is so common for clients with substance abuse problems in detox treatment to experience depressed mood that they are often given antidepressants in anticipation of their having depressive symptoms. Steve's frequent relapses seemed to find him more and more depressed. It seemed likely that he had a comorbidity of depression that acted as a trigger for his substance abuse. He often sat staring at the floor, looking sad, and usually led with a seemingly depressed part that rarely talked. When addressed, Steve gave short, one-word answers that at times were barely audible.

Bob presented at first as a little shy but showed a good sense of humor once oriented to the group. Bob was one of the few members with whom Steve seemed comfortable enough to take a risk. Surprisingly, Steve agreed to be the Poet after Bob volunteered to play the translator. After the audience chose the poet's name (Baba Choo) and his homeland (Mars), Bob introduced Steve. Rolling a toothpick around in his mouth, Steve smiled as he looked toward Bob and recited the first lines of his poem in gibberish with minimal tonal variety and no gestures. Looking back over his shoulder, Bob smiled and then turned to the audience to translate the lines. Steve seemed to loosen up a bit as he waved his hands while reciting his next line. Bob then mimicked Steve as he, too, waved his hands around while giving the poetic translation. As Steve gave further lines he became more animated, increasing the variety of inflections and gestures. After the eighth line, Baba Choo could not think of additional lines, so they ended the poem with a smile to audience applause. Both players smiled, pleased with the audience response.

In the postenactment feedback, Steve said that he had been worried about performing adequately but felt supported by Bob. For his part, Bob reported having had fun, although being also worried whether he was reading Steve's cues correctly, reflecting his own pattern of being a people-pleaser. He said, "This was fun. I want to do it again. This time I would like to play the poet." Steve was then asked if he was willing to play the game as the translator and agreed.

The therapist saw this as an opportune time for Steve to assume another role and to grow more comfortable with expressing himself in the group setting. It was also a chance for Bob to take some new risks by pleasing himself rather than others.

They switched positions, and Bob, as "Vladimir from Poland," started reciting quite animatedly as he delivered the poem using gibberish with a Polish accent. As he spoke, Steve responded first by copying Bob's movements and then adding new movement. As each player increased his own movement, the other player added to the movement.

They were so synchronized with verbal tones and movement that it was hardly noticeable that they were speaking in different languages.

As the action advanced, Bob pretended to apprehend a pesky animal that was destroying his property. Steve picked up on this and escalated his movement and voice tone to express frustration with the animal as it scampered up a pole to get away. The pesky animal became trapped in a burlap bag. Bob and Steve took turns wrestling with the animal until Bob took the bag to the woods, where he released the animal into the wild. The audience laughed, whistled, and applauded loudly.

During this game, the players seemed to achieve mutuality of energy and purpose as though they had both experienced this event together in real life. The cocreation of this new reality was so believable that players and audience became as one in the drama. It was also noteworthy that, while both Bob and Steve accepted each other's offers in action and voice, each felt free to add their own individual touches, which enhanced the poetic presentation. Whenever clients attempt an enactment something is learned, but when a performance works so well esthetically, it creates a memorable and transformative event for players and audience both.

When asked to contrast his experience in this performance with the first, Bob replied, "This was more real than the first. It reminded me of when

I was a little boy, and I watched my father chasing a squirrel out of our attic."
Steve laughed, saying to Bob, "I just chased a raccoon out of my yard two
nights ago. I thought that you either knew about my experience or that you
had experienced the same thing." Smiling as he chewed on a toothpick, Steve
said, "I was caught up. It was so real." Invited to share their experiences as
audience members, Barbara said, "It made me think about the time my brother
and his friends tried to get a skunk out of our yard, and they got sprayed." Bill
said, "You guys were good! It was so believable that you made me laugh."
Mae said, "Are you sure that you didn't rehearse this?" Bob then commented,
"I'd like to teach this game to my children. Maybe I can start connecting
with them through this game." The therapist agreed to work with Bob during
the break after group.

*A testament to the beneficial impact of RfG exercises and games is that players
often want to share their play experience with a loved one. Clients in recovery from
substance abuse problems very often are anxious to improve strained relationships
with their loved ones but do not recognize that the nonabusing family members are
also healing or working through pain and suffering endured by living with them.
Oftentimes, nonabusing family members are angry with the client and are not able
to connect with them as desired. Instead, they themselves need time to heal before
they can interact positively with the client. Hence, Bob was cautioned not to become discouraged if his family's reaction to the game was not what he hoped.*

Presents

The exercise Presents (Wiener, 1994, p. 105), or its many variations, is
used frequently in RfG Groups. The versatility of Presents is due both to the
simplicity of its instructions and clients' familiarity with the social rituals of
giving and receiving presents universal to all cultures.

In the basic form of Presents, a giver and a receiver face one another.
The giver is instructed to hold out his or her hands, palms up and together, in
a gesture of offering a present to the receiver. Unlike realistic gift-giving, the
giver does not know what the present is. The receiver is told to look at the
giver's outstretched palms and imagine a gift for himself or herself appearing
there. Once he or she "sees" the present, he or she mimes picking it up and
using it, ending by signaling acknowledgment of the giver's act of giving it to
him or her. Imaginary presents can be either material (e.g., flowers) or conceptual (e.g., love).

When used in couples or family therapy, Presents allows players with a
relationship history to bring out or intensify feelings and expectations that
they have toward one another (Wiener, 1997). In brief group settings, where
relationships are less established, the more frequent form is that of receiver-
as-self playing opposite a giver in the role of a significant other in the receiver's
life.

Jarid had talked about his father who was never at home, saying that he resented his father's giving him gifts and yet never spending time with him. Jarid reported that he always politely thanked his father for the gifts but that he really wanted to return them and let his father know how he really felt. The therapist invited Jarid to enact this in a Presents exercise with Bob, who volunteered to play Jarid's father. Without looking at it, Jarid threw the gift down on the floor and said to his pretend Dad, "You are never here for me. You think that you can just give me token presents in place of spending time with me. Just keep your presents." Bob, as Jarid's pretend Dad, without any coaching, apologized to Jarid and promised to start spending time with him, starting that weekend, by taking him to lunch and a basketball game.

Because the receiver of the gift determines what the present is, the giver is assured that the receiver will accept responsibility for getting that particular gift and for how to acknowledge the giver. To a far greater degree than in psychodrama, auxiliary players in RfG games and exercises are free to improvise dialogue and stage action as their characters.

Jarid said that it felt good to be able to express his true feelings and to have his (pretend) father apologize and offer to start spending time with him.

Pretense has the power to elicit and rehearse clients' expressed feelings. Presents evokes issues and enacted scenes that depict not only real-life situations but also wished-for changes from the often painful reality.

Bob, who portrayed Jarid's father, seemed to connect readily with Jarid's feelings; he reported that he needed no coaching to play this scene. This enactment allowed these two group members to connect with each other more intensely than in a talk-only group.

During a group session between Thanksgiving and Christmas, the therapist used guided imagery to invite group members to get in touch with their holiday experiences when they were between age 7 and 12. Holidays frequently trigger powerful memories of both pleasant and unpleasant times. Members were asked to focus on imaginary presents in the center of the room, to envision what was happening at that time and, when ready, to share with the group what presents they received and would have liked to have received. Timothy went first, showing how he opened his presents, only to be disappointed in not getting what he really wanted, a piano. Then he showed us what it would be like if he had gotten his piano. He pretended to play a song for us on his new piano. Being offered the opportunity to enact and experience his wish fulfillment helped Timothy to have and to share an intimate side of himself with the group.

Another member, Ann, knelt on the floor by her imaginary presents and said that she felt sad opening them. She said that she could not enjoy them or even remember what they were because she was then being sexually abused and could only think about that. The present she wished for her 9-year-old Self was the end of her sexual abuse.

Wished-for emotional gifts can be more powerful when received than physical gifts. If the therapist desires, he or she can use RfG enactments to let clients explore what it would be like to receive the emotional gift that they long for.

For Ann, the Presents exercise had brought up unhappy childhood memories, as well as the hope of offsetting this pain that had eclipsed any happiness in receiving ordinary Christmas gifts. Through this exercise Ann was able to feel safe enough to share the depth of her pain within a caring and supportive group atmosphere. Unfortunately, this was the client's last RfG group, and there was not enough time to do further work. The therapist could only encourage Ann to continue her work on this issue in private therapy.

During a Presents exercise between Barbara and her partner Mae, Barbara took the "gift of love from her father" as a present from Mae. Mae was impressed and pleased as Barbara embraced and thanked her. Having brought it up before, Barbara tearfully explained to the group that her father is an alcoholic who has never told her that he loves her; she wants to hear him say this more than anything. Barbara's mother spent most of her time going to support groups and visiting Barbara's father in detox. Barbara said that she felt emotionally and physically abandoned by both of her parents. According to Barbara, her mother would say to her "I love you, but I must go to save your father." To help Barbara and the group experience this description more vividly, the therapist invited Barbara to participate in an activity in which she asked some group members to play her mother, her father, and her brother. This type of activity is a "Family Sculpt."

Family Sculpting

Family sculpting, an action method originally developed at the Boston Family Institute (Duhl, Kantor, & Duhl, 1973) and adopted by Virginia Satir (Satir et al., 1991), can be done with or without using words or movement. A client sculpts his or her family by having actual or role-played family members placed in physical space positions in relation to each other as the client experiences the family. The therapist can choose to have the client stop the exercise here and verbally process the sculpt with the client, sculpted family members, and the audience, or the therapist may ask the client to give movement to family members to further define each family member and their interrelationships. Finally, the client may be instructed to give dialogue to pretend family members who voice the words that the client perceives or remembers real family members uttering. Family sculpting can be very powerful in evoking client emotions while giving the therapist, the role-players, and the audience a vivid experience of the family as experienced by the client. A further use of family sculpting is to ask or encourage the client to change the Family Sculpt to represent the way he or she would like the family to be or to have been.

Barbara agreed to play herself in the pretend family and was invited to place each pretend family member in the position that she envisioned for her real family's counterpart, including herself. In her Family Sculpt she faced her parents, who were placed slightly to her left, standing close together, and her brother to her right. No one was touching anyone else. She stepped out to observe her sculpt and made small adjustments until she was satisfied. The therapist then invited Barbara to tell pretend members what to say and show them how to move to simulate the real family members they were playing. She gave them the following dialogue and movements:

Father: (with one hand on hip, looking off into space) I'm an alcoholic. Gotta go to my meeting.

Mother: (to Barbara) I love you, honey, but I gotta see about Dad. (turns and takes Father's arm)

Brother: You know, I love you and will always take care of you. You can come and hang out with me and my friends. (reaches out both arms toward Barbara)

In response to the therapist's invitation to respond to each family member, Barbara responded as follows:

Barbara: (to Brother): I know you love me, Ken. (snuggling up under his arm)
(to Mother, reaching out her hands in a pleading gesture): But I want you to spend time with me, too!
I just don't feel you care about me, Dad. (looking directly at him, eyes tearing up, standing stiffly, fists closed).

The pretend Father spontaneously looked down and began to walk away. When asked if this fit, Barbara nodded yes.

After they had moved and spoken in the ways instructed, the therapist asked Barbara if she wished to have the pretend family members act and speak the way she would like to experience them. Turning her pretend father toward her, she had him hug her and say, "I love you, honey." She had her pretend brother say and do the same. Then she had her pretend mother say, "I will spend more time with you today," while taking Barbara's arm. This had such a powerful effect that Barbara started to sob; the whole pretend family became emotional and embraced each other. This ended the session and the group's week for the program. It was also Barbara's graduation.

At the beginning of the following group week, Barbara's real father came to the family support group for the first time. Barbara's husband, who had attended two sessions prior to this, also came. There, Barbara's father engaged in dialogue with that group about his love for his daughter and his inability to say "I love you." Using a variation of the Presents exercise near the end of the group, that therapist invited each group member to extend his or her hands and to offer a present to either a group member or the entire group. Another member, Grace, who had a daughter in the program, gave Barbara's father "The gift to find a way to say to your daughter 'I love you'." At this point, Barbara's father started to cry. He wiped his eyes and said humorously, "Do you think it's okay to start by saying it to her on the phone first?" Grace nodded "yes" and smiled approvingly.

Address the Telephone

Address the Telephone was devised as an effective and nonrepetitive warm-up exercise. Earlier, the therapist had noted that a real telephone was already mounted on a wall in the group room. Because of the seating arrangement, most clients would have to leave their seats to talk on this phone. This circumstance led to inviting group members to move from a familiar activity, talking on the telephone, to performing the act of speaking to an imaginary person on stage, using the telephone as a theatrical prop.

Clients seem more willing to participate in action methods if there is safety and familiarity in performance.

A similar version of this exercise was developed by Renee Emunah (1994): "Like drama itself, the telephone as a prop is almost real, treading that thin line between the actual and the imaginary—a line at which such powerful theatre and therapy can take place" (pp. 185–189).

Jarid presented a tough-guy image in the group. He bragged about getting kicked out of another substance abuse program because he refused to participate. He then said, "Don't get me wrong. In my mind I want to participate, but I can't make myself get out of my chair." After thanking Jarid for his willingness to share the feelings of some of his parts, the therapist asked him to reassure his parts that he would not get kicked out for not participating. She then asked him, "What would it take for your parts to feel safe enough to step back and let you participate in the Address the Telephone game?" Jarid said, "My girlfriend would need to be on the phone." The therapist obtained his permission to ask for a volunteer to play his girlfriend.

It can be very effective to a use displacement to help create safety for clients by allowing them to try out the desired action without consequences. Because an RfG enactment is framed as a rehearsal and not the real performance, participants typically feel less threatened. For some clients, even the thought of performing an act feels real enough for them to decline the invitation to pretend.

Ann volunteered and the therapist had her hold the telephone receiver.

Accommodating Jarid's fearful part, the therapist chose to minimize his risk further by having him perform from his seat, as himself, with a surrogate for the actual other person.

The therapist asked Jarid to coach Ann so that her enactment resembled his girlfriend Diane's. Ann caught on quickly. From his seat Jarid said to Ann, "Hey Diane, we need to talk. I've changed." Said Ann (holding the phone and looking down), "I can't hear you. Please come closer." Said Jarid, "I need to know that you are going to forgive me." Ann replied, "I can't hear you!" Walking over to the phone, Jarid answered, "I want us to work it out. Can you forgive me?" Ann answered, "I forgive you, and I want us to work it out, too!" Ann stepped back as Jarid, smiling, took the phone from her. Ann's performance as Jarid's girlfriend on the phone empowered Jarid to take a risk to perform. Jarid's and Ann's success in this enactment contributed to them participating together in later RfG exercises.

Although Ann had not been coached to draw Jarid to the telephone, she did so quite effectively, to his therapeutic benefit. Very frequently, although not always predictably, other group members function as effective cotherapists when they are in Self. The therapist needs to intervene selectively in interactions between group members to ensure therapeutic progress.

Bob feared that his marriage was headed for divorce if he continued to use cocaine. Yet, although he was in sobriety, he and his wife were having difficulty resolving marital problems effectively. When group members were invited to address the telephone, Bob stood up and walked to the phone, pretending to call his wife. "Hi, Nina, it's me," said Bob. "We need to talk about something that's really bothering me. You know how I told you that it bothers me that my parents never listened to me or valued my opinion when I was growing up. Well, I feel that you are treating me the same way. Whenever we decide to go out for dinner, we always end up going to the places you pick out. Even though I suggest a different place, you say 'no' or pout until I agree to go where you want. When you do that, I feel like you don't value my opinion and you're treating me just like my parents did. That hurts!" The therapist then asked Bob if he would be willing to enact a scene showing what happens when he and his wife discuss where to go for dinner. Bob readily agreed and asked for a volunteer to play his wife. Bill stepped forward. After coaching Bill on how his wife talked and behaved, the scene began. The first scene was structured to show what happened in Bob's actual experience. The group seemed to feel Bob's frustration. In the next scene, the therapist asked Bill in playing Bob's wife to let Bob successfully negotiate to accept his choice of restaurants. This scene had so powerful an effect on Bob (because his pretend wife had valued and accepted his choice of a restaurant) that he hugged Bill in appreciation.

Fulfilling a long-standing desire or overcoming its pain can have this impact on a player. It allows a needy part to experience satisfaction, even though gained in a pretend enactment. Using dramatic enactments in this way allows clients to discover, explore, and work on clinical issues rapidly.

With tears in his eyes Bob said, "I cannot tell you how good that made me feel." The therapist then speculated that this second enactment soothed both Bob's childhood and marital wounds around feeling valued. This hypothesis was validated when the group performed its ending ritual of sharing their thoughts that evening. At that time, Bob thanked the group for helping him address a long-standing problem from childhood that was now threatening his relationship with his wife.

Evelyn used Address the Telephone to express to her children her sorrow that they had been taken away from her by the State. She said, "Mommy really misses you. I am getting help for my disease of addiction so that it will be safe for you to come back to live with me. I am so very sorry." Next, Bill walked up to the phone and yelled, "Shut up! You drive me crazy all day at work. When I leave work I don't want to hear you." He motioned as though to put a pillow over the phone to silence it.

In another group, Barbara used Address the Telephone to pretend that her drug dealer had called. She told the drug dealer to never call her number nor contact her again. When she hung up the phone she said, "I'm going to change to an unlisted phone number to be sure that drug dealer can't call me." The applause, louder than usual, signaled that the audience felt that Barbara was speaking for them also.

It is common for the audience to react emotionally to performances on the telephone, as the form of this game evokes projective identification. The turn taken by one group member acts as a warm-up for others to express parts of themselves and bring up life issues.

Barbara used the game to concretize her desire to be proactive in ending her addiction. Judging from the group's applause and cheers, several other members strongly connected with the heroism of Barbara's enactment.

In recovery, clients with substance abuse problems struggle with their shame and self-devaluation when recollecting their addiction-controlled prior conduct. RfG games offer them an opportunity to enact scenarios as they wish themselves to have been, to be, or to become. "The improviser is simultaneously a potential hero and the storyteller, whose performance will either confirm or disconfirm the performer as heroic" (Wiener, 1994, p. 15).

Outcomes

The program is operated from a small, mental health agency that obtains funding through a mix of insurance reimbursement, community funds, and state appropriations. As is typical of such agencies, the program's resources are wholly devoted to vital administration and direct services. The view "from the trenches" is short-term; funding is heavily contingent on the number of clients serviced and the number of billable hours of service and not on the effectiveness of treatment. Consequently, not even rudimentary data useful in effectiveness evaluation are compiled. Initial measures of psychosocial functioning are not part of the intake process. There is no follow-up procedure in place to track recidivism or relapse of former clients, nor are data collected bearing on client acquisition or improvement of social skills during their participation. Hence it is not possible to offer quantitatively supported conclusions concerning the effectiveness of either the program as a whole or the RfG groups. Anecdotal and indirect evidence supporting the effectiveness of the RfG groups is presented later in the chapter.

Postgroup Functioning of Members

What follows are brief anecdotes concerning postgroup functioning of the five group members introduced in this chapter.

Barbara reported in her last group that she had attended many alcohol and drug treatment programs in the past, but this time she felt differently about her experience. She added that her family was more involved in her healing and that this felt good, and she thanked her fellow group members for their help with her Family Sculpt. She requested that RfG be offered in the aftercare program.

Timothy started to open up more and to talk more honestly about his parts. He thanked the group members for helping him to stop being phony and to face who he is. Timothy also shared that he plans to use some of the RfG games to induce fun into a future seminar that he will be running for salespersons.

Jarid commented that his relationship with his girlfriend was improving. He also thanked the group for making him feel safe in participating in the RfG exercises. He said that he hoped to get up the courage to start mending his relationship with his father. Jarid started the aftercare program but did not like the clinicians and the talk-only format, so he left.

Bob seemed more open and outgoing by the time that he graduated from the program. He attributed this in large part to the safety created by his RfG group experience. He also expressed a desire to find and use more action method games to help him start relating better to his wife and children.

Ann joined an all-women aftercare group so that she could work more intensely on healing from the sexual abuse she endured in childhood. She is also undergoing individual therapy and hopes to eventually involve her family in therapy.

Generic Changes Noted in RfG Group Participants

RfG group members regularly participated more enthusiastically in subsequent sessions and offered reassurances of safety to new members of the group. They also talked more about themselves in relation to others, making such comments as, "I am not going to let my fearful part keep me from trying new things that might help me;" "I am more outgoing and willing to take a risk now;" "I am more open to accepting how other people feel;" and "I am more willing to do and say what I need to without worrying about what others will think of me." Many thanked other group members for making it safe enough for them to get up and experience another way of expressing themselves. Some members expressed appreciation to specific others for their support as partners during an RfG enactment that led to growth. A large majority commented spontaneously that they felt closer to the group. Some graduating members challenged remaining members to carry on their outgoing roles so that new and shy members would be encouraged to take a risk that might help them.

Not all RfG group members experienced growth to the same degree. Some commented on the enjoyment that they had but added that they were still struggling with parts that kept them from being comfortable enough to participate fully. One member had been a parentified child in an alcoholic family and had not been allowed to play like other children. Another member expressed a strong shy part that kept her from getting up in front of people and performing. These members did, however, participate in those games and exercises that could be done from their seats both with and without partners. A final datum gained from clinicians' reports on members who relapsed and reentered the acute phase program is that most spontaneously requested attending the RfG group.

The authors retained a strong impression that there had been noticeable gains in psychosocial functioning in many RfG group members by the time they graduated. Of the 236 clients serviced by the program over the two years that RfG groups were run, 66 (28%) did not complete the program, while 170 (72%) did so. This latter number includes 23 clients who dropped out of the program a first time but subsequently re-entered and completed it.

PSYCHOSOCIAL FUNCTIONING AND SKILL IMPROVEMENT CRITERIA

Relying on available case records, the authors made retrospective, rough estimates of the psychosocial functioning of the 170 clients who completed the program based on 8 criteria (described below). Insufficient information was available regarding the 66 clients who left without completing the program.

1. *Well-connected to family:* Refers both to the absence of emotional cutoffs between program clients and members of their immediate family (parents, siblings, spouses, children) and to predominantly constructive communication occurring in the

presence of program clinicians. (Rough estimate: one quarter improved.)

2. *Experienced turning unwanted situations into desired situations through exercise of enactments:* Refers to instances of constructive departures from habitual social patterns during RfG enactments. (Rough estimate: one quarter improved.)

3. *Demonstrated ability to connect socially through nonverbal behavior:* Refers to instances of social connection observed during and following nonverbal RfG enactments. (Rough estimate: one third improved.)

4. *Displayed ability to share control with others via role expansion:* Refers to observations of behavior during RfG enactments in which clients assume stage character identities. (Rough estimate: one half improved.)

5. *Increased enjoyment of social interaction in non-drug state:* Refers both to observed enjoyment during RfG group sessions and reports of outside-group experiences clearly occurring in non-drug states. (Rough estimate: three quarters improved.)

6. *Confident and non-anxious generally in non-drug state:* Refers both to observed behavior during RfG group sessions and reports of outside-group experiences clearly occurring in non-drug states. (Rough estimate: one half improved.)

7. *Increase in popularity and acceptance within action group:* Refers to comparisons in social behavior between initial and subsequent RfG group interaction. (Rough estimate: one third improved.)

8. *Increased verbal participation in non-action group therapy:* Refers to reports from verbal-only group therapists. (Rough estimate: three quarters improved.)

Although based on retrospective estimates, these data support the impression that clients who completed the program significantly improved in their psychosocial functioning. However, these gains cannot be attributed unambiguously to RfG group participation.

CONCLUSION

The application of dramatic, playful action methods in a supportive group milieu appears to hold considerable promise as a tool in that reintegration of clients' personality and social functioning necessary to prevent relapses from substance abuse detoxification. By a coupling of enactment followed by verbal sharing, group members explore alternatives to avoidance, manipulation, and reliance on psychoactive substances to feel better about themselves, experience drug-free enjoyment, create trustworthiness among group members, and deal honestly with life problems. Therapists who can project nurturing leadership, playfulness, and an aptitude for flexibility will be able to use these methods effectively.

REFERENCES

Duhl, B. S. (1999). A personal view of action metaphor: Bringing what's inside outside. In D. J. Wiener (Ed.), *Beyond talk therapy: Using movement and expressive techniques in clinical practice* (pp. 79–96). Washington, DC: American Psychological Association.

Duhl, F. J., Kantor, D., & Duhl, B. S. (1973). Learning, space, and action in family therapy: A primer of sculpture. In D. Bloch (Ed.), *Techniques of family psychotherapy* (pp. 47–63). New York: Grune & Stratton.

Emunah, R. (1994). *Acting for real: Drama therapy process, technique, and performance*. New York: Brunner/Mazel.

Grinspoon, L. (Ed.). (1991). Dual diagnosis: I. *Harvard Mental Health Letter*, 8(2), 1–4.

Johnson, D. (1991). The theory and technique of transformations in drama therapy. *Arts in Psychotherapy, 18*, 285–300.

Lefcourt, H. M. (2001). The humor solution. In C. R. Snyder, (Ed.). *Coping with stress: Effective people and processes* (pp. 68–92). New York: Oxford University Press.

Miller, W. R., & Heather, N. (Eds.). (1986). *Treating addictive behaviors: Processes of change*. New York: Plenum.

Moffett, L. A., & Bruto, L. (1990). Therapeutic theatre with personality disordered clients with substance abuse problems: Characters in search of different characters. *Arts in Psychotherapy, 17*, 339–348.

Regier et al. (1990). Comorbidity of mental disorders and other drug abuse. *Journal of the American Medical Association, 264*, 2511–2518.

Rollnick, S., & Miller, W. R. (1995). What is motivational interviewing? *Behavioural and Cognitive Psychotherapy, 23*, 325–334.

Satir, V., Banmen, J., Gerber, J., & Gemori, M. (1991). *The Satir model: Family therapy and beyond*. Palo Alto, CA: Science & Behavior Books.

Schwartz, R. C. (1995). *Internal family systems therapy*. New York: Guilford.

Thoren, P., Floras, J. S., Hoffmann, P., & Seals, D. R. (1990). Endorphins and exercise: Physiological mechanisms and clinical implications. *Medical Science Sports Exercise, 22*, 417–428.

Velasquez, M. M., Crouch, C., Maurer, G. G., & DiClemente, C. C. (2001). *Group treatment for substance abuse: A stages-of-change therapy manual*. New York: Guilford.

Wiener, D. J. (1994). *Rehearsals for growth: Theater improvisation for psychotherapists*. New York: W. W. Norton.

Wiener, D.J. (1997). Presents of mind. *Journal of Family Psychotherapy, 8*, 85–93.

5

DEVELOPMENTAL TRANSFORMATIONS IN GROUP THERAPY WITH HOMELESS PEOPLE WITH A MENTAL ILLNESS

KIMBERLY C. GALWAY, KATE HURD, AND DAVID READ JOHNSON

Editors' Introduction: The developmental transformations approach arose from explorations of the therapeutic effects of dramatic play. Improvisation in the form of ever-shifting play is at the core of both theory and practice in this approach. Its emphasis on here and now process as an end in itself (akin to gestalt therapy) stands in contrast with most psychotherapies. To an extent greater than in most approaches, developmental transformations therapists assume an understated leadership social role, playing ever-shifting dramatic roles alongside their clients. Group leadership is emotionally demanding, requiring the therapist to be playful yet purposeful, permissive yet directive.

This chapter describes the action method developmental transformations and its use in group therapy with homeless people with a mental illness. Developmental transformations is a form of drama psychotherapy that is based on the use of improvisation and free play among the participants, including the therapists (Johnson, 2000). Using developmental principles, group sessions begin with simple and structured forms and then progress in small increments toward developmentally more complex and less-structured forms. Throughout, the images and scenes arising from the group are allowed to transform fluidly as the thoughts and feelings of group members change. The therapist helps these transformations remain organized and relevant to the group's issues. Many aspects of this method are consistent with other forms of drama therapy (Emunah, 1994; Landy, 1986).

 The aim of this method is the achievement of an "embodied encounter in the playspace." It encourages clients to interact with the therapist while experiencing ongoing bodily movement and physicalization, which allows more authentically felt experiences to arise into awareness. For clients who have difficulty putting feelings into words, as well as for those whose use of words has become too facile, this emphasis helps to access more grounded experience. The method is conducted within the "playspace" of pretend and dramatization, in which scenes are constantly transforming. The method tends to loosen the participants' reliance on restrictive, linear self-narratives, opening them up to new possibilities and increasing their curiosity about others' perspectives.

This chapter describes (a) the major concepts of developmental transformations, including establishment of the playspace, processes of embodiment, encounter, and transformation; (b) interventions and techniques that enhance these processes; (c) the rationale for using this method with homeless people with a mental illness; and (d) a case study illustrating these concepts and techniques.

THE PLAYSPACE

The playspace is the container of the entire therapeutic action. The *playspace* is not a physical area or section of the room but rather a state of playfulness, imagination, and pretend (Johnson, 1991). The therapist helps the clients play with real feelings and issues. Inevitably, thoughts and feelings arise that do not seem playable to the client. The therapist's job is to help the client maintain the state of play through these moments, often by shifting away from them temporarily. Over time, the goal is for the client to be able to play with what had seemed unplayable (Dintino & Johnson, 1996). Verbal discussion or processing occurs within the playspace, not at the end of the session outside the state of play.

The therapist's job is to preserve the playspace by maintaining a state of playfulness. The therapist is an active participant and guide throughout the session. He or she participates in the play and should be comfortable playing with whatever the clients bring up. The therapist follows the clients' energy and offers structures to explore the multiplicity of meanings within the movement, sound, image, or role-play. If the therapist chooses to explore something that does not have energy for the clients, there will usually be a disruption in the flow of the play. The therapist attempts to be open to the client at all times and faithfully render characters, feelings, or issues that the client projects onto the therapist. The therapist thus becomes a client's "playobject."

The therapist uses a variety of improvisational techniques that are intended to facilitate transformation, heighten or diminish intensity, and increase or decrease cognitive distance in the session. A more detailed description of these techniques is found in Johnson (1992).

EMBODIMENT

In developmental transformations, the body is considered the essential source of thoughts and feelings (Johnson, Forrester, Dintino, James, & Schnee,

1996), while the mind is viewed as an aspect or component of the body. Whereas in many therapies the meta-awareness that comes with mental comprehension of events is seen as the last chapter, as it were, of a therapeutic discovery (the "why I do what I do"), here the flow of the bodily impulses and mental imagery in the moment are paramount.

ENCOUNTER

The intersubjective encounter between the therapist and the client is one key component. The play is a collaborative effort to aid the client in revealing blocks that narrow his or her experience of the encounter with another. The client is asked to engage in this encounter using only his or her inner impulses and his body. The therapist offers himself or herself to the client in a direct fashion, acknowledging that he or she can be affected by the client in the playspace. The therapist's countertransference reactions are thus treated as material for the clients' play and can be valuable in the further development of the relational encounter.

TRANSFORMATION

In this work, flow is emphasized over narration, multiplicity of meaning is favored over one truth, and irony is invoked by the acceptance of incongruities. Spontaneity in the here and now becomes paramount. The focus is not on a linear progression of events or a story line that unfolds within the session. The interest is not on developing and building a story or even on fully developed roles. Rather, the emphasis is on emergent bodily impulses and images that diverge from linear story lines. Instead of looking for through-lines to create or discover a meaningful story, the therapist deconstructs the story to break up constraining narratives. Therefore, the emphasis in this model involves the removal of obstacles rather than a gathering of insight or skills.

Developmental transformations, therefore, is a form of psychotherapy in which the therapist(s) and client(s) seek to achieve the continuous transformation of embodied encounters in the playspace (Johnson, 2000). The aim is to re-engage clients in their natural developmental process, by reducing fear of the instability of being. The focus of the method is on flow and discovery, in the letting go of blocks that have been impediments to desires and impulses, thoughts and perception, images of self and others, and roles and identities.

Dimensions

Developmental transformations may be conducted in individual or group therapy, depending on client preference and goals of treatment. As this chapter deals with group applications, we delineate below the five basic developmental dimensions in group therapy (Johnson, 1982). These dimensions correspond to stages of cognitive development described by Piaget (1951) and Werner and Kaplan (1963). In these dimensions the therapist can intervene in the session through action methods, by altering his or her instructions to offer the group a particular level of each dimension. The therapist intervenes to titrate the developmental demand on group members so that the ongoing flow of the play is maintained.

1. *Ambiguity* refers to the degree to which the therapist offers a clear structure in terms of task, space, and role. A low level of ambiguity means that the clients are being told what to do (task), in what formation (space), and how to do it (role). A high level of ambiguity in task, space, or role occurs when clients are allowed to determine their own structure. Most groups need to start with a low level of ambiguity and, as the group progresses, are able to tolerate higher levels of ambiguity. This is parallel to the infant needing structure from an external source (the mother) in early stages of development and progressively learning to structure his or her own experiences.

2. *Complexity* refers to the degree to which structures of task, space, and role are differentiated, determined by the number of unique elements required of each. Thus, the task of unison movement and sound is less complex than having each individual move and make sounds or speak in a different way. The most complex task is when each individual in the group is directed to act in a different way. The simplest structure of space is a circle. The simplest structure of role is to direct each individual to play the same role; the most complex is to direct each to play a unique role.

3. *Media* is the representational form of expression. Media used in therapeutic sessions are movement, sound, image, role, and word. These correspond to an infant's progressive level of development, through sensorimotor, symbolic, and reflective stages, according to Piaget (1951), Bruner (1964), and Werner and Kaplan (1963). Generally, sessions begin in pure movement and sound, then images are developed and, finally, verbal interaction emerges.

4. *Interpersonal demand* refers to the degree to which the impro-visation places a demand on the participants to relate to oth-ers. The form, or type of character the individual is asked to portray, is important. Higher forms (i.e., humans) usually re-quire more complex portrayals. Inanimate objects, forces of nature (i.e., "the wind," "the sun"), and animals are less com-plex. The level of interaction among the characters or group members is also a dimension in which the therapist can inter-vene in heightening interpersonal exchange, varying from no interaction to complex improvisations.

5. *Affect expression* refers to how personal and intense the imag-ery in the session is. Generally, sessions move from imper-sonal and low-intensity topics toward more personal and evocative images. The therapist will make alterations in this dimension in order to maintain the group's ability to play.

It is within these five dimensions that the therapist intervenes, increas-ing or decreasing the levels of ambiguity, complexity, media, interpersonal demand, and affect expression to facilitate group participation, involvement, and discovery. These interventions arise spontaneously during interaction with the clients and cannot be planned.

Other Action Methods

Additionally, other action methods illustrated in the case study include

1. *Faithful rendering:* The therapist plays out a scene or role in a way that matches the client's inner experience.
2. *Defining:* The therapist asks for more details of an image to help the client to further clarify an image that is still ambigu-ous and may hold meaning.
3. *Transforming to the here and now:* The therapist makes a ver-bal commentary on the action within the scene and relates it to what is going on in the group in the moment.
4. *Intensification:* The energy of a scene or dramatic structure is heightened to enhance awareness.
5. *Act completion:* The therapist completes an act that the client may be afraid to go through with.
6. *Pre-empting:* The therapist takes on an acknowledged or fa-miliar role of the client to encourage him or her to choose an alternative role.
7. *Repetition:* An image is brought back or repeated to explore its multiple meanings.
8. *Action interpretation:* A scene is transformed into elements of the client's real life to explore connections among images.

Stages of a Group Session

In general, a group session begins at the earliest developmental level, in which there is little ambiguity, little complexity, pure movement and sound, low interpersonal demand, and a minimal level of affect. Gradually, the therapist begins to introduce more complex developmental interventions. The goal is not to get to the highest developmental level, rather, to be able to travel throughout the levels (both forward and backward) with greater ease. While different populations feel comfortable beginning at different levels (i.e., more rigid personalities may feel comfortable beginning with words rather than unison movement and sound), there are typical stages that most clinical populations go through (James & Johnson, 1996b).

The typical stages of a group session include the *greeting*, whereby the group members are invited into the playspace; *unison movement and sound*, during which the clients are asked to stand in a circle and repeat movements and sounds made by each individual, as if mirroring the individual; *defining*, when images emerging from the kinesthetic experience are defined by the group; *personification*, in which organized roles and images emerge; *structured role-play*, when the therapist sets up dramatic enactments exploring core issues; *unstructured role-play*, when the group enacts scenes in an improvised, spontaneous manner with little or no direction from the therapist; and a structured *closing* (Johnson, 1986).

CASE EXAMPLE

The following group therapy session took place in a day treatment program for homeless people with a chronic mental illness. They have lived on the streets of New York City—some for years, others for only days. Diagnosed with schizophrenia, schizoaffective disorder, or bipolar disorder, many have been plagued by auditory hallucinations, paranoia, thought disorder, and depression. They have withdrawn from the world, creating a space for themselves that is often devoid of human contact. They have experienced feelings of worthlessness, despair, hopelessness, shame, and humiliation. Most have been in and out of hospitals.

Clients are brought into the program by outreach workers. Although they come voluntarily, often they come with great trepidation. Looking someone in the eye is a frightening prospect to someone who has been isolated by their homelessness and mental illness, let alone speaking of their fears, desires, and hopes in a psychotherapy session. A significant characteristic among these clients is their rejection of services, including offers of shelter, from helpers. They demonstrate a profound interpersonal aversion to others and maintain a protective social withdrawal even when contact may improve their situation (Schnee, 1996). They experience not only a loss of resources but also meaning in their lives, hovering between human and inhuman levels of existence. One client equated himself with the "trash" with which he surrounded himself. With great frequency, these characteristics derive not only from the thought disturbances of mental illness but also from devastatingly traumatic childhood experiences of abuse, neglect, and violence.

One of the major goals of treatment programs with this population is to increase their capacities for attachment through the reduction of their interpersonal fears, to directly address the loss of meaning in their lives, and to reanimate their sense of humanness (Forrester & Johnson, 1995; Johnson, 1999). Only through these measures will the clients be able to stay involved in the various programs and services offered them.

The Other Place (TOP) is a day treatment program that focuses on psychosocial rehabilitation. TOP takes referrals from Project Reachout, New York City's first mobile outreach team, and a homeless Assertive Community Treatment team. All programs are part of Goddard Riverside Community Center, a settlement house that has been serving the Upper West Side of Manhattan for more than 100 years. TOP was developed to work in conjunction with the outreach and community work. The clients attending the program typically have failed elsewhere. They were unable to tolerate the structures of a rigorous hospital day treatment program and were unable to live up to the level of independence expected at most psychosocial clubs. The focus of rehabilitation lies in building skills of socialization, self-expression, independent living, interpersonal relationships, and vocational abilities. The goal is to help the clients achieve and sustain permanent housing, a supportive social network, and psychiatric stability.

The group described below consists of 10 members who have been together for nearly 2 years. The group meets weekly for 1 hour. Members come voluntarily and are usually regular in their attendance. The issues that have been explored over the years have centered largely around homelessness, poverty, loneliness, and the stigma of having a mental illness.

The Session

The therapists, Kim and Kate, gather the group into a circle. Greg, Hank, Manuel, Diego, Jose, Natasha, Keith, Joseph, and Jolene warm up with a stretch and a growl.

> Greg: Quiet on the set!
> Kim: OK. Let's make as much noise as we can and then Greg will say, "Quiet on the set!" Ready? (the group lets out a big sound)

The leader here is going with the resistance in a playful way and trying to get Greg to enter the playspace by reframing his behavior into a role. The group is in its initial greeting phase and getting warmed up for the session.

Kim: You have to be louder than us, Greg. OK. Again. (the group repeats, even louder)

There is a sense of playfulness already in the group while acknowledging Greg's need to assert himself. Through repetition, the leaders are beginning to structure the warm-up and engage the members in unison movement and sound.

Greg: The sky is falling.
Kate: Lift up our arms. (the group then begins to lift their arms) Let's say hello to Natasha. Hello, Natasha. (everybody waves) Who else should we say hello to, Keith?
Keith: Manuel. (the group says hello to Manuel; Manuel then selects another member to say hello to and so forth, until they have said hello to everyone in the group; the wave changes, from a one-handed wave to a two-handed wave to a little wave with both hands)

In this way the group begins warming up to one another, taking in others, making eye contact, and getting in touch with their physical bodies.

Greg: Can I ask the group something? Did anyone see "Cats" this morning?
Kim: "Cats" . . . this morning?
Greg: Yes, this morning, on channel 13.
Kate: Hmmm. He's very cultured. (she says in a playful refined voice)

The leader is noting that, as the group members are getting in touch with their bodies, Greg is not. Instead, he is more comfortable in a verbal discussion. The leaders could view this as a departure from the group structure; instead, they incorporate it into the structure of the group.

Kim: Meow.
Jose: (responding to this in a bigger voice) Meow. (he uses a little hand motion similar to our last hello wave, hands close to the body, like paws; the group begins some meows)
Kate: Let's all curl up like a cat and then stretch like a cat. And curl up like a cat and stretch like a cat. (everyone does this as they say meow)
Kate: Let's take our long cat nails and give ourselves a scratch. (everyone does this in an imaginary way, on faces, neck, and legs)
Kim: And just stretch all the way out. (the group stretches fully with a loud, pleasurable sigh, similar to the very beginning of the group)

The leaders are trying to establish the playspace. Also, here the leaders are developing the material presented to them, even though the imagery is evocative. They do not come in with a preconceived plan. They are providing structure with a low degree of ambiguity. This brings the group together. The image of the cat carried with it the sense of autonomy and interpersonal distance many of these clients felt in their lives, being "alley cats," as one of them often commented.

Kim:	Keith's got a little feet thing going.
	Let's all do what Keith is doing. (Joseph slightly alters the movement by marching with his knees high up; the group starts to chant the names of each member as they come into the center; members are snapping their fingers rhythmically as they are "bopping" to the rhythm)
	Let's bring down the magic curtain by snapping our fingers.
Greg:	The curtain's stuck.
Kate:	Uh-oh.
Kim:	It's stuck.
Kate:	OK. Everybody grab that curtain. (she grabs the imaginary curtain at a midway point in front of her)
Kim:	And yank it down. (the group yanks the curtain all the way down and then parts the curtain and steps inside; the leaders instruct each member to begin a movement, while the rest of the group mirrors it; group movements consist of snapping, marching, taking a big breath in and out, Keith's signature moves of turning around in a circle, Greg's stroking his chin and giving a kick with one foot; Manuel alters the movement, then Kim)

The magic curtain is a structured ritual that this group has incorporated into most of their sessions. Also, the leaders continue to provide a low level of ambiguity, complexity, and interpersonal demand, as the group continues to make various sounds and movements. More spontaneous variations are introduced by the members, requiring less direction from the leaders. Members are exploring eye contact and movement, the beginning stages of encounter and embodiment. Manuel comes into the center and starts a soldier-like arm swing while chanting "Umm," a familiar sound and movement of his; he then turns to Kim and nods for her to change the movement. This can be seen as Manuel's discomfort with the encounter and the embodiment and his need for more structure. We are back to simple sound and movement, each person taking his or her turn. Although Manuel was expressing his anxiety about the encounter, the rest of the group appears to want to see each other and make contact.

Kate:	Everyone look at someone across the room while they do this.

The leader notices that there is a lot of lip pursing on the hmm sound; she asks everyone to purse their lips on a count of 3. The leader is increasing the interpersonal demand by asking members to look at one another. Also, here, instead of following a linear progression, Kate is following the energy and interest in the embodied experience of pursing the lips. She defines this and lowers the ambiguity while increasing the interpersonal demand. There is energy in this exploration of the emergent images, which Kim follows through on, defining the impulse even more.

Kim:	Again, 1–2–3, everyone take their hand and throw a kiss into the center of the room.
Kate:	Let's all give Greg a kiss. (Greg ducks)

Kim: Greg, we're all going to rain kisses on you whether you like it or not. (the group throws him another collective kiss)

Kate: We need to give Keith kisses. (he responds quite differently, evidently enjoying them)

Greg has been trying from the beginning of the group to keep himself separate. The play around kissing acknowledges his fears. To a group of homeless clients, a kiss is certainly antithetical to their usual orientation: no one has kissed them, they desire to stay away from others, their appearance keeps others at bay. A kiss is basically inconceivable, yet at the same time it symbolizes the aim of treatment: to enter human relations again. The group's familiarity with each other allows them to tolerate playing with this evocative image. The leaders are intensifying the moment by singling out Greg in a playful way.

Kim: Keith, who should we give kisses to next? (Keith chooses Manuel to give kisses to; Manuel puts his hands up in a stopping motion, but he is also smiling and nodding his head "yes")

Greg: Smother, smother, smother.

Kim: (to Manuel) We are going to smother you with kisses.

Here, again, the leader is increasing the level of interpersonal demand while making it clear that each person can have a turn if he or she so chooses. Also, the leaders are picking up on the emergent theme, taking material offered by the participants and using it as a means of exploration. The leaders have begun to define images, which have emerged from the sound and movement and which the group seems interested in. To work with the increasing levels of affect expression and interpersonal demand, the leaders must provide structure, a low level of ambiguity and complexity, and a strong sense of the playspace. The fact that this group of homeless individuals with mental illness are expressing this level of intimacy is quite exciting. This can be attributed to the cohesiveness of the group (most of the members have been working together for years) and the level of trust in the playspace. The double meanings evoked here—to be smothered (i.e., abused) with kisses (i.e., human relationships)—are the first signs of the deep confusion in the group about love and hate, which will take up most of the rest of the group session.

Kim: Manuel, who else should we smother with kisses? (Manuel points to Hank; Hank raises his arms in a strong man salute; Kate asks him to step into the center, saying he's going to "take it," all the kisses)

Kim: He needs to protect himself from the kisses! Hank, get ready to protect yourself from the kisses. (Hank gets a group kiss)

This is an action interpretation. The leaders are noting how Hank's response is different than the ones that have gone before and incorporating it into the improvisational structure of the group.

Kate: He can take it. He's a man. (he gets another kiss; Jolene then enters the center for kisses, moving her hips a bit)

Kate:	Jolene's warming up for her kisses.
Kate:	You are being very stingy with your kisses, Greg.
Kim:	Greg, give us your kisses. (she notices something that Greg has done) Oh, he's giving them to himself. Oh my!
Kate:	Everyone give yourself a kiss.
Kim:	Oh. We are going to keep our kisses just to ourselves.
Greg:	(singing) You must remember this, a kiss is just a kiss, a sigh is just a sigh.

The group joins in, but there is no energy to the song; Kate asks the group to breathe in a big sigh, reminiscent of a breath that Natasha had initiated earlier; everyone breathes in and exhales on an "Aaaahhhh" sound. Kate is noticing a divergence in the way one member is responding to the group activity. Also, the therapists pick up on this divergent action and incorporate it into the group. The group is no longer going along with the structure of giving and receiving kisses. The leaders are noting this and faithfully rendering the shift in interest and involvement. Kate enters the center, shakes her whole body while she raises her hands, and says "Ooooohh, wah!" Kate asks everyone to do this; they repeat it Kate is returning to sound and movement, another shift in media, as a response to the drop in energy. It appears as if the members want to dabble in their emotions but are still guarded against it. By returning to the sound and movement, the therapists are again establishing a clear and simple structure. The therapist also places herself at the center of the action to offer herself as the group's playobject. This simplifies the interpersonal demand on the clients.

Kim:	Why don't you go in, Greg?
Greg:	I'm scared of that thing.
Kim:	You're not scared of the feelings, are you?
Greg:	I'm scared of that thing (as he gestures to the center of the room).

The group begins to enter the personification stage. Greg is able to project his fears onto an imaginary object in the center of the room. However, the leaders do not choose to define this projection at this time because of Greg's initial resistance to entering the playspace. Natasha enters the middle of the circle; she has her hands out, like cat claws, and says "ooohhhhhhh" as she slashes the air; everyone does this gesture toward the center of the room, yet there is a divergent element in the various individuals' movements; people are twitching their fingers as they do a pouncelike move saying "wooooo"; momentum increases toward the center, everyone coming in closer. Suddenly, Jolene pushes Kim back into the center of the circle; Kim acts scared, holding on to the hem of her dress as she tries not to step on anything.

Kate:	Quick, pull her out, everybody. (the group pulls her out with an imaginary rope)
Kim:	Oh, my God! That was really scary, that was really scary in there!

The energy has increased. We have returned to the personification of that scary thing in a safe way, and it is clear that there is group interest. Jolene has indicated that it is the therapist who should take on and embody the feelings and images that are beginning to be projected into the middle of the room. Someone starts pointing to the center of the room; soon everyone is pointing, saying "Shhh!"

Kim: You see that? What is it?
Greg: It's a green-eyed monster.
Kate: It has fangs.
Kim: Fangs! Mighty fangs!
Greg: It has wings.
Kim: It flies!
Kate: What else?
Greg: It's hungry.
Joseph: It has four legs.
Greg: And a long tail.
Kim: A long, nasty tail. (Kate jumps in as the monster, and energy increases; Keith starts jumping up and down.)
Kim: Get back, everybody. Back.

The group finally begins to reveal the personification. The image takes on more detailed characteristics. Kate becomes the playobject here. She offers herself up to the group as the scary monster to intensify the play and increase the affect expression within the group.

Kate: Let me just grab my tail. I am going to swing my tail three times, and I am going to capture someone with it. (Greg hides behind Keith; Kim and Jolene huddle together; Natasha turns toward Diego; other group members stand back; Keith appears to be enjoying this the most)
        One! Two! Three! (Kate captures Keith; he readily comes into the center of the circle)
        I am going to give you fangs! And I am going to give you wings! (Keith responds by changing his body posture; he flaps his wings)
        And a long tongue. And a long tail! (Keith seems fully engaged in this; he turns in circles)
        Wonderful! (Keith has his tongue out, flapping his wings as the monster; Kate duplicates his move; they say "Ha, ha ha")

The images of intimacy are now pushed back by the images of danger, personified here as a monster, at once both the concretization of group fears and perhaps the symbols of the actual perpetrators within their families from the past. Thus, projections of group fears as well as transferential components of early family relationships begin to emerge.

Kate: And we are going to capture someone. (both Keith and Kate do a tongue move out of the mouth and back in; they capture Natasha, who pretends to shake)
Kim: Oh, she's scared. She's very, very, very scared. (Kim takes Natasha, who is getting "scared" more and more and puts her arm around her)

Kim is transforming to the here and now, making a comment on what is actually going on for one of the group members.

Kim: Oh, it's too much for her!

Kate: Oh, no. I don't think so. (Kate starts to move closer, as Kim continues to protect Natasha) I want Natasha.

Because there are two leaders, they can take opposite stances and allow members to play with their desire to be taken in, devoured, and even consumed by the group. If the leaders were really at odds with one another in terms of an appropriate action method, this intervention would not succeed. The leaders in fact take on different transferential components of early parental images, so that they can be played out, explored, and altered in various ways during the course of the session. The emphasis will be on passing through these roles, as the leaders stay with these existent roles until something new emerges through the improvisational play.

Kim: No. We need to protect her. Help me. (She addresses other members of the group, who begin linking arms to form a barrier between Natasha and Kate; they start chanting "No! No! No!" Kate meanwhile has enlisted fellow "monster" Keith, as well as Manuel and Hank, and they start chanting "Yes! Yes! Yes!" Natasha has started to march, and the group begins to pick up on this, the "yes" group joining in a train and marching around the "no" group; they capture Natasha.)

The group has entered the arena of structured role-play. The media of expression and complexity have changed dramatically. The group is no longer in a circle. They have divided into two. Kim's enrollment as the protector of the "children" presumably is consistent with her current role as therapist in the program, as well as the parental figure that tried or should have tried to protect the children from abuse. In this sense, Kim plays both a hero and a failure at the same time. Soon everyone is "captured" except Kim.

Kim: Oh, I know you are going to smother me with . . . with . . . . with . . .

Kate: What are we going to smother her with?

Greg: Kisses! (The group starts throwing Kim pretend kisses as she pretends to scream; Kim starts shimmying in the middle of the room and circling, again reminiscent of earlier moves, and is transformed by the kisses, smiling and happy and calm; she puts her arm on the two members next to her; the group applauds, and she moves into the center and takes a bow.)

Kate: Welcome to the love fest, everyone! A round of applause!

Greg: Ooh, a love fest!

Kim: And in just a minute, we are going to talk about how wonderful each one of us is. What a wonderfully perfect group we have here together.

Greg: It's like Woodstock.

Kim:	Come into the center, Greg (he does). We're going to say only wonderful things about this man. What can we say about Greg?
Joseph:	He's very intelligent.
Kim:	(with an arm flourish) He's very intelligent. Let's all say that. (The group repeats the phrase, incorporating the arm flourish.)
Kate:	Let's give him a kiss. (The group throws him a kiss with an elongated "mmmwha" sound.)
Kim:	What else can we say about Greg?
Hank:	He's marvelous. (The group repeats this phrase, raising their arms.)
Kate:	Let's give him a kiss. (Again, the group throws a kiss to Greg.)
Kim:	What else can we say about Greg?
Manuel:	He's active.
Kim:	(repeats) He's active. Ooooh. (The group spontaneously "Ooohs" and extends their hands.)

Kim uses repetition to feed a previously related image back into the group's play. Kate restructures the story line, lowering the ambiguity and following the enthusiasm with which people are applauding. Moreover, while the group remains in a circle, having each individual come into the middle heightens the interpersonal demand. Having them speak personally heightens the affective expression. Kate is using repetition of an earlier embodied image.

Greg:	Enough about me. Enough about me. (His hands are on his heart, and he begins to leave the center.)
Kim:	He can't take it. He can't take it.
Kate:	Keith said he's funny.
Kim:	He's funny!
Greg:	Awww. (He returns to the center and the group throws him a kiss.)
Greg:	(hands on heart) Enough. Enough about me. How about Joseph?

Kim transforms to the here and now, making a comment on what is actually happening. Further, Greg takes the focus off himself here and turns to another group member. If he were not able to do this on his own, the therapists might have intervened and shifted the focus off Greg. The purpose here is not to concentrate on any one individual but to incorporate all group members in the play.

Kim:	Oh, Joseph. Step into the center (he does). What can we say about Joseph?
Greg:	He's attractive. (The group repeats this and throws him a kiss; Joseph bows.)
Kim:	What else can we say about Joseph?
Hank:	He's marvelous, too. (The group repeats this and throws Joseph a kiss; again, he bows deeply.)
Kate:	He goes to more groups than anybody else in the whole wide world. (Joseph raises his fist triumphantly, and the group sends him another kiss.)

Greg: A real go-getter. A real go-getter. (Joseph bows to Greg.)

Although this part of the session is largely a defensive retreat from the previous engagement with victimization, the resulting exercise of giving each other positive feedback is itself a huge achievement for these clients who, prior to treatment, could barely acknowledge each other's presence.

Kim: What else about Joseph?
Jolene: He's a nice baby.
Kate: A nice baby!
Kim: He's a nice bébé. (She mirrors Jolene's French pronunciation.) OK! (Joseph shakes Jolene's hand.)
Kate: (begins to snap her fingers; the rest of the group follows) He's a nice bébé. He's a nice bébé. (This is rhythmic and has a sing-song quality; Joseph, too, remains in the center, snapping his fingers and bouncing to the rhythm.)
Kim: Ooooooh. (looking at Jolene) Do we have another bébé here?
Jolene: Baby. (She moves into the center, taking on the role of a baby, and heads toward Kim.)
Kim: (In "motherese") Is this the little baby who needs to be taken care of? (She puts her arm around Jolene, as Keith and Jose spontaneously pat her on the shoulder and Natasha throws her a kiss.)
Jolene: Hungry.

This contribution of Jolene's seems to come "out of the blue." It does not follow the plot that is being developed. Rather than redirecting her back to the plot, Kim heightens what Jolene said through repetition. The group has resumed its prior journey in full force, as the image of the baby and their early childhood abusive experiences again rise up in the group. As before, the playful environment will give room for the representation of conflicting, contradictory acts and desires: to hold and protect, and to harm and neglect.

Kim: Oh, the little baby is hungry. Let's all feed baby Jolene.
Kate: (begins a chant as group members join in and advance toward Jolene, mixing up imaginary food) Let's feed the baby, let's feed the baby, let's feed the baby.
Greg: (begins to sing, over the chant) Feed the Baaaaay-by! Feed the Baaaaay-by! (the rest of the group joins in) Feed the Baaaay-by! Yeah, yeah. Feed the Baaaaay-by!
Greg: (to Jolene) Has the baby got her food? Did you get enough, baby?
Jolene: Yes. (She nods and leaves the center, returning to her place in the circle.)
Greg: She's happy!
Kim: Everyone, pick up a little baby. (Group members begin rocking their babies.)
Jolene: Rock the baby.

Kate: (Begins a gentle chant, as each member continues with the rock-ing movement.) Rock the baby. Rock the baby. (The entire group joins in.) Rock the baby. Rock the baby. Rock the baby.

There is energy in the rocking and holding of the babies, which the members are exploring fully and actively with their bodies.

Kim: Welcome all of you to the parenting class! (She moves into the center.) Welcome. I know you're all new parents.

Greg: I want to stay far away from it.

Kate: I want him to take full responsibility for the child.

Greg: Aawww.

Kim: We're here to take responsibility and take care of our babies. And the first thing we must do—does everyone have the baby in their arms? The correct holding position for the baby is as such.

The therapists note the quality of gentleness and caring that is being explored by the members. They both are touched by this and are aware of their desire to give these members the care and attention that they have been denied. Kim's shift into the parental educator is one that is congruent with her desire to teach, educate, and foster the members in their ability to care for and love themselves. Thus, her countertransferential reactions are structured into the role-play.

Manuel: Can the baby have chocolate milk?

Kim: You want to feed your baby chocolate milk? All right, that's a good question. (to entire group) Can we feed our babies choco-late milk?

Greg: Choc-o-lat-ay for the ba-bay. (The group begins to sing this, bouncing up and down as they feed their babies.)

Kate: What else can we do with the babies?

Kim: Well. We've got to change the babies.

Greg: Burp the babies.

Kim: Oh, yes. First we should burp the babies. Then we need to change the babies. Alright, can we put the babies over your shoulder and . . .

Kate: (begins to sing, all join in) Burp the Baaaay-by! Burp the Baaaay-by! Burp the Baaaaay-by!

Greg: (makes a burping sound, the rest of the group follows) Bleeeehhhh.

Kate: Everybody. (the entire group) Bleeeehhhh.

Kim: Let's hear that big baby belch.

Everyone: Bleeeehhh!

Asking the question "What else can we do with it" deconstructs the plot line and encourages variation in meanings. From simply caring for the baby came the parenting class and then the chocolate milk and then the burping and belching and (soon) defecating. The baby is being transformed into the frustrating, problematic, deni-grated object that soon will need to be punished.

Kim:	Now, put the babies on the changing table. (all place the babies down) And feel the baby's diaper. It should be very full. (most group members make sounds of "ooohhh")
Joseph:	Phew.
Kate:	What was that? Phew?
Kim:	Alright, now open the diapers quick! Open! (The entire group starts fanning their hands in front of their noses.)
Everyone:	Phew!
Kim:	Oh, my, the babies sure make a mess!
Everyone:	(in disgust) Eeeeeewwww!

The therapists are following the interest of the group without making specific interpretations because there are multiple meanings in this image. Shame dynamics, interest in nurturance and taking care of another, and regressive aspects of dependency may all be contained in this image. At this point, it is best to trust the momentum of the play.

Kate:	What should we do with it?
Greg:	Throw it away!
Kate:	Throw it away.
Manuel:	Let's put them in the basement. Down, in the basement.
Joseph:	Put it in the basement.
Leshon:	Flush it in the toilet.
Keith:	Throw it in the basement.
Kim:	Basement. All right, let's put them all in the basement.

At this point, it is unclear to the leaders whether or not the group wants to throw the diapers or the babies in the basement. The leaders choose to let this remain ambiguous, acknowledging images of abuse that rise to the surface. Members of the group make direct references to their own histories which, due to the pretend nature of the action, are not entirely known to the group. Thus, Leshon had his head pushed into the toilet bowl and held there by his foster mother; Manuel was removed from his parents' home due to repeated and extensive physical harm.

Greg:	Let's wipe the baby's bottom.
Kim:	Damp cloth. (Members take their time in wiping their babies' bottoms; this is done very gently by all.)
Hank:	Throw it away.
Kim:	In the basement?
Joseph:	Yes. (The cloths are thrown away.)
Greg:	And powder the babies. (Everyone powders the babies; this, too, takes some time and is done carefully and gently.)
Kate:	Let's give a little tap on the bottom everybody. Ready?
Everyone:	Tap, tap, tap. Tap, tap, tap. Tap, tap, tap.

Kate moves into the center and takes on the role of a baby, to the delight of the group; members are fully engaged; Joseph even begins to clap.

| Kate: | Waaaaa! |

Kate:	Waaaaa! Waaaaa!
Greg:	That baby is a spoiled brat.
Kim:	(repeats) This baby is a spoiled brat.
Leshon:	(laughs) Throw the baby in the basement.
Kim:	Throw the baby in the basement? (This brings laughter from many group members; there appears to be much energy around this.)
Kim:	(begins to chant, others join in) Throw the baby in the basement. Throw the baby in the basement. (She lifts her hands, as the group follows.) Throw the baby in the basement. Throw the baby in the basement.
Kate:	(as she is being lowered into the basement) Waaaaa! Waaaaa! (She lies on the floor.)
Kim:	(emphatically) Throw the baby in the basement!

Here the therapist is embodying the role that holds so much interest and energy for the group. She is acting as their playobject and will take in the group projections both through her bodily expression of the role and through her encounter with each group member. She does this in part because she anticipates an increase in the intensity of affective expression, specifically aggression. The projection is taken in, and the therapists begin to play with it. Kate will now behave as if she were a spoiled brat. Following the group's energy, Kim provides a low level of ambiguity and complexity to help the group achieve act completion.

Greg:	(to Kate) Now what do you have to say for yourself?
Kate:	I'm very selfish.
Greg:	You're a spoiled brat, too.
Kate:	I'm a spoiled brat. (Leshon leans in close; many other members laugh or make sounds indicating a release of tension.)
Greg:	Are you going to behave?
Kate:	Nooooo!
Greg:	Well, then, you're going to stay down there!
Kate:	I need you so much! Feed me!

Perhaps Greg was called a spoiled brat when he was a child. According to self-report, he has been homeless since he was a child, being abandoned by his mother at age 6 and eventually winding up in the foster care system. Kate is faithfully rendering her role. She is playing the child who needs to be punished. Perhaps this is how many of the group members feel about themselves, as if they are not worthy of receiving the love and nurturance but rather should be punished for their illness, for their homelessness, for not being good enough. Keith reaches his hand out to her and pulls her up off the floor. Keith has difficulty tolerating the intensity of the negative affect expression as displayed by the rest of the group. He makes this clear by rescuing Kate from the basement. Kim, acknowledging this, uses repetition as she returns to the previous structured role-play, to maintain the safety in the playspace. She is also faithfully rendering their feelings. If Kim had stayed with the intensity of the act of perpetration, members may have become overwhelmed and retreated from the play.

> Kim: (enters the center) All right. Class, that was not the way to take care of your babies.
> Greg: Who did that?
> Kim: You did that! (pointing to Greg) And you, and you, and you, and you! (She goes around and points at each group member.)
> Hank: You told us to.
> Kate: You told them to!
> Kim: We have to take care of the babies! Who else is going to take care of them?
> Greg: (quietly) Let's *sell* them.
> Kate: (repeats, louder) Let's *sell* them.
> Kim: (shocked) Wait a minute! Wait a minute!
> Greg: Let's sell them.
> Hank: (raises his hand) Let's sell them.
> Greg: Let's sell them . . . to some rich families. They'll be wealthy.

Again, pertinent personal information is emerging through projection. Perhaps Greg felt "sold off" as a child, when he was abandoned by his parents. His ability to explore affective issues related to this through improvisational play is noteworthy. Greg rarely mentions his personal history and has shared little about his early life. He has stated that his parents beat him until he was black and blue and that he does not remember much.

> Hank: They'll shine your boots.
> Kate: They'll shine. . . . They can be our servants!
> Joseph: Put them in an orphanage.
> Greg: No!
> Keith: Yeah, that's a good idea. Put them in an orphanage.
> Kim: Put them in an orphanage!
> Greg: I say sell 'em.
> Kate: Put them in an orphanage, sell them.
> Leshon: Orphanage.

Kate is able to incorporate Hank's association into the play, illustrating the flexibility of this method. Throughout this remarkable section of the play, the members of the group—homeless, thought-disordered individuals—have been playing directly with their own experience of neglect and rejection; Joseph's exclamation, "put them in an orphanage!" demonstrates his ability to play with material and affective content that normally he would not be able to address.

> Kim: (in a gravelly, high pitched, mean voice) All right! We're in the orphanage now. (she comes into the center) All of you rotten children deserve to be here! (Greg, Natasha, and Kate begin to stick out their tongues and wave their fingers by their ears at Kim)

Kim:	(to Kate) That's it! No food for you for a week! (to Keith) And you, look at you shaking like a baby! (Keith begins to exaggerate the shaking in his body, as if he's very, very scared) I'm not changing your diaper! (to Jose) And you, I can't even communicate with you! (to Manuel) Aaaaarghh! (he covers his face with his hands) I don't even want to say what I think about this one! (Pointing at Leshon.) And you, look at you, you should be ashamed of yourself coming into this orphanage! (Immediately spins around to face Greg, pointing in his face.) Hey! Keep your mouth closed!

Kim becomes their playobject and faithfully renders their internal drama. Kate further enhances the sense of play with such uncomfortable material by giving the members permission to ridicule a figure that normally would hold great power and control over their lives. The group members are fully engaged in this structured role-play. Kim exaggerates the character she is playing, making it more safe to explore feelings in the scene. The energy is extremely high, and all members are fully engaged in their bodies as they respond to Kim. Of importance is that they have shifted from the perpetrator roles to the victim roles. In this encounter they can explore their neediness and feelings of abandonment without the definition that this is "what it is about."

Kate:	We want food! We want food! (she begins to jump up and down; the rest of the group joins in)
All:	We want food! We want food!
Kim:	All right! All right! Old, stale fishbones for you. (She extends them toward Greg.)
Greg:	After you, after you.
Kim:	Oh, no, I'm quite full. Here you go. (She shoves them in his mouth.) Ah!
Leshon:	(laughs)
Kim:	(to Keith, whose hand is outstretched) What do you want?
Keith:	(he is smiling) Just a small portion.
Kim:	(pretends to spit into his hand)
Everyone:	(with laughter) Oooohhhh!
Greg:	Want some fishbones? How about food?
Kim:	All right. Listen all of you. What do you want?
Greg:	We want some food!

The subtext here seems to be "we want to be nurtured," something they rarely received. The therapists, however, continue to play with the withholding role, so as to intensify the moment. The level of play is very high and members clearly feel safe in engaging in these images. At the same time, Kim is experiencing discomfort in her role as the sadistic director. She allows this discomfort to become playable by exaggerating and elevating the sadism even further, going so far as to feign spitting into a member's hand. By heightening the transferential role, she is allowing everyone, including herself, to explore the disquieting power dynamics of the perpetrator.

Kim:	(pointing at Diego) What do you want? (Diego shakes his head)
Kim:	(putting her arms around Diego) This is the *perfect* orphan. He doesn't want a thing. He doesn't want food, he doesn't want shelter, he doesn't want love. (looks at Diego) Am I right?
Diego:	(nods his head)
Kim:	(patting Diego's hand) He can be my assistant.

This remarkable interaction suggests an intriguing possibility: that, as neglected and denigrated human objects, these clients had adapted by denying their own needs, for their neediness evoked the abuse and violence of their caretakers. The best way to survive was to not be needy, not to demand, and not indeed to be a human, so as to help maintain the insecure stability of their abusive caretakers. If so, then this imagery reveals a possible meaning of their interpersonal aversion, chosen homelessness, and rejection of services.

Kate:	(with a cockney accent) We just want to go to sleep, ma'am. Truly. We just want to go to sleep. We'll be no bother. No bother at all. We'll be no bother.
Greg:	(sing-songy) We just want to sleep, we just want to sleep, we just want to sleep.
Kim:	All right. If I make a nice big bed for you, will you all sleep nice? And not make any noise?
Greg:	Yaaaay! (Kate, Joseph, Keith, Jose, and Natasha clap; Kim begins to pass out the pillows, silently; after she gives Greg his pillow, Greg mimes coming after her with it, as if to smother her)
Kate:	It's a pillow. A pillow to go to sleep with.
Kate:	(after Kim has finished giving out the pillows, she begins to sing softly, as each group member starts swaying with a pillow tucked under their heads) Sleep babies, sleep babies, sleep orphans, sleep orphans . . . . (Kate, noticing that Kim, too, is pretending to fall asleep, gathers most of the group members around her and brings their attention to that fact; Keith, Joseph, and Jose begin to feed Kim sleeping pills)
Kim:	(as she descends to the floor) I'm feeling very sleepy . . . very woozy . . . oh, my, what have you done to me? (she is now lying on the floor)
Greg:	We have to kill her with our pillows.
Kate:	Oh yes! (she comes forward, singing) Sleep, baby, sleep, baby, sleep baby.
Kim:	Oh, oh no. I was mean and so horrible to you all! I deserve it! I deserve it! I was so horrible! So horrible! (Jolene is laughing as Greg steps forward)
Greg:	(advancing with his pillow) Shall I take the honor?
Kate:	I think maybe you must.
Kim:	Oh, no! Oh, I'm so sorry!
Greg:	Ha ha ha ha ha ha ha! (he bends down to smother Kim's face with the pillow)

Kim:	Oh, please!
Keith:	(jumping in and grabbing the pillow from Greg) Noooo!
Kate:	Did we go too far?
Keith:	Almost.

The sense of aggression returns. Also, Greg voices the aggression, and Kate further structures its expression. Further, Kate transforms to the "here and now," aware of the fact that Keith had previous difficulty tolerating such dark and emotionally laden material. In this manner, Keith is able to manage his anxiety within the playspace. He says this "almost" in a very playful manner.

Kate:	We almost went too far! (She raises her hands above her head.) Everyone, take your pillows—we will not go too far, though— take your pillows, but do not go too far.
	Ready, and . . . (She brings the pillow down near Kim's face, pretending to smother her while keeping the imaginary pillow far enough away from Kim so that the members see that she is not "going too far"; the members respond by duplicating this motion with her.)
Manuel:	She fell.
Kate:	We gave her a sleeping pill, Manuel. And she fell, yes. Now what should we do with her?

Here, the therapist offers structure and a low level of ambiguity, so that there can be act completion. It is a moment of playing with things that are usually rendered unplayable, due to the nature of the impulses and the trauma that are being explored. It is now safe for the members to express their anger for being neglected and abused, within the simple action that Kate offers.

Kim:	(coming awake with the wicked, gravelly, high-pitched voice) No more for you!
Kate:	Get away from us!
Kim:	You! You! You! (pointing at Jose; Jose extends his hand to Kim as if to help her up)
Kate:	Let's zap her into something else. One, two, three, zap! (they all throw their hands at Kim)

The members have explored their angry impulses and are now seeking some reparation. It still seems somewhat threatening to fully engage in their feelings toward the therapists, toward their role, toward their neediness, or toward their feelings of worthlessness.

Kim:	(as if she is waking from a dream, in normal voice) Oh. Oh my. Where am I? What happened?
Greg:	We got Kim again. (The members seem relieved that she has dropped this role.)
Kate:	She's with us again.
Joseph:	You passed out.
Jose:	It's OK.

Kim:	I had a very odd dream. (Manuel and Natasha help her up.) Oh my God, it was horrible. We didn't have food to eat, and there was an awfully mean lady there.
Kate:	There's nobody mean in here now, though. Is there?
Kim:	Is there? (There is silence in the group.)
Hank:	We had fishbones.
Kate:	Fishbones?
Kim:	Are we still in the orphanage, or have we left? Where are we? Huddle! (She draws all the group members into a tight circle.)

The members are reassuring the therapists that they are still in the playspace. The killing or elimination of the abusive parent gives rise to guilt and anxiety in the group, for many of them indeed were defined not as victims but as problems within their original or foster families. Hank's final comment, "we had fishbones," seems to encapsulate the scene: There was very little to eat, what we ate was dangerous, and we were treated like cats.

Kate:	I think we need to create a special concoction and drink it to come back to The Other Place. (members begin a ritual of putting ingredients into a mixing bowl; they put in many things, including apple cider, a couple of cigarettes, chocolate, and cream; they then stir it up)
Kate:	Everyone take a glass and drink. (The members begin drinking, making gulping sounds, all but Greg.)

The group members were so embodied in the role of orphans that there needs to be some de-roling, or structured transition.

Kate:	And now, just to check, each person needs to come into the center of the circle, say their names and then come out.
Manuel:	(enters the middle of the circle) Manuel, back to normal life. (Each member, picking up on Manuel's response, comes into the center, says their name, and repeats, "Back to normal life.")
Kim:	Everyone take a deep breath and let it out. And again. One last time. Now reach up and pull down the magic box. Three turns to the right. (they open up the box) What are we going to put in this week?
Jolene:	The movements.
Greg:	The green-eyed monsters. (Other members of the group and the facilitators mention the "yes, yes, yes, no, no, no," the "baby food," "the kisses," "Natasha being afraid," "smelly diapers," "getting locked in the basement," "the emotions of it.")
Keith:	That's good. (The ritual of putting the top back on the box, and storing the box up above, is enacted; then the magic curtain is raised back up to the ceiling, and the group ends. Everyone applauds.)

The magic box is an image that is brought up toward the end of this group. It is used weekly, serving as a metaphorical container for the group movements, images, roles, thoughts, and feelings. In putting images back into the box, the projections and transferences that have manifested themselves over the course of the session are named by the members, although they do not recognize them as such. They are naming images that they remember, because they held the members' interest. For the therapists, there is a recognition that the group played out transferential relationships through the drama and that, by the therapists' enactments of such roles as the green-eyed monster, the smelly and spoiled baby, and the evil director of the orphanage, the members could fully engage and explore their emotions.

Discussion

In this group session with 10 homeless clients with a mental illness, the therapists facilitated a flow of playful improvisation that allowed feelings and images related to these clients' early childhood experiences and current difficulties to emerge. The level of engagement among these clients was high, and their immersion in the play allowed for processing of these issues. Because this group had been working together for approximately 2 years, members by this time were comfortable with this type of exploration. Trust in the play and leaders had to be established before these issues could be tolerated and expressed through the play.

In the beginning of the group's formation, it was not unusual to spend more time in the sound and movement stage; exploring half-defined images; and playing with "safer," less personal stories. When developmental transformations was first introduced, the therapist leading the group took a strong supportive stance and structured the session in a way that modeled and encouraged a playful atmosphere. There were no expectations as to the content of the group's play, and the exploration of personal issues was not a focus. Group members often played out their own defenses, and sessions consisted of members building walls around themselves, creating their own fantasy worlds, and expressing grandiose wishes. The therapist not only tolerated this type of play but also encouraged it.

It was only after the group members felt sufficiently supported that they were able to explore more disturbing images and issues. Recent images leading up to this session included "walking through the fire," being bathed in "healing" waters, finding lost treasures, and looking for food and eating sumptuous meals. Over time, the group became able to integrate more personal content in their play. This was not true for all group members, however. This group session offered good examples of how sound, movement, and seemingly disconnected images became warm-ups for metaphorical explorations of greater depth. In this session, the layers of meaning and affect for each image reverberated in the session as they were repeated again and again. For example, the important dynamic of group members suppressing their own needs so as to avoid further rejection by the parental figure was clearly represented. Elements of their larger story as homeless people emerged, providing pieces with which they can begin to construct a sense of meaning in their lives.

Greg offered his tell-tale resistance and need for differentiation in a group that was beginning to deal on more personal levels each week. It was no surprise that he introduced a question that could normally be considered resistant ("has anyone seen Cats?"). He has been homeless on and off since age 6, when he was abandoned by his parents. He grew up in and out of foster homes and on the streets. He would not speak of his early childhood, simply stating "I don't want to talk about it," and had left other groups when childhood recollections were introduced. This was Greg's second time in the program, and only recently had he become able to trust enough to use his supports and make connections with other people. Since becoming involved in this group and others like it, he obtained permanent housing, enrolled in a GED program, and became involved in a competitive employment program. His defensive posturing, when incorporated into the group, became less rigid. His awareness of this guardedness became more pronounced, and he was able to laugh about this with the group. As his trust in the group developed, his capacity to share the complexities of who he is emerged. His posturing became just that, mere role-playing of an attitude that once had strong protective roots.

Greg's behavior in this particular session, while playful, posed some challenges to the group leaders. In most group therapy approaches, departures from the group theme can be construed as resistance. Rather than directing Greg back to the topic at hand when he took another point of view, the therapists attempted to incorporate his comments into the play. For example, when the group members were caring for their babies in a nurturing manner, Greg's discomfort with this quality of role-play led to his refusal to participate. It could be viewed as stopping the play when he stated "that baby is a spoiled brat." Instead, the spoiled baby, the one who receives all the love and attention it requires, was punished for being so demanding in the ensuing scene. Rather than trying to re-focus Greg, the therapists incorporated the image he offered, which led to another level of exploration for the entire group. Thus, therapists must be careful not to hold on to what is happening in the moment but rather allow themselves to be open to whatever "resistances" or divergent feelings and images arise.

In a similar manner, the therapists did not direct each group member to change their tendencies in role-play or even movement. For example, when Keith first began the group, he compulsively made the same movements and sounds at the beginning of the group. He rotated in a circle and said "hello" in a monotone, with no eye contact with the other members. However, during his 2 years with the group, he began to show more flexibility in this area. Although he still did the same movements, he took in the other members of the group while he did this. He allowed other members to "borrow" his movement, something that previously upset him a great deal.

Keith began showing more spontaneity in other ways as well. He allowed himself to fully enroll as the "monster," exhibiting a full range of affect and expression that is normally difficult for him in reality. He may have been identifying with the aggressor here (i.e., the abusive parent) or even allowing his own anger and aggression to take form in a manner that was tolerable for him. His inability to smother Kim as the wicked orphanage director and his impulse to "rescue" Kate as the abused baby may have reflected his fear of losing a love object, whether abusive or nurturing. In fact, this role-play indicated multiple levels of meaning occurring simultaneously: Keith related to Kim in role as the wicked orphanage director and out of role as the actual program director of TOP. Keith's participation in the group since this session has increased, and he has begun to show leadership qualities as he engages in more complex and affect-laden roles. In addition, he has made progress in the vocational program and has begun to look at goals for his future, commenting that he would like to be more social and connect with others.

Overall, the group members were able to practice positive interpersonal skills and be recognized as human beings with unique attributes. They had a successful group experience. The therapists' interventions were largely determined by the aim of maintaining a state of embodied play rather than shaping the enactments in line with the developing issues. The therapists attempted to provide less engaged members extra support when needed and to contain more energetic members. They allowed themselves to become playobjects for the group, playing various roles and transforming these roles according to the rapidly shifting energies of the group members. Most telling were the rapid transformations near the end of the group around the images of victims/perpetrators (children/parents), demonstrating simultaneous presentations of contradictory figures around anxiety-provoking issues.

The therapists were challenged when they elected to enroll as negative figures that embody the projections of the group. Kate's choice to enroll as the monster and Kim's choice to play the wicked orphanage director were evocative for both therapists. They were acutely aware of the magnitude of neglect and the need for love and attention that these clients experienced, and stepping into these roles was uncomfortable for them. However, as facilitators of this group process, they realized that they must take on such roles for the members to fully explore their feelings.

This group session demonstrated that severely disturbed clients can participate productively in a relatively unstructured, expressive, and evocative group environment. The reason for this lies largely in the inherent structuring power of attuned play, in which the dramatic flow is closely geared to the interests of the members (Johnson, 1984). It is the therapists' aim to establish and sustain such attunement, which in itself becomes the safe container for the clients' process. The stereotype of the homeless person with a serious mental illness and hampered by a variety of negative symptoms and side effects of psychotropic medications does not prove to be our experience.

In this and other sessions that followed, these clients were able to make connections with each other while exploring difficult personal material.

EMPIRICAL SUPPORT

Drama therapy has been applied to the full range of psychiatric populations, although there have been no experimental studies specifically examining the effects of drama therapy on homeless people with a mental illness. Support for these approaches has consisted of detailed case studies (Forrester & Johnson, 1995; Johnson, 1984, 1999; Schnee, 1996; Smith, 2000) and descriptive studies (Emunah, 1994; Landy, 1986). Drama therapy appears to most often affect clients' self-esteem, current levels of distress, hopefulness, compliance with treatment, and social skills (Johnson, 1999).

CONCLUSION

Developmental transformations is a form of drama psychotherapy that relies on improvisational play. Limitations of its use are based on (a) the need for in-depth training of the therapist and (b) preferences for this type of activity among clients. Although this method can be used with virtually any population, certain conditions need to be taken into consideration. For example, if a client is in crisis (e.g., floridly psychotic, suicidal, or under the influence of drugs), the deconstructive aspects of the play may be confusing. Interestingly enough, clients with looseness of associations, delusions, depression, and somatic complaints are able to participate actively and the method helps to connect their worlds with others, reducing isolation and avolition. This method of intervention demonstrates the power of improvisational play, bodily movement, and interpersonal encounter within the playspace. Its reliance on indirect, even divergent, processes in the session, guided by the energetic flow of the play rather than the developing meanings of the issues, is unique and deserving of further study.

REFERENCES

Bruner, J. (1964). The course of cognitive growth. *American Psychologist, 19*, 1–6.

Dintino, C., & Johnson, D. (1996). Playing with the perpetrator: Gender dynamics in developmental drama therapy. In S. Jennings (Ed.), *Drama therapy: Theory and practice* (Vol. 3, pp. 205–220). London: Routledge.

Emunah, R. (1994). *Acting for real: Drama therapy process, technique, and performance*. New York: Brunner/Mazel.

Forrester, A., & Johnson, D. (1995). Drama therapy on an extremely short-term inpatient unit. In A. Gersie (Ed.), *Brief treatment approaches to drama therapy* (pp. 125–138). London: Routledge.

James, M., & Johnson, D. (1996a). Drama therapy in the treatment of affective expression in post-traumatic stress disordered patients. In D. Nathanson (Ed.), *Knowing feeling: Affect, script, and psychotherapy* (pp. 303–326). New York: W. W. Norton.

James, M., & Johnson, D. (1996b). Drama therapy in the treatment of combat-related PTSD. *Arts in Psychotherapy, 23,* 383–396.

Johnson, D. (1982). Developmental approaches in drama therapy. *Arts in Psychotherapy, 9,* 183–190.

Johnson, D. (1984). The representation of the internal world in catatonic schizophrenia. *Psychiatry, 47,* 299–314.

Johnson, D. (1986). The developmental method in drama therapy: Group treatment with the elderly. *International Journal of Arts in Psychotherapy, 13,* 17–34.

Johnson, D. (1991). The theory and technique of transformations in drama therapy. *International Journal of Arts in Psychotherapy, 18,* 285–300.

Johnson, D. (1992). The drama therapist in role. In S. Jennings (Ed.), *Drama therapy: Theory and practice* (Vol. 2, pp. 112–136). London: Routledge.

Johnson, D. (1999). Creative arts therapies in an era of managed care. In D. Johnson (Ed.), *Essays on the creative arts therapies: Imagining the birth of a profession* (pp. 85–90). Springfield, IL: Charles C Thomas.

Johnson, D. (2000). Developmental transformations: Towards the body as presence. In P. Lewis & D. Johnson (Eds.), *Current approaches in drama therapy* (pp. 87–110). Springfield, IL: Charles C Thomas.

Johnson, D., Forrester, A., Dintino, C., James, M., & Schnee, G. (1996). Towards a poor drama therapy. *Arts in Psychotherapy, 23,* 293–308.

Landy, R. J. (1986). *Drama therapy: Concepts and practices.* Springfield, IL: Charles C Thomas.

Piaget, J. (1951). *Play, dreams, and imitation.* New York: W. W. Norton.

Schnee, G. (1996). Drama therapy with the homeless mentally ill: Treating interpersonal disengagement. *Arts in Psychotherapy, 23,* 53–60.

Smith, A. (2000). Exploring death anxiety with older adults through developmental transformations. *Arts in Psychotherapy, 27,* 321–332.

Werner, H., & Kaplan, S. (1963). *Symbol formation.* New York: Wiley.

6

GROUP ART THERAPY WITH SELF-DESTRUCTIVE YOUNG WOMEN

BARBARA F. COOPER AND ILO B. MILTON

Editors' Introduction: The approach of Barbara F. Cooper and Ilo B. Milton to art therapy is distinctively improvisational, with interventions developed in response to the client's immediate concerns rather than to an agenda predetermined by the therapist. This orientation, although not unique to art therapy, demands of therapists a high level of flexibility, empathy, and willingness to participate in a reflexive process, where the client's response shapes successive art directives. The theoretical underpinnings of this method are based in ego psychology and object relations, whereby art-making, as the bridge from the client's private inner world to external relationships and realities, becomes the vehicle to psychic maturation.

This chapter describes group art therapy with six young female patients in a residential treatment facility. These patients were self-destructive; all had a history of problems with substance abuse, and the majority also experienced eating disorders or self-mutilation. As art therapists, we have been professional collaborators for more than 10 years. The theoretical orientation featured in this chapter is a result of our collaboration.

ART THERAPY DESCRIBED

As a treatment modality, art therapy permits the expression of unconscious and conscious emotions, thoughts, sensations, fantasies, conflicts, and experiences through the creation of visual images that are their symbolic equivalents. These images and the process by which they are created function as a form of symbolic discourse between patient and therapist. Patients' reactions and responses to their own artwork can then be used to help them find more compatible relationships between their thoughts and actions. Thus, the art process aids in developing higher functioning to replace nonadaptive functioning.

It appears that the more severe the difficulty patients have with interpersonal relationships, reality testing, and impulse control, the greater may be the relative advantages of action modalities (e.g., art therapy) over verbal ones. Art-making provides these patients, so often overwhelmed by their anxiety, with a safe outlet for constructive tension reduction in place of such maladaptive alternatives as self-mutilation or substance abuse. Additionally, the image-making process can help an individual come to terms with losses and other painful experiences they have endured. One premise of art-making is that it can give concrete and observable form to psychic pain. "The capacity for creativity seems closely interwoven with the alchemy of the ego to bring order and meaning out of chaos and distress" (Vaillant, 1993, p. 2). Unlike verbal exchanges, the visual language of art crosses cultural, economic, social, and intellectual barriers. It also provides a bridge from the unconscious to the conscious and from the nonverbal to the verbal.

Art therapists work from their chosen theoretical orientation, be it psychoanalytic, object relations, ego, self, gestalt, cognitive–behavioral, phenomenological, Jungian, or eclectic, as it applies to different populations, treatment settings, and the therapist's training. Descriptions of the variety of ways that art therapists work is beyond the scope of this chapter; for an excellent overview of a variety of theoretical positions, incorporating many art therapy techniques, see Rubin (1987).

Art therapy is often complementary to other treatment modalities, with the result that art therapists need to be flexible to contribute to the varying goals of the therapeutic team, with an understanding that therapeutic goals shift throughout treatment. Accordingly, not only do we work differently with different patient populations, but also each population requires that therapists accommodate fluctuations in the psychic organization within each patient. Art therapists assess the patient's current level of ego organization and tailors their interventions in an attempt to match the patient's internal experience. This style of practice assumes that art therapists have familiarity with a variety of developmental theories and hold the belief "that the phenomena that provide the basis for drive, ego, object relations, and self theories are inherent in the life of the developing individual" (Pine, 1985, p. 72).

THEORETICAL CONTRIBUTIONS TO OUR APPROACH

Ego psychology focuses on how people handle their anxieties. Each person develops characteristic adaptive and defensive patterns, which are used to relieve anxiety and conflict arising from thoughts, feelings, impulses, or fantasies. Ego functions can be sufficiently or insufficiently developed and unfold as one matures physically, cognitively, and so forth. Horner (1984) suggested that ego functions unfold according to the quality of object relations.

Winnicott's (1965) idea of the "environmental mother" relating to her 2-year-old child is relevant here, as the art therapy session has many similarities to this period of development. The environmental mother makes available to her toddler the "objects of the world" that the child is then able to "discover" while the mother watches. The mother structures the child's exploration and functions as a container for the frustrations of the child, serving as an "auxiliary ego." As such, the mother, functioning with a high degree of organization, temporarily lends to the child her own ego strength whenever his or her ego strength is inadequate to the task that confronts him or her. Through this process the child becomes able to organize his or her inner world by internalizing the mother's model of organization.

Winnicott believed that creativity develops here, when the mother is a "good-enough" one. The good-enough mother creates a holding environment, or psychological security, by finding the balance point among impinging on, flooding or overwhelming, and abandoning her child. She allows her child to play in her presence without being intrusive or disappearing.

The internalization of this holding environment is not developed exclusively in early childhood. It can be achieved through maturation and a therapeutic environment that models it and permits it to be internalized (Vaillant, 1993).

Therapeutic play is a way for an action-oriented therapist to create a holding environment of "relatedness and resonance within which deficits in early object relations can be repaired" (Robbins, as cited in Rubin, 1987, pp. 71–72). Different forms of holding are necessary for patients functioning at different developmental levels. The holding environment can make the pain of working through unmet stages of development "bearable and can allow progress and growth to proceed" (p. 73).

The art therapist functions as the good-enough mother to the group, in which the art materials are those objects of the world that the patients can discover. New materials can be received with fear, enthusiasm, caution, or rejection as a result of how they are presented. The therapist's familiarity with a wide range of art materials is critical to offering the sense of security and holding while presenting a new material, idea, or construct. It is asking too much of patients having weak egos, lacking a sense of self, and experiencing overwhelming anxiety to require that they "express" themselves using materials they find unfamiliar or intimidating. A competent art therapist "holds" his or her patients by how he or she presents materials and directives. "Different media provoke different kinds of messages in individuals. Some materials tap deep libidinal levels and still others have an exploratory quality" (Robbins, 1987, pp. 106–109). Attention to textures, malleability, and chromatic stimulation are important considerations in choosing what materials to offer patients in art therapy.

All the patients described in this chapter had difficulty managing their affects and impulses. Therefore, they were offered a combination of paint, pastels, and clay that helped them initially make contact with their feelings while simultaneously providing structured boundaries to prevent regression. These patients need active intervention and instruction that has been tuned to their level of experience as well as their current affective state. The women in the group used ego defense mechanisms that have been insufficient to help them integrate, make sense of, and master conflict. Therefore, the art therapist provides "ego building techniques for the understructured personalities within a therapeutic climate that affords opportunity for structuralization" (Blanck & Blanck, 1986, p. 19).

Essential to this process is helping clients express their internal experiences in art-making and then translating their artwork into words. Robbins (as cited in Rubin, 1987) stressed that "secondary process thinking, with its foundation in words, must be evoked if the ego is to gain mastery and understanding of primitive material" (p. 68). Robbins continued, "The art form, then, organizes object relations and mirrors them back to the patient" (p. 68).

Both the lack of self formation and a denial of a sense of self in an individual stem from being intruded on or neglected by another who perceives that individual as a narcissistic object, ignoring those needs that are constitutionally and developmentally unique to that individual. The women in this group had in common childhoods in which they were "bought" with material things and not validated for who they were. Expectations of "success" impinged on them so that the validating social mirrors that might have helped them connect to their self-identity and self-worth were grossly distorted. Their normal development of a consistent sense of self had been impeded.

The feelings of "I am" can be viewed from an attachment vantage point as postulated in the works of Bowlby (1988); Mahler, Pine, and Bergman (1975); Ainsworth, Blehar, Waters, and Wall (1978), Cassidy (1999); and other attachment theorists. The sense of I am originates in the relationship to another; only then can separation be viewed as a positive developmental step and not as a negatively tinged, rebellious act. The reparative process can take place within the relationship between the patient and his or her own creativity. That is, the basic attachment deficit can be repaired through patients' relationship with their artwork, leading to a more cohesive sense of self, because "creativity also transmutes pain and restores a sense of self" (Vaillant, 1993, p. 27).

If the ego or "self" is viewed as a container, and that container is leaking, damaged, or hasn't developed, then the container first needs to be reinforced, repaired, or developed before a secure-enough internal structure exists to hold one's affective experiences. For patients who have not developed a sense of, or solid connection to, their experience-containing selves, particular art therapy interventions (as exemplified in the case material that follows) can provide substitute containers that permit affective experiences to be known from a more distant and therefore safer vantage point. Inherent in the art-making process is the potential for exploration with messing, merging, creating, and dismantling boundaries, all outside of the creator. Once outside, both original and novel structures and relationships are safer to view, probe, rework, and eventually to own. Therefore, the art-making process offers these patients the opportunity not only to create self-symbols but also to attain ego mastery, which is very much akin to "how the mind manipulates experience which is at the core of ego development" (Vaillant, 1993, p. 3).

THEORETICAL FRAMEWORK FOR UNDERSTANDING SELF-INJURING PATIENTS

Why is it that many therapists do not want to treat self-injuring patients? These patients require a tremendous amount of support because of their intense anxiety and strong impulses crying out for expression. They appear chronic and acute at the same time and have long histories of feeling they have not been seen or heard. The etiology of this "being unheard" is not on a verbal level but on a more primitive, preverbal level. In looking at the backgrounds of the patients in this group, there is evidence of early, preverbal trauma and disturbed object relations. For the most part, the trauma was not the kind one finds in criminal court cases or publicized in the media. "In the lives of these individuals there was an accumulation of discrete traumatic experiences" (Krystal, 1978, p. 90). As Breuer and Freud wrote in 1893, "any experience which calls up distressing affects—such as those of fright, anxiety, shame or physical pain—may operate as a trauma of this kind" (p. 6).

It is theorized that these patients had primary caretakers who failed to protect them in infancy from psychic traumatization. Impinged on, flooded, or overwhelmed, these patients quickly regress to a time of timeless mortal terror (this refers to infancy when basic needs were not met and the infant was overwhelmed in a timeless state). This childhood trauma in adults "is a lifelong *dread* of the return of the traumatic state and an *expectation* of it" (Krystal, 1975, p. 198). "There is a fear of one's emotions and an impairment of affect tolerance" (p. 98). Accompanying this trauma is lifelong anhedonia and masochistic problems. These patients exhibit what Freud (1926) called "automatic anxiety," in which affective responses become overwhelming and initiate the traumatic state (Krystal, 1978). The patient feels helpless and surrenders to this flooding, and her anxiety changes to "cataleptic passivity" (p. 92). "Anxiety is the signal of the perception of *preventable* danger. Helplessly surrendering to the peril changes the affective state from the hyperalert and hyperactive response (anxiety) to one of the blocking of emotions and progressive inhibition" (p. 92).

This "catatonoid reaction," or "freezing" (Stern, 1951), becomes a threat to one's survival.

In the catatonoid state we are dealing with the very moment of the self being overwhelmed with a phylogenetically determined surrender pattern which is also a potential "self-destruct" mechanism. When people experiencing this reaction do not die, they spend long periods of time in a robotic, depersonalized state; psychically closed off. (Krystal, 1978, p. 93)

"In the traumatic state there is a psychological paralysis which starts with a virtually complete blocking of the ability to feel emotions and pain as well as other physical sensations, and progresses to inhibition of other mental functions" (p. 101). This numbing and closing off, which brings relief from anxiety, is also experienced as the first part of dying, which is accompanied by cognitive constriction. Because of the threat in beginning to die from the catatonoid state, the patient is jolted into adaptive action. Due to the characteristic effects of the catatonoid state, these actions are not planned and thought out but are "reflexive in nature and self-destructive in outcome" (p. 104).

"Self-mutilations may represent a means of interrupting the traumatic state" (Simpson, 1976, p. 72). The self-mutilation "may (paradoxically) be life saving in that the individual asserts mastery, thereby interrupting the state of helplessness and surrender" (Krystal, 1978, p. 104). Thus, the self-destructive act is really a coping or survival mechanism, albeit a dangerous and maladaptive one. The blocking off or constriction of mental function in this catatonoid state reduces self-observation and cognition to a minimum. Schneidman (1976) has made the same point about suicidal patients, stressing that they cannot write a "full and explicative note" (p. 90). He asserted that, if they could write it, they would not have to kill themselves.

Why do these patients need to cut, mutilate, and use intensely aversive means for making contact that tend to push others away, including therapists? These are patients who need to *see* the feeling that they exist. The feeling of I am is often achieved by seeing their blood flow. Their self-mutilation does not primarily result in experiencing physical pain but, more importantly, in feelings of humiliation and shame. For these patients, their early attachment relationships are fraught with associations to these very same feelings of shame and humiliation. This understanding guides the art therapist to offer image-making as an alternative to self-mutilation that provides patients with the opportunity to explore their early feeling states in a concrete, mirroring way. The creative process and the images become safe transitional spaces where the patient can "be."

Due to the deprivations and trauma experienced by these patients during the preverbal phases of their development, their inner lives are rich and full of symbols, yet their verbal abilities fall short of effective expression. Art enables the patient to use materials symbolically to communicate feelings and experiences and to develop coping mechanisms. This process also affords the patient the opportunity to neutralize his or her propensity for acting out his or her aggression destructively. The art process helps to promote comfort with and acceptance of feelings of aggression, so as not to allow these feelings to become overwhelming. In this approach we help the patient to first recognize his or her aggression and then help him or her acquire a more effective ego structure that first is manifested externally in the creative process, for example, mastery of art materials or forming authentic symbols (Deri, 1984).

Patients who act out destructively present a challenge to a purely verbal treatment approach, in which the expectation is for the patient to replace action with words. That is an unrealistic expectation when a therapist needs to engage patients quickly and reduce their self-destructive actions before they kill or injure themselves. Action-oriented treatment (in this case, art therapy) offers these anxiety-ridden and self-destructive individuals techniques that provide immediate, constructive alternatives to their self-destructive actions, right from the first session. Although other forms of therapy may complement and be conducted simultaneously with such action interventions, there is no time to wait for these patients to develop better coping mechanisms through verbal treatment methods alone.

In verbal therapy, metaphors or analogies often arise that relate to affective states and conflicts that the patient and therapist visit and revisit throughout the treatment. These metaphorical images are often the profound touchstones that are mutually shared and worked through in treatment. However, self-injuring patients find it extremely difficult to hold on to these verbal metaphors because of their severely fluctuating ego states (due to splitting, dissociation, denial). Therefore, art-making with directives often produces physical images that are concrete reminders of their affect states and relationship to the therapist, to themselves, to their peers, and to their core conflicts. The permanence of the art pieces serves as a tangible representation of consistency and provides a fertile ground for integrative work in verbal therapy.

Art productions help shift the focus or direction of emotional energy as well as stimulate or decrease the intensity of that energy. Sometimes therapists may not know the impact of the piece created during the group art therapy session. The patient can be relatively quiet verbally in the group in both the art-making and processing. When a patient seems uninvolved and disconnected to his or her artwork, the therapist needs to give that patient the space and perhaps permission to cut, slash, void, and vacate with the art materials. Often, in verbal therapy afterward, the primary therapist reports an increase in verbal connectedness and positive shift in energy. This is an example of how the patient's social relatedness can increase through his or her engagement in the creative process.

The women in this group were used to "performing" their lives for others rather than living their lives for themselves. Therefore, a major focus of these groups was the search for individual authenticity. For some of these women, the idea that they lived a performance life, with a mask on, was new to them. Some of these patients knew their lives were "false" but felt helpless to change because of their fear that there was really nothing inside. They feared that the mask, or what had been mirrored for them throughout their lives, was all there was.

The following questions arise in group art therapy: For whom does the patient make art? Who is the audience? Is art-making for the self, the therapist, the group? Is it to impress each other? Is it to comply with "the right" therapeutic goals? The art therapy methods selected for use with this group were designed to help these patients connect to their authenticity, which aids in their acquisition of identity.

CASE PRESENTATION

Milieu

The art therapy groups described in this chapter took place at a residential treatment facility for adults situated in a rural, farmlike setting. The patients occupy either single or double rooms in a house with a living room, kitchen, dining room, art room, and clinical staff offices. Patients generally come to this residence following an acute hospitalization so that they can continue their therapeutic process in a milieu that encourages expression, family living, attachment, and peer support. The minimum length of stay is 3 months, although patients frequently stay for longer periods and may remain for up to 1 year. These patients are generally from upper-middle-class families with the financial resources to continue treatment after insurance coverage ends.

The unit, or house, is not locked; although patients can move about freely, clear limits are set about their participation in the program, with most of their waking time scheduled for treatment of various types. Treatment is varied and intensive: daily individual verbal psychotherapy (cognitive and psychodynamic), daily community meetings or women's group, semiweekly group art therapy (the subject of this chapter), semiweekly expressive group therapy (chiefly therapeutic holding and anger release), semiweekly "work" program (e.g., farmlike chores, cooking), weekly puppetry, and semiweekly psychodrama.

Many patients choose this facility because of the staff's success with individuals experiencing eating disorders, self-mutilation, dissociative disorders, substance abuse, and depression. The primary therapeutic stance is a relational one, in which all levels of interpersonal relationships are opened for examination in the therapeutic process. A maximum of 10 patients can be treated at any one time, and the average census is 6 to 8 patients. Most often the patients are women, although occasionally male patients come into treatment.

The therapeutic team consists of three primary therapists, a psychiatric nurse, and two mental health counselors in addition to an art therapist and two expressive therapists as adjunct team members. A psychiatrist is on site for 1 day a week and is always on call. An arrangement exists with the local hospital for patients having an acute episode and needing a more secure level of care. The team works closely together, meeting frequently both formally and informally to discuss each patient's progress, the pulse of the patient groups, and the emotional climate of the house (e.g., agitated, peaceful, collapsed, engaged). Team members believe in the critical importance of processing together their own reactions and countertransferences (frustration, disbelief, rage, protectiveness, sadism, rescue fantasies) that this population powerfully elicits. Staff processing is essential, benefiting patients by reducing the likelihood of these countertransferences being acted out.

The art therapist is present on this unit for approximately 6 hours per week, offering two 1 1/2-hour art therapy groups each week. Because of time constraints, the art therapist rarely is able to see a patient individually. Most of the therapeutic work is accomplished in group therapy sessions.

Patients

This chapter tracks the art therapy group during a period of 4 months when the patient population was unchanged, with six White female patients living at the house and attending art therapy groups twice weekly. Four of these patients engaged in self-mutilation (e.g., cutting and burning themselves), all engaged in substance abuse, and five had eating disorders. All but one had come from acute hospitalizations into this facility for continued treatment.

Pam, age 19, spent 2 weeks in an acute hospital during her first year of college. This was her first hospitalization, and she was sent to our facility for longer term treatment of her long-standing difficulties with substance abuse (marijuana, LSD), anorexia/bulimia, and cutting.

Shiela, age 21 and adopted at birth, was first hospitalized for a suicide attempt during her final semester of college and then sent to this facility. She, too, has a history of substance abuse (drugs and alcohol) and cutting. She hears voices and dissociates.

Lee, age 35, was hospitalized following a suicide attempt when her parental rights for her two young children were terminated. She has been addicted to alcohol and Valium for more than 15 years. Her alcoholism began at age 12; her addiction to Valium began at age 20, when she had surgery that had left her in chronic pain.

Jo, age 22, entered the program voluntarily to "change her life." Specifically, her history of multiple daily purging and cutting episodes was causing her great distress. She reported that she began burning herself at age 5 and continued to create burns by scraping her arms on rugs and rough sur-faces. She is an athlete in an aggressive and sometimes violent sport.

Risa, age 19, was hospitalized for the first time during her initial year of college because of suicidal thoughts, the severity of her eating disorder (an-orexia/bulimia), and substance abuse (drugs and alcohol).

Darcy, age 19 and adopted at birth, deferred her first year of college because of the severity of her eating disorder (anorexia/bulimia). She was hospitalized for 3 months in an eating disorder program and then transferred to our facility for follow-up treatment. She had difficulty engaging in our program because of her anger and sadness over leaving her prior treatment program. She describes cutting herself at her first treatment facility to fit in with the other patients.

Treatment Planning

After initially reviewing the histories and meeting these patients, it became clear to the therapeutic team that they shared common modes of self-destructiveness, either self-mutilation or drug and alcohol ingestion. Therefore, the overriding goal for art therapy would be to help these patients express their feelings out onto art media instead of into their bodies. In other words, the objective of any intervention or directive presented would be to externalize or redirect their feelings of pain, shame, and humiliation into the art-making. This was considered the priority in treatment because of the dangers inherent in their self-destructive behaviors (cutting, purging, and substance abuse). On a secondary level, attention would be focused on ad-dressing items such as "core" self-issues, body image, differentiating sources of sensations (internal or external), the development and use of the creative self, self-esteem, group dynamics, object relationships, and coping skills.

> The work of art is certainly not merely a projection and direct reflection of our inner world through self expression as it is often assumed. It re-ceives the fragmented projections of our inner world only to nurture and transform them. (Ehrenzweig, 1979, p. 223)
>
> Treatment centers around the management of reality and the rein-forcement of more effective, ego-based coping mechanisms. Included in this orientation are such techniques as offering therapeutic contracts, supporting and improving ego skills and creating models of identifica-tion which improve social effectiveness. (Robbins & Cooper, 1994, p. 66)

Recognition of the patient's developmental level guides the art therapist in offering appropriate developmental tasks and emotional support so that the patient is not overwhelmed by inappropriate expectations of her skills and cognitive or emotional integrative ability.

Art therapists work in many ways, depending on their personal style and theoretical orientation. How they approach a group is guided specifically by their view of the etiology of the illness of the patients coupled with their experience of the impact that specific art materials have on different psychological states. We strongly believe in approaching each group session with an openness that allows us to perceive the needs of the patients in the here and now. Therapists who enter a group on any given day with a planned agenda (e.g., a body image art experience because these patients have eating disorders) may miss the mark of other potent issues that may have surfaced, such as the climate on the unit, news from the outside world, or a crisis facing one group member. It is important to understand what these patients are currently experiencing in addition to their developmental, structural, historical, and relational histories.

Pragmatics of Group Art Therapy

Given the primitive defensive structure of their psyches (especially the defense of splitting), these patients challenge the art therapist to provide experiences that will truly "hold" or contain the group. This challenge is caused by many factors. First, facilitating a group with a focus on group dynamics is difficult when patients are in a regressed, collapsed, or very resistant state. When the individual egos of all group members are weak, the group ego is weak. Winnicott's (1965) previously described environmental mother had one toddler at a time on whom to focus her attentions. In these groups, there are often six needy, regressed women to "parent" all at once. Rather than working dynamically with the group-as-a-whole as we would with clients functioning at a higher level, facilitating this group more as if working individually with patients in a shared space (akin to parallel play in toddlers) made sense from this developmental perspective. In this way, patients can witness one another's work and learn much-needed social and relational skills. They sometimes become role models for one another in their approach to art-making and verbal processing of their creations.

We believe that the modeling and energy-sharing that occurs in such groups is valuable. Individual art therapy, although valuable in other ways, cannot replicate the benefits of group modeling and energy-sharing. Working individually on art-making in a group setting also implies permission to work on one's issues in the group and challenges resistance in any group member. The group interaction is nonverbal, as the patients resonate with each other during art-making. Issues around bonding, connection, and lack of connection may be worked through in this nonverbal, holding space. As some patients become more highly ego-organized, a ripple effect occurs in which less organized patients "borrow" ego strength from the more organized and can function on a higher level, which is evident in their behavior, the organization of their artwork, and the quality of verbalization about their artwork. At the outset, most patients predictably demonstrate selfishness and a lack of empathy toward other members. As it is desirable for the patients to eventually be aware of others and able to play in their presence while expressing emotions such as anger constructively, it is necessary to progress slowly. It is almost as though the therapist has to provide individual womblike containers in which the art form can develop and identifications can be explored through self-nurturance and play. Only then can the more social aspects of play and creativity emerge.

To propel the group toward achievable goals, it is important to take the pulse of the group as well as of each individual. This is done by starting with a "warm-up" consisting of a "go-around" in which participants are asked how they are feeling or what is on their mind at that time. The participants are asked to respond with only a word or a short sentence to avoid spending too much time on this activity. Talking at length about how or what each person is feeling can cut short the art-making time of the group, which usually angers members because of their limited ability to attend to the needs of others. The art therapist listens to the answers that participants give during the go-around, seeking a common thread in what she hears that can unite the group on a shared theme. Throughout this warm-up process, the art therapist functions as a "funnel," first collecting a variety of components and then synthesizing the components into one that shares common ground. Reports from unit staff about any issues brewing that might not be brought up by the patients are obtained before group sessions. These reports also are poured into the art therapist's funnel and then integrated into her thinking.

In a typical go-around, patients' responses when asked how they are feeling might include "anxious," "tired," "edgy," "sad," or "jittery." The therapist's assessment might be that all these feelings are heavy and difficult for the patients to feel. The therapist must choose how to proceed in creating a directive; in this example, she might decide to have each group member go deeper into their feeling state and, within the structured group, to explore the feeling in an art piece. The therapist is asking the patients to express their feeling states in an image. Group members might relate to each other by exploring whether their feeling states changed during the exercise. The common ground here is experiencing one's ability to alter or transform affective states.

Psychosocial Development During Therapy

In keeping with both the self-as-container and art-as-substitute-container metaphors expounded earlier, both the art therapist and the group can function as a container from within which a patient can view him or her self. Peers in different stages of recovery and those who have been in treatment longer can offer valuable mirroring and feedback to others. Peers and the art therapist can demonstrate techniques and interesting uses for art materials, sparking a sense of adventure and creativity for all.

For example, a self-mutilating patient new to the residence might witness another patient, who used to cut herself, instead cutting into clay in a satisfying way. The new patient can be encouraged to try that alternative or find some other way of using art materials to contain her impulse to cut. The therapist, at the same time, might do a collage, cutting into paper and magazines, which might also appeal to this new group member. Throughout this session, the structure of the space and group process serves as an external safe container. Group participants witness the healing power of creative expressions to transform their anxieties into healthier forms of expression than self-mutilation. Thus, the external container provided by the art therapist and group may eventually become internalized as a self-structure or container.

Over time, working with this population in groups, an expectable and repetitive range of themes emerges. Therefore, calling on an idea that has been previously used to address the current needs of the group is not unusual. For example, a collection of both ordinary and unusual keys is kept in a box. The box can be passed around, asking each group member to choose the key that "jumps" out at her, one to which she is immediately attracted. Participants are asked to visualize the object that their particular key opens and then to draw the object and what is inside of it. This activity is useful when the group is unfocused and no particular common issue surfaces, becoming an exercise in accepting one's creativity and allowing uncensored projection. All too often, both authenticity and a sense of genuine surprise emerge from directives like this that offer both structure and the opportunity for indirect and nonthreatening self-exploration.

Once a patient has been attending art therapy groups for a few months and has progressed in her work to the point at which she no longer self-destructively acts out, the approach changes. Patients are encouraged and empowered to take their treatment somewhat into their own hands. The therapist asks the participant what she needs to do with the art materials to help herself move toward her treatment goals. This way, participants are encouraged to separate from the art therapist through the formation of their own directives. The art therapist helps them with this process very carefully so that they do not experience this shift as a break in trust or as abandonment. The therapist reassures participants that they now have a new awareness about themselves that will guide them in using art in a personal way.

Competition

The variation in art abilities across group members, combined with their inter- and intrapsychic issues, produces an additional undercurrent of anxiety throughout all the group art therapy sessions. For example, Pam's reputation as an "artist" inhibited other group members from making their own art. Such competitively based inhibition frequently occurs in art therapy groups with all populations and age groups. Raising the issue of competition was helpful on many levels because these women were quite competitive in all aspects of their lives, particularly about their weight, appearance, clothing, and severity of self-mutilation. Rather than view the use of competition as a resistance, the art therapist chose to persevere in pushing them to do the art directive, believing that they could tolerate their feelings of aggression by becoming involved in the art-making process. Once the art pieces were created and shared by group members, their initial uncomfortable, competitive feelings were diminished enough to allow them to be aired collectively, resulting in connecting to a deeper level of personal meaning.

Very often these issues mirrored sibling or family issues that could be explored and then worked through in family sessions. Competition can be a defense against feeling empty and inadequate for these patients, who expect not to be seen or heard but rather assume they will be criticized or judged, resulting in feelings of humiliation and shame. Accordingly, they often try to take control through stopping the creative process by using competition as a defense to prevent themselves from expression. All members shared the fear that if they truly expressed themselves, they would be rewounded, because no one would "see" them. A great struggle for the art therapist was to make sure everyone was validated in some way in every group. When negative acting out occurred, it was acknowledged but not made a focus of attention. Any movement toward *creative expression*, by which we mean the reconfiguring of something old, archaic, and dysfunctional, was mirrored in an obvious, direct, and positive way.

Use of Directives

The key to successful practice lies in finding an art directive that addresses the unique element unifying the group in the present moment. That directive is then offered in such a way that it can be interpreted by each patient in any way she chooses. The art therapist needs to have no investment in how participants respond to the directive, which offers enough latitude so that each can use it as a springboard for her own individual emotional work. A nondirective approach is less successful with these patients; the lack of structure and boundaries often increases the patients' anxiety to an overwhelming degree. At times, patients became so disorganized and regressed that a focused directive lowered their manifest anxiety, even when it was disregarded. Stated another way, patients need the auxiliary ego from the art therapist so that they can have a place from which to begin to take action. These patients desperately need structured directives and interventions that specifically relate both to their overt and covert here-and-now emotional states. Appropriate directives are thus essential to the transformation of their destructive impulses toward their bodies into structurally integrative changes that promote healthy self-expression.

VIGNETTES FROM GROUP SESSIONS

First Group: Joining Through Art

The art therapy group was the first group Barbara Cooper had run in this unit, being a new employee at this facility.

I was understandably nervous, knowing that these patients had issues with trust and anxiety.

I brought with me a "goody box" filled with assorted art-making materials and supplies, described later in greater detail, to entice the patients and give them a positive first group experience. I began by introducing myself, explaining what art therapy is, and describing the overall goals that I hoped to help them achieve. The patients introduced themselves by giving their names and saying how long they had been at this facility. Some also talked about why they were there.

Each participant was offered a small piece of colored plasticene, an oil-based colored clay that does not harden. Working it in one's hand causes it to become soft and malleable. I put on some calming instrumental music and asked the patients to hold the colored clay in their hands and let their hands shape the clay in any way. I stressed that they wouldn't be judged by what they made. I further explained that this was an event to experience and not product oriented at all. I guided them in grounding themselves by putting their feet on the floor and breathing deeply and slowly as they shaped the clay. I asked them to put the piece down in front of themselves when it was done.

At that point, I offered the patients different-sized white boxes, from 1 inch to 6 inches square. I asked them to choose a box to house their clay piece and to rummage through my goody box to find things with which to embellish these boxes, such as feathers, fluffy pom-poms, tissue paper, sequins, pearls, yarn, ribbon, small animal figurines, and images cut out from magazines. I also had paints, markers, and crayons.

The patients spent a good deal of time choosing objects and making homes for their clay figures. Of the six patients, three had sealed their boxes so the inside could not be seen. I had told them that they could do that if they wished, respecting their need for privacy with a relative stranger (me). They were surprised at how much they enjoyed the experience and were actually eager to show the group their boxes. The three who had sealed their boxes decided to open them and find a way of closing them so that they could be opened and closed more easily. Each patient displayed her box, both inside and out.

I encouraged them to show these boxes to their primary therapists. The subsequent feedback I received from the treatment team revealed how powerfully illuminating this work was, because many of the patients had processed their work with their primary therapists. These therapists found that they learned more about their patients from this one art object than from most of their verbal work to date. Using these objects as springboards, the patients more readily verbalized their feelings and experiences to their therapists.

The boxes became a bridge from the unconscious to the conscious, from the nonverbal to the verbal. Fortunately, the therapeutic team was appreciative of this sharing of modalities and used it well.

Smearing Plasticene: Pam

In one of the earliest groups, while doing the warm-up go-around, Pam was collapsed on the couch. She was either unable or unwilling to speak. She had a glazed, distant look. The group decided to work with collage that day around the theme of bridging where they were "at" to where they wanted to be. Pam stayed collapsed. I helped the others get started while thinking about how to work with Pam. She looked like a rag doll.

I felt helpless.

I cut a piece of tag board into a large circle and brought some colored plasticene clay over to her.

I chose the circle for its containing and healing qualities (Jung, 1973) and the plasticine because of its soft, smeary quality.

I began smearing the plasticene inside the circle. I placed some into her listless hand and gently guided her onto the floor with me and helped her hand push the plasticene to begin smearing (see Figure 6.1).

The use of plasticene on paper was chosen because it takes some physical energy to make the plasticene stick and creates a physical external sensation in the arm and fingertips.

Pam had trouble beginning but was eventually able to work with the plasticene. She trembled and cried. Small animal sounds came from her. She gained momentum and filled a good portion of the circle with the plasticene. I kept encouraging her to push the plasticene, which she did until she was perspiring. Eventually, she stopped and curled up again on the couch. She was still unable to speak.

At the time I was discouraged but later (the next week) was able to speak with her about her passivity and fear of her own aggression.

Her passive–aggression was something that, she declared, was "new" to her; this acknowledgment was an important step in her treatment.

Figure 6.1. Smeared plasticene on 24 × 36 paper, by Pam.

I had hoped this intervention would let her know that I wasn't frightened or put off by her catatoniclike state. Rather than leaving her alone in this state, which had historically led her to cut herself, I wanted to engage her in a nonverbal, action-oriented way. The plasticene and the use of smearing and pushing had assertive and aggressive qualities. I believe that, had I not offered such an opportunity to accept, encourage, and promote a safe way to channel her aggression, her next action would have been to cut herself. We have observed that, even though these patients present themselves as timid and collapsed much of the time, their self-mutilation is evidence of their rageful power. As art therapists we accept and appreciate the polarity of experiences that exist on a continuum, such as passivity and aggression, helplessness and power, and love and hate. By letting ourselves feel the emotional tone of the patient we are able to offer an art experience that will encourage the patient to explore and eventually accept the dimensions of her own affective world.

From Regression to Integration With Clay: Jo

During an early group, the warm-up uncovered a sense of free-floating agitation in the group. The patients were unfocused and resistant. I brought out clay.

Although some art therapists find clay work too regressive and "loose" for patients who are acting out, I tend to disagree. I feel very comfortable using this medium to promote integration because of my long experience with, expertise in, and mastery of clay as an art medium. Professionally, I have used clay in all settings with a wide range of populations and found that how the clay is presented and used largely determines the patient's experience of the medium. Clay can be experienced as a structured, solid building material as well as a mushy, regressive material, depending on the therapist's presentation of the medium and directives for its use.

When I want to offer an expressive, manipulative material, I choose clay. Clay differs from other modeling materials (e.g., plasticene, modeling dough, sculpey) in that it mixes with water and actually comes from the earth. Holding and working with clay can bring the patient into the here and now by the inherent nature of its earthiness, which is often experienced as soothing and calming. Although clay can stimulate early oral and anal process, using clay in a structured, prescribed way can contain regression while promoting symbol formation and sublimation.

When I offered clay to this group, everyone had a tray to work on, which provided a tangible boundary. Each group member was given a palm-sized ball of clay, a selection of sponges, and clay tools. I was in charge of a spray bottle of water. Many therapists make the error of putting bowls of water on the table, which gives regressed patients who are acting out the opportunity to make smeary mud. This usually has the effect of disorganizing them and weakening the ego, which is antithetical to the goal of the group. By retaining the spray bottle I can aid the participants in keeping their hands wet while not letting too much water turn the clay to mud. Thus, my function became that of an auxiliary ego, helping patients organize their inner world by internalizing my model of organization.

I put on some gentle music and asked the women to pinch, punch, pound, and explore their piece of clay. All but Jo seemed relaxed and comfortable as they began to chat and form the clay into various shapes. Jo sat apart, agitated and unfocused. She had cut the sides of her face the evening before and had some long cuts on the undersides of her arms. She took the clay and began rubbing it into the cuts on her face. I moved my seat to be next to her and gently asked her to stop. She asked, "Why?" I quickly said, "It can't be good for those cuts to have clay rubbed into them." She responded by briefly continuing to rub the clay on her facial cuts but then switched to rubbing clay on her uncut arm. I sat next to her, watching her do this.

I was concerned that she would become more disorganized and so sat next to her, watching carefully so I could intervene if she regressed further.

When the clay covered her hand and was packed onto her arm midway to her elbow (about 1 or 2 inches thick), I playfully asked her if she could stop and see if she could wiggle her hand while it was inside the clay. She tried this and could. I asked her if she could slide her hand out of the clay without disturbing the shape. She was intrigued by this and did so with my help. I stayed in very close contact with her during this time.

When her hand came out, I challenged her to take this hollow shape and make it into something.

As she worked, I felt her ego strengthening as organization and solidity emerged from smearing and hollowness. Jo began purposefully working; asked for tools; and was more energized, focused, and relaxed than she had been before. I believed that Jo was working with conscious deliberation rather than being driven by impulse. She initially had begun to work the clay much as a toddler might and then developed into a young adult before my eyes. It was an amazing process to witness as Jo turned this shape into a manatee.

When she wanted whiskers for it, we looked around the room, saw a broom, and broke off some of the straw to make the whiskers. She then transformed the back half of this creature into a snail shell. She called her figure a Snail–Manatee. The manatee is grotesquely huge, although not scary, and a rather gentle and vulnerable creature. Jo stated that this manatee cares for its young in a special way by always having a safe place to curl into, the snail shell, when it is wounded or scared. She named this creature "Mr. Whiskers."

Jo was very nervous about the kiln firing of Mr. Whiskers ("Will he withstand the fire?" she asked) and was somewhat surprised that he did make it. She then painted glaze on him and waited for the second firing. Jo was extremely pleased with his yellow speckled glossy coat. I suggested that Jo make a home for Mr. Whiskers so that he could safely travel home with her when she leaves. She immediately said it needs to be a nest that is soft.

Softness has not been a part of Jo's life at all. She was raised by an emotionally absent mother and a rageful, overbearing father.

Jo collected items from nature during the weekend between sessions: seed pods; leaves; feathers; grasses; dried flowers; and thick, mossy pieces of bark that she wanted to use to make a "nest" for Mr. Whiskers. Together we drilled holes in the bark for her to tie together a secure box, which she then filled with the treasures she collected in nature (see Figure 6.2). The creation of a home for her ceramic piece further shored up her boundaries and conveyed a sense of structure, strength, and softness.

Jo expressed much pleasure with the outcome of her effort. We reviewed and reflected on the 5-week evolution of this piece.

She could step back, take distance, and appreciate her therapeutic process. Left to her own devices, formlessness, accompanied by regression, most likely would have occurred. I see my repeated active interventions as promoting a personal expressive outlet for healing and integration through symbol formation supported by an increase in judgment and planning skills.

Following this review of her accomplishment, Jo asked me for some ideas of work she could do over the upcoming weekend. I suggested she write Mr. Whiskers' autobiography as if it were a children's book—to take the

Figure 6.2. Clay and glazed ceramic with found objects, by Jo.

voice of Mr. Whiskers and tell his story. She made an amazing hand-sewn book with the story written inside that was so moving I had tears in my eyes while reading it. It is Jo's own story, of course, written in a most tender way—a wonderful example of going from the nonverbal to the verbal in therapy. As Robbins (1987) wrote, "Secondary process thinking, with its foundation in words, must be evoked if the ego is to gain mastery and understanding of primitive material" (p. 16). This is precisely what happened for Jo.

Sculpting Out of Collapse: Risa

During another group session, the emerging theme, based on the warm-up, was "collapse." The group members were all "collapsed." They were angry and resistant about being asked to participate in yet another group that day. I gave each person a sheet of thick white Bristol board paper, a heavy-duty, weighted paper that can be used in creating paper sculpture. I demonstrated manipulating the paper in various ways, narrating as I went along.

My objective was to have the group take the two-dimensional piece of paper and create a three-dimensional piece in any way they wished.

182   COOPER AND MILTON

They could rip, tear, cut, fold, curl, pleat, or bend the paper. Scissors, tape, glue, and staplers were made available. I asked them to check in with themselves as they went along to make sure that what they were making was true for them at that moment.

My purpose was to help them curb their desire to "make something pretty," which had been an ongoing issue for this group.

Because they were so collapsed, I encouraged them to have the paper speak for them.

I wasn't sure how this would go, because I was asking them to do something active, and they were presenting themselves as passive. I wondered if they could own their aggression. I keenly felt and appreciated the underlying aggressive edge to their passivity and was hopeful that they could direct it into the creative process.

As they all began to work with the paper, I watched. One of the women began biting her paper and sculpting it with her teeth. Others were cutting and folding.

Risa, who had presented herself up to this point as a "princess," incapable of making anything that wasn't "cute" or "pretty," crumpled her paper up into a dome shape and worked on it for quite some time. She ripped the edges into a ragged edge, then asked if she could add color to her piece. I offered her various drawing and painting materials. She chose red and black chalk pastels and explosively added color to her sculpture (see Figure 6.3). She was angry and aggressive with this piece, behavior I had not yet witnessed from her. Her hands were dirty, something she proudly showed the group because it was so unlike her.

She was unwilling to talk about her piece at first, as it surprised her that it was so "ugly." The group, curious about this piece that was so different from her earlier cute and pretty images, encouraged her to speak. Risa slowly and fearfully spoke about her anger toward her therapist, who she felt was treating her unfairly, just like her father did. She told the group about her life as a "doll" and a "princess" and the wrath she incurred when she tried to be "myself. . . whatever that is." She was encouraged both by me and the group to take the piece to her primary therapist. She was afraid to and asked if I would show it to him.

This image was helpful both for her and her primary therapist in beginning to explore not only different dimensions of her relationship to him but also to her father and others.

My decision to present the Bristol paper to the group was the result of first acknowledging the collapsed state of the group and selecting a material with a sense of sturdiness, which can be viewed as the opposite of collapse.

As I allowed myself to experience the collapsed group that day, I found myself thinking about sturdy things. I remembered that I had this wonderful, sturdy paper that could stand up by itself when folded in half. From there, I gave my directive.

Figure 6.3. Bristol paper and chalk pastels, by Risa.

Each person that day created a piece that spoke about his or her experience. The patient who chewed her paper was amazed to find that I admired her work, because it so aptly conveyed her experience of herself at that moment! For these women, who have been treated as narcissistic extensions of their parents and who are materially wealthy but spiritually starving, these experiences with both the materials and the environmental mother/therapist are richly satisfying. There are moments of real contact, which sometimes seem fleeting and sometimes are sturdy enough to be built on during treatment.

Coaxing Participation: Sheila

With the exception of the first art therapy session with this group, Sheila stayed in bed for the sessions I facilitated for 6 weeks. She was overwhelmed by the idea of participating in an art therapy group. I attempted to encourage her, and she was always receptive. She was a creative writer who seemed in theory eager to participate in the group but was unwilling when it came time to do so. A few times she showed up for a minute or two and then disappeared.

One morning, her therapist told me that Sheila had cut herself badly the evening before and was in distress. This therapist asked Sheila to just show up at art therapy and try to stay, even if she didn't participate. Sheila agreed to do this. Fortunately, that day, the group had chosen to finish collages they began during the previous group, allowing me to sit with Sheila and talk her through an art experience. I asked her if she wanted to make a collage so that she would feel part of the group. She agreed; she sifted through some precut magazine images, chose a large-size word, and pasted it in the middle of a sheet of white paper. The word was "Uh-oh." She didn't want to add to it. She was smiling as she handed it to me. I smiled back and said "Uh-oh" in a rather dramatic way. This caused her to giggle. I asked if she felt like doing something that would demonstrate the idea of "Uh-oh." She was intrigued.

I took a sheet of paper and demonstrated using chalk pastels to draw abstractly in a flowing way. I told her as I worked that I was scanning the pastel box with my eyes and letting myself pick up the color to which my eye was attracted. Once in my hands, I would take that color and move my arm around the paper, leaving the color on the paper. Then I would put it back and choose another color, not thinking about what I was making. I told her that it didn't matter if her work was "nice," addressing a concern she had. I told her it was an experiment in a visual form of "Uh-oh."

Sheila, who had previously refused to make anything in art therapy, proceeded to work very intently on her picture.

With art materials, the creator has the potential to be in sole control of these materials. What we have experienced over and over again is that our patients derive pleasure from working with the material. When given needed structure and guidance, their anxiety is reduced; there is often an increase of optimism (a sense of "I can," which fosters the sense of "I am") and the opportunity for positive feedback for constructive self-expression. All too often, these are patients who have been able to obtain reactions from others only in response to their negative, self-destructive expressions.

I encouraged Sheila to turn the page upside down or sideways every time she felt "stuck" or when she felt that she was controlling the picture. She became more and more aggressive with the chalks, putting increasing pressure into her drawing. I offered her plasticene to smear into the picture, to provide it with some dimension and to push more of herself into it (see Figure 6.4).

Sheila created her picture and received many compliments from her peers, who were surprised that she was able and willing to do this. She shyly showed her picture to the group. I asked her to title it. She called it "Better than Suicide" and then commented that she must be really sick to do this. Knowing that she lived in a city renowned for its art museums, I suggested she take herself into any one of those museums when she returned home and look for kindred spirits living there. She liked that idea and smiled.

Sheila wanted the piece to stay in her primary therapist's office for safekeeping. She was amazed at how well she felt after making it. When her anxiety returned a short time later (a couple of hours), she was encouraged to use art once again. Subsequently, she has become one of the patients at this

Figure 6.4. Oil pastels and plasticene on paper, by Sheila.

facility who asks for art materials to be left for her use over the weekends, asks for homework assignments, and so forth.

My feelings throughout this group session ran the gamut. I was anxious at first because I wanted to engage Sheila in art therapy. I was frustrated that it had been so difficult, and I wanted to show the therapeutic team that what I did could work! I also felt empathy for Sheila in her state of despair and anxiety and wanted to give her a way of externalizing and looking at those feelings. I was very excited when she became invested in the drawing and expended energy drawing it. Her title was the "icing on the cake," reflecting her perception of the power of the creative process.

Visualizations as a Bridge: Lee

Guided visualizations can expand this population's opportunity first for self-awareness and then for healing in a personally unique form. During a guided visualization of "going to an old barn," one of the patients, Lee, who had not really "taken" to art therapy, visualized her children's toys inside the barn. Her children had been taken away from her due to her substance abuse and her neglect of them. In treatment, she repressed her feelings about her losses while pleading for cigarettes and Valium. She first drew her children's toys and then cried and cried. At first she was self-deprecating, expressing feelings of shame and humiliation at her crying in the group. When the group rallied around her and expressed their sorrow for her situation, Lee was positively surprised at how her feelings and tears were accepted and understood by her peers and by myself.

This episode marked the beginning of Lee becoming a part of the group in a more related, authentic, and spontaneous way.

Removing the Mask: Jo

In a previous group, the theme of "taking off one's mask" had come up. To follow this theme, I brought plastic face molds, plasticene, and plaster-infused gauze strips to the group. I demonstrated how to use the face molds and plasticene to build up a face shape, followed by use of the plaster strips to cover the face. A hardened mask would be the end product. Rather than give a specific directive, I asked the group members to think about the theme of masks discussed in the previous group and to think about what type of mask would be relevant for each of them to make and explore. I also asked questions such as whether it would make more therapeutic sense to look at what was under the mask or at the mask itself. I let the patients know that they would be working on these for two or three group sessions, so that they could take their time. Two group members were far along enough in their treatment that they could take the materials and work confidently and independently, while the remaining group members needed my help.

Jo was one of the patients who eagerly engaged in creating her mask at her own inner direction.

I was pleased, as she had become overwhelmingly anxious and unable to ask for help over the previous weekend and had hurt herself by rubbing the side of her face around her eye on the rough couch fabric, causing friction burns. I knew, from previous work with Jo, that working with three-dimensional materials helped lessen her anxiety.

Jo built up a frightening, robotic, and alien looking face with plasticene. She carefully covered it with the plaster. She didn't have much to say about it at the end of the first session. She was, however, very satisfied with her work. During the next session, she was offered paints and various three-dimensional materials (e.g., fake hair, feathers, colored tissue paper) to embellish her mask. She painted her mask, cut some holes and slashes in it, and added feathers to it. Other group members said it reminded them of a phantom.

Toward the end of the group, I asked Jo, along with the other group members, to speak *as* their masks, starting with the statement "I am _____." Jo had trouble coming up with a statement that she could say was true for her. I asked her if she needed to change the mask so that it could speak from a truthful place. After carefully considering this, she decided to cut it. The group watched as she cut the mask so that it covered one of Jo's eyes, the one without the burns around it, and diagonally moved over her nose and mouth, ending at her chin opposite to the covered eye. The result of her holding it up to her face was to frame the eye with the burns. When looking at her face, the hurt eye area became the most prominent part of her face. She claimed that now the mask was true for her, and her "I am" statements were about finding inner balance and acceptance. I responded by commenting on how the mask almost forced me to look at her burns. She became quietly tearful and spoke about how, since she was a little girl, she would hurt herself in hidden places on her body. Now she felt that she wanted us to see her pain.

I asked her to work with the parts of the mask that were cut out and discarded. In Jo's voice, they "spoke" as the pieces of Jo that hid her pain, isolation, and hopelessness. The mask not only forced us to see Jo in a genuine way but told us she was ready to relate more honestly and directly. I said to her that I could see her pain even when she had no injuries on her face, that by knowing her and listening to her, I could recognize this pain in her. Jo was surprised and relieved. She stated, "what I've done my whole life, isolate and hurt myself, doesn't work. I can now see that I have to find another way to live." I encouraged her to let the pain come up and to ask for support from the staff. She had fought that up until now. She said, again, that she now had no choice, because what she had always done no longer worked. She then chose to take the mask and discarded pieces with her to the expressive group therapy session later that day and then to her primary therapist for further exploration.

Drawing to Authenticate Self: Pam

Pam, a gifted artist, was hospitalized during her first year of art school. Her drawing style at the beginning of treatment was stylized, defensive, and technically well-executed. She was eager to show me her artwork the first day we met. Her sketchbooks were filled with black-and-white line drawings that were provocative and yet devoid of self-expression. When I looked at them, I had no idea who Pam was. I knew she had technical skill and imagination, but I didn't see the person of Pam in this work; I saw a performance. In the art therapy groups, she could draw the directive while half asleep, displaying no emotional investment in her creation. I spoke with her about this as we got to know each other, encouraging her to try different materials and to use color.

When Pam first entered this facility she was cutting herself with pieces of glass on a regular basis. She was ingenious in the ways she found to cut herself, which enraged the staff, who felt powerless to stop her. I encouraged Pam to use her art instead of a piece of glass. I left materials for her to use in her room such as pastels and paper. Her primary therapist gave her a journal and asked her to write about a particular topic he gave her each day. She used the journal both as a place to write and to draw.

Pam subsequently began approaching me with drawings she had done in her room. The more she drew and wrote, the less she cut. The large piece (Figure 6.5) was completed over several weeks. Every time Pam thought of

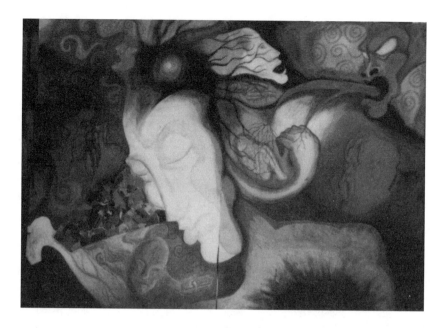

Figure 6.5. Oil pastels and collage on 36 × 48 paper, self-portrait by Pam.

cutting herself, she would work on this image. She talked about how drawing in this way was very new for her.

Pam had always done her art to obtain acknowledgment and praise from others. However, she rejected and devalued this praise. For example, her artwork won high school awards, yet she refused to put any of her work in the senior show at a local museum because she did not want to give the teachers, her parents, or herself the satisfaction of receiving public accolades for her accomplishments. I interpreted this refusal as a powerful plea to "See me! I am more than an artist!" Therefore, my stance with her was that the work was for no one but herself. She did not have to show it to anyone if she did not want to do so. She was doing it for herself alone.

Pam explored that concept for awhile. When she worked on a large piece, she kept it hidden under her bed. She would not let anyone see it for quite some time. Eventually, she invited me to see it and then brought it down into the living room of the house to share with her peers and with the staff. She revealed that, when she had layered the colors thickly, it was a new way of working for her. She explained that the more agitated she felt, and the more she wanted to cut herself, the harder she pushed the color onto the paper. The images, she said, "just flowed out of (her); these are images that float around in (her) head all the time."

She had not put these internal images into visual form in quite this way before; they were always more disguised and stylishly drawn. Her other self-portraits (Figures 6.6, 6.7, and 6.8) became more and more a reflection of

Figure 6.6. Oil pastels on 8 × 10 paper, self-portrait by Pam.

how she felt inside rather than a representation of the "pretty" picture out-side.

I looked at these self-portraits and began to feel the pain inside of Pam, which I reflected to her. Although her self-portraits became successively more disturbed and disorganized, I saw this as a step forward for Pam. She was finally able to strip away her social veneer to express authentically her true feelings toward self. Whereas she had been used to authority figures responding to her skill level, I, along with her primary therapist, were the first people to respond to her emotional self through her communication in her imagery.

Use of Self of the Therapist

Noted art therapy pioneer and psychologist Arthur Robbins (1982) has written extensively about the artist as a therapist and the therapist as an artist: "We require a complex theory of treatment that integrates psychodynamics and aesthetics. . . . Psychological theory must be recast into the language of art so that psychodynamics can be felt and comprehended within a nonverbal frame" (p. 8). We agree with Robbins when he stated, "My professional identity as an art therapist is no longer static, but ebbs and flows with each session and patient" (p. 8).

Another noted art therapy pioneer Harriet Wadeson's chapter in *Approaches to Art Therapy* (Rubin, 1987) applies to our clinical work as well: "The instrument of the therapy is the self of the therapist in concert with the self of the patient. Our basic tools are not paint or brushes any more than they are words. Whatever happens in art therapy occurs within the container of the transference relationship." And,

I believe, as well, that the therapeutic endeavor is a creative enterprise. Since the selfhood of each therapist is unique, each clinician's creative work in this realm will bear the imprimatur of the self, with all its life

Figure 6.7. Oil pastels on 8 × 10 paper, self-portrait by Pam.

experience influencing each moment of the therapeutic relationship. Just as my painting will be different from yours (even though we may have attended the same art school), so we will practice therapy differently, each according to our own style, even though we may share similar views of psychodynamics and treatment objectives. (as cited in Rubin, 1987, p. 299)

For most of the young women in the featured cases, the therapist's external validation, appreciation, and support of their genuine and emerging self-knowledge are new experiences. Their rage against not being heard or seen that had, until now, been acted out on the self now was being acted on in art-making, resulting in a growing and enhanced sense of self. As the environmental mother/therapist, the art therapist functions as the mirror of the distressed self and an ally for a multidimensional self. A healthy self can be enraged, but how that rage is expressed is another matter. Early in treatment with this group, the therapist followed the advice of Levenkron (1998), who believed that the therapist must be willing to look at the patient's cuts and scars and not be put off by them, to accept these marks as the best that the patient can do under certain circumstances as she sees them. During a later stage in treatment in which attachment and trusting relation to the art therapist has developed, the desire to self-harm can be brought out in the open, underlying anxiety can be explored, and alternatives to self-harm that are personally meaningful can be created.

The vignettes of Pam and of Jo and Mr. Whiskers illustrate how the therapist needs to recognize and redirect the destructive impulses of these patients. For instance, Pam's stealing and hiding glass shards from broken bottles for use in private self-mutilation and Jo's facial slashing and self-smearing were channeled into art-making. Unlike Jo, for Pam, privacy was important to her experience of being genuine, which is why I gave her materials and encouraged her to use them in the privacy of her room. The art therapist remains continually aware of how different patients require different art di-

Figure 6.8. Oil pastels on torn 18 × 24 paper, self-portrait by Pam.

rectives and interventions. Jo required something different than Pam (e.g., accepting Jo's smearing yet redirecting it, first to a safer part of her body and eventually away from her body altogether so that she could create an externalized and satisfying form).

Patient Follow-Up

Pam entered the facility looking well put-together; however, she had been secretly cutting and purging. During treatment, she was eventually able to let her symptoms be seen by everyone (the group during which she smeared the plasticene was the beginning of her revealing her symptoms) and then begin to work through her feelings of anger. Unfortunately, her parents had discharged her from the facility before she completed treatment, claiming a lack of financial resources. Pam was well enough at discharge, however, to obtain a job at home and transfer to outpatient treatment.

Sheila entered the facility in a nonverbal, "collapsed" state. At first, she was curled up in bed for most of the time. She gradually began to attend groups, tentatively and briefly at first and then for longer periods of time. Her art piece, "Better than Suicide," marked the first art therapy group she attended for the entire session. Sheila became able to express her anger rather than hurt herself or stay in bed. She came to understand, through the relationship-based treatment we offer, that she has a voice to which others will listen and respond. Sheila is not yet ready to leave the facility but may need only another 2 months or so if she continues working in therapy.

Lee entered the facility drug-dependent, angry, and closed down. She was grieving the loss of her children and angry that she had to change her life to get them back. She displayed typical substance abuse behavior, such as lying, somatizing her drug craving so that she could receive any medication, and so forth. Lee was able to withdraw from substances and engage in therapy very gradually. Mirroring in the art therapy groups was a valuable intervention for her in that she was able to accept previously unacceptable feelings (such as anger and sadness) that emerged as a result of sobriety. Lee was discharged from the facility in a very positive, high-functioning state. She had successful weekend passes for 2 months before discharge and had a solid discharge plan.

Jo came into the facility eager to change her life. She had been living alone and was unable to leave her apartment because of the number of times per day she was purging, cutting, and burning herself. Jo was verbally closed down and mistrustful on entering the facility. She was sure that no one there could help her. Art therapy and the outdoor work programs were especially valuable for Jo. These action-oriented modalities enabled her to physically move about while anxious. She was absolutely unable to sit through a verbal discussion. Even in art therapy, when time came to process the artwork, Jo often needed to leave the group. After about 2 months she was able to tolerate more of her own inner anxiety. This was evidenced by her ability to stay in the group; to verbalize her feelings about her work; and to give constructive, insightful feedback to others. Jo became able to trust treatment and was optimistic about the prospect of recovery. After being discharged, Jo joined a local art therapy group that I had recommended and on her own, secured a job assisting a puppet maker and producer of puppet shows. In this way she continued creating 3-dimensional artworks.

Risa came into the facility after a serious suicide attempt. She appeared to be just fine and looked "perky" and put-together, although she was purging daily and spoke about being depressed. Risa maintained this persona for about 2 months and then began to let her inside feelings of depression show. As she became better able to express herself, somewhat in art therapy but mostly in psychodrama and expressive groups (she has aspirations of being an actress), Risa has become more "real" as evidenced by her ability to search for who she is inside and to let herself cry. Risa will soon begin the discharge process, which consists of having weekend passes and working toward an aftercare plan.

Darcy came into this group only 2 months ago and has had difficulty engaging in treatment because of her idealization of her previous treatment facility (she was discharged from this facility, which does not treat psychiatric illness, when she was diagnosed as having a bipolar disorder). We have had difficulty adjusting Darcy's medication levels; she has left our facility for acute inpatient treatment and has come back during that 2-month period. She is just now establishing herself in the art therapy group.

EMPIRICAL SUPPORT ON ART THERAPY EFFECTIVENESS

Unfortunately, there has been a serious lack of outcome research in the field of art therapy. Existing research has been focused on art-based assessment, such as the Diagnostic Drawing Series (Cohen, Mills, & Kijak, 1994), the Formal Elements Art Therapy Scale (FEATS; Gantt & Tabone, 1998), Kinetic Family Drawing (Burns & Kaufman, 1970), and the Silver Drawing Test (Silver, 1996). Gantt and Tabone have used the FEATS assessment to assess the outcome of electroconvulsive therapy (ECT) during hospitalization. Outcome research on art therapy with patients who self-harm or who have eating disorders seems to be nonexistent in the professional literature.

"Although we probably all believe that art-making is inherently therapeutic and that the creative process is healing, the investigations necessary to support these simple beliefs have not been completed" (Malchiodi, 1995, p. 218). This can be, in part, attributed to the education of art therapists. The terminal degree for an art therapist is a master's degree, a 2-year, clinically-based course of study with very little time devoted to teaching research methods. Because of the current cost containment focus in health care, art therapists are more aware of the need for outcome-based research, and the American Art Therapy Association changed its education standards in 2002 to give greater emphasis to research in graduate art therapy programs.

CONCLUSION

We have attempted to demonstrate how group art therapy offers therapeutic benefits and has the potential to add a deeper dimension to the struggle for healing. By recognizing the specific reactions the art therapist experiences in response to each individual patient and to the group, appropriate materials, structure, directives, and interventions may be selected that foster awareness of polarities of affect and reduce fear, terror, helplessness, rage, and disorganization. Recognition and appreciation of both current and past ego states allows the therapist to flexibly model, encourage, and support the more mature defenses and coping mechanisms.

The art therapy group can serve as an arena to safely experiment with options for new and more adaptive patterns of behavior through art-making in a structured, contained, nonjudgmental environment. We have tried to illuminate how much of the persistent engagement efforts of the therapist described in this chapter have been based on our appreciation that these patients have not only the ability but also the desperate need to use their energy to create meaning out of their lives. The therapist's effort to use his or her own vitality to engage very emotionally distant women who often present as helpless, angry, withdrawn, depressed, compliant, vengeful, demanding, and self-deprecating is challenging and demanding. By first allowing himself or herself to use his or her own sensations and imagery in response to the patient's presentation, the therapist can more effectively mirror the patient's emotional energy and then help the patient find personal and constructive forms of expression. The vignettes presented reveal how the process of creating works of art as well as the images portrayed are key to achieving treatment goals. And, as Sheila so aptly stated, "art-making is certainly better than suicide."

REFERENCES

Ainsworth, M. D. S., Blehar, M. C., Waters, E., & Wall, S. (1978). *Patterns of attachment: A psychological study of the strange situation*. Hillsdale, NJ: Erlbaum.

Blanck, R., & Blanck, G. (1986). *Beyond ego psychology*. New York: Columbia University Press.

Bowlby, J. (1988). *A secure base*. New York: Basic Books.

Breuer, J., & Freud, S. (1893). Studies on hysteria. *Standard edition of the complete psychological works of Sigmund Freud*. London: Hogarth.

Burns, R. C., & Kaufman, S. H. (1970). *Kinetic family drawings (K–F–D): An introduction to understanding children through kinetic drawings*. New York: Brunner/Mazel.

Cassidy, J. (1999). The nature of child's ties. In J. Cassidy and P. Shaver (Eds.), *Handbook of attachment: Theory, research, and clinical applications* (pp. 3–20). New York: Guilford Press.

Cohen, B. M., Mills, A., & Kijak, A. K. (1994). An introduction to the diagnostic drawing series: A standardized tool for diagnostic and clinical use. *Art Therapy, 11*, 105–110.

Deri, S. (1984). *Symbolization and creativity*. New York: International Universities Press.

Ehrenzweig, A. (1979). *Hidden order of art*. Berkeley: University of California Press.

Freud, S. (1926). Inhibitions, symptoms and anxiety. *Standard edition of the complete psychological works of Sigmund Freud*, (Vol. 20, pp. 77–174). London: Hogarth.

Gantt, L., & Tabone, C. (1998). *The Formal Elements Art Therapy Scale: The rating manual*. Morgantown, WV: Gargoyle Press.

Horner, A. J. (1984). *Object relations and the developing ego in therapy*. New York: Jason Aronson.

Jung, C. G. (1973). *Mandala symbolism* (R. F. C. Hull, Trans., Bollingen Series). Princeton, NJ: Princeton University Press.

Krystal, H. (1975). Affects tolerance. *The Annual of Psychoanalysis, 3*, 179–219.

Krystal, H. (1978). Trauma and affects. *Psychoanalytic Study of the Child, 33*, 81–116.

Levenkron, S. (1998). *Cutting*. New York: W. W. Norton.

Mahler, M., Pine, F., & Bergman, A. (1975). *The psychological birth of the human infant*. New York: Basic Books.

Malchiodi, C. (1995). Does a lack of art therapy research hold us back? *Art Therapy*, *12*, 218–219.

Pine, F. (1985). *Developmental theory and clinical process*. New Haven, CT: Yale University Press.

Robbins, A. (1982). Integrating the personal and theoretical splits in the struggle towards identity as an art therapist. *The Arts in Psychotherapy*, *9*, 1–9.

Robbins, A. (1987). *The artist as therapist*. New York: Human Sciences Press.

Robbins, A., & Cooper, B. (1994). Resistance in art therapy: A multi-modal approach to treatment. In A. Robbins (Ed.), *A multi-modal approach to creative art therapy* (pp. 63–86). London: Jessica Kingsley.

Rubin, J. (1987). *Approaches to art therapy: Theory and technique*. New York: Brunner/Mazel.

Schneidman, E. S. (1976). Suicide notes reconsidered. *Psychiatric Annual*, *6*, 90–91.

Silver, R. (1996). *Silver Drawing Test of Cognition and Emotion* (3rd ed.). Sarasota, FL: Ablin Press.

Stern, M. M. (1951). Pavor nocturnus. *International Journal of Psychoanalysis*, *32*, 302–309.

Vaillant, G. (1993). *The wisdom of the ego*. Cambridge, MA: Harvard University Press.

Winnicott, D. W. (1965). *The maturational processes and the facilitating environment*. New York: International Universities Press.

RECOMMENDED READING

Dalley, T. (Ed.). (1984). *Art as therapy*. London: Routledge.

Herman, J. (1992). *Trauma and recovery*. New York: Basic Books.

Johnson, B. (1999). Three perspectives on addiction. *Journal of the American Psychoanalytic Association*, *47*, 791–815.

Landgarten, H. B. (1981). *Clinical art therapy*. New York: Brunner/Mazel.

Schwartz, H. J. (1988). *Bulimia: Psychoanalytic treatment and theory*. Madison, CT: International Universities Press.

Shengold, L. (1989). *Soul murder*. New Haven, CT: Yale University Press.

Stern, D. (1985). *The interpersonal world of the infant*. New York: Basic Books.

van der Kolk, B. A., McFarlane, A. D., & Weisaeth, L. (Eds.). (1996). *Traumatic stress*. New York: Guilford Press.

7

USING THE NORDOFF–ROBBINS APPROACH TO MUSIC THERAPY WITH ADULTS DIAGNOSED WITH AUTISM

ALAN TURRY AND DAVID MARCUS

Editors' Introduction: For most people, although to varying degrees, music is a significant medium of expression. To those most attuned, music rivals verbal language in its variety, subtlety, and power to effect communication in the emotional realm. Yet music's meaning can at best be only partially understood through verbal language. Therefore, understanding and appreciating the work of music therapists through reading alone can be challenging. Alan Turry and David Marcus present convincingly the utility of music in working with clients whose disorders include greatly impaired verbal expression. It seems likely that these clients can be reached therapeutically in no other way than by mutual music-making. This approach is based on the use of improvisation as the core method by which communication and social interaction are elicited.

The American Music Therapy Association (AMTA) defines *music therapy* as "the prescribed use of music by a qualified person to effect positive changes in the psychological, physical, cognitive, or social functioning of individuals with health or educational problems." AMTA (1999) states that

> Music therapists assess emotional well-being, physical health, social functioning, communication abilities, and cognitive skills through musical responses; design music sessions for individuals and groups based on client needs using music improvisation, receptive music listening, song writing, lyric discussion, music and imagery, music performance, and learning through music; participate in interdisciplinary treatment planning, ongoing evaluation, and follow up.

This chapter demonstrates application of a specific music therapy approach to working with a group of adult clients diagnosed with autism. We describe distinctive features of the Nordoff–Robbins (N-R) approach and offer theoretical rationales for its use with this client population, particularly in the context of group therapy.

MUSIC THERAPY

Music therapy as a profession originated in work with special populations whose difficulties proved particularly intractable to verbal and other interventions but were found to respond to music. The attempt to understand these initial results and refine and expand the techniques that produced them gave rise to the formal discipline of music therapy. Today, music therapists work effectively with an ever-expanding spectrum of conditions and in a widening variety of settings (Bruscia, 1998).

The methods music therapists use vary according to the condition or situations being addressed, the particular strengths and deficits of the client, and the training of the therapist. Theoretical approaches may derive psychologically from behavioral, psychodynamic, humanistic, or transpersonal theory. The music used may be prerecorded (audiotapes and compact disks), precomposed by the therapist or others, or improvised. The course of therapy, which may be with individuals or groups, can be long-term or short-term depending on the population and the setting. This chapter presents a case of long-term group music therapy.

THE NORDOFF–ROBBINS APPROACH

Description

The Nordoff–Robbins (N-R) approach to music therapy, also known as "creative music therapy," was developed through the partnership of Paul Nordoff, an American pianist–composer, and Clive Robbins, an English special educator. This approach is music-centered, in that it views music as the essential feature of the therapy.

In most approaches to group music therapy, music has been used as an important adjunct to the therapy process itself, functioning as a reward to reinforce positive relating, as a stimulus to bring up memories or associations, as a nonthreatening means to promote interaction or socialization, as a means of expression of unconscious or challenging feelings, and as a way to furnish positive or successful experiences. Because music is seen as an aid to or a part of the overall therapy process this type of music therapy is described as "music in therapy" (Bruscia, 1987, pp. 8–9). Rather than "music in therapy," the N-R approach would be more accurately termed "music as therapy" (Bruscia, 1987, pp. 8–9). The musical activity between therapists and clients *is* the therapy; change is accomplished in and through musical processes and transfers from these into the life of the client outside the therapy room.

In practice, N-R music therapy involves active and creative music-making by therapists and clients, much of it improvised. The most distinctive feature of this approach as compared to other forms of music therapy is the degree to which it is both a musical and an improvisational process. The music that is created spontaneously by and for the clients in each session is a vibrant interpersonal interaction in which music is the major—sometimes the only—means of communication, regardless of the population. With the skillful intervention of the therapist, this ongoing collaboration and the songs and improvisations that are its products become the basis of the therapy and define its course. Gains in areas such as socialization, communication, motor skills, or self-esteem can ensue and be mirrored in personal and family life.

One of the key observations of N-R was that pathology is reflected in musicality. Difficulty in finding and keeping the music's beat, playing consistently at various tempos, playing comfortably at varied dynamic levels, and in using the singing voice for personal expression may not merely be reflective of lack of "talent" or of debilitating physical conditions. These musical "symptoms" may be reflective of weaknesses or inflexibilities in the underlying personality. The process of identifying and addressing these musical tendencies in the series of musical encounters that make up a course of music therapy can result in behavioral and personality change that extends far beyond the sphere of musical behavior.

It is important to bear this in mind when considering the case material presented later in this chapter. The presenting behavior of clients is assessed functionally, in terms of its effect on their ability to be freely, consciously, and responsively involved in music. The therapy is not directed at the extinction of behavior that is impulsive, compulsive, perseverative, or otherwise pathological, although such extinction may well be a duly noted and much appreciated product of the therapy. It is rather through deepening musical involvement that change is effected. Such change is interpreted as transcendence of the pathological by clients whose motivation has been strengthened and whose range of expression has been broadened through participation in a creative process.

N-R Action Methods

The following section discusses two action methods used in the N-R approach.

Realization

In its early years, N-R group music therapy relied strongly on the use of precomposed pieces. Compositionally, these pieces usually involve a piano accompaniment played by a therapist and parts for instruments or voices realized by clients with the facilitation of the cotherapist, who usually has committed the various parts of the piece to memory. These precomposed pieces employ a wide variety of instruments that are struck, and more rarely shaken or blown. They are relatively easy to get sound from, and are generally of professional quality. Together, they are capable of playing in all rhythms and keys.

We call the action method that uses precomposed pieces in the process of N-R group music therapy *realization*. In actualizing the potential of working in a musical environment, the action method of realization offers the following particular benefits:

- *Stimulation:* The most obvious aspect of the realization environment that makes it a unique source of stimulation is that it is an aural/tonal environment. Hearing can be every bit as important as sight in functioning in this environment, and often the former supersedes the latter. In fact, many of the cues for musical participation can have a threefold nature: They can be aural, visual, and verbal. This overabundance of directive stimulation can have several beneficial effects. The intensity of such stimulation can motivate clients to be more active. It can help in diverting the attention from internal preoccupation and self-stimulation and focusing it on outside stimuli. It also can help sustain and increase the intensity and duration of concentration. Finally, the clarity of such stimulation can be reassuring to the client, leading to greater confidence and higher levels of activity.

- *Socialization:* Realization necessitates a basic social awareness of other members of the music therapy group. The initial awareness of the leader as the person who facilitates by giving musical directions expands to include the therapist at the piano and the other group members. Awareness of others may reach the point at which it is independent of the leaders' activities and persists in the absence of music. Clients become aware of each other as people and peers as well as fellow musicians.

- *Community:* A sense of belonging, of camaraderie and cohesion, develops with the memory of the successful completion of pieces and the anticipation of new experiences. The aspects of participation that are common to all help to form a bond: the risk of facing the challenge of attempting things that are untried, the willingness to work to overcome individual difficulties for the sake of the group, the willingness to persevere in one's efforts in order to experience a sense of musical completion, and the ability to tolerate and appreciate differences in levels of participation.

Group Clinical Improvisation

The second major action method, most used in working with this case, is group clinical improvisation. This method possesses all of the clinical benefits inherent in realization as well as additional benefits that are discussed below. Typically, in clinical improvisation group members are offered the opportunity to choose instruments and play together without a predetermined musical plan. The music created is spontaneous as each member brings forth self-determined sound from his or her individual instrument; this music is being created while fellow members are exploring their own instruments to create a group sound. The therapist at the piano plays a vital role, creating music that simultaneously supports the continuing efforts of the group members, while integrating and giving structure to their disparate voices. The cotherapist may contribute musically by playing instruments or by directing others to create and sustain form and expression.

The most important consideration in the creation of an improvised piece is that the clients have a maximum role in determining its onset, sound, and duration. To the spontaneous expressive efforts of the clients, the therapists bring a thorough grasp of the aesthetic principles by which such expression may be given form and context. This makes the contributions of each member clearer to the others and enhances the possibilities for meaningful responsive interaction. The resultant counterpoint preserves each individual voice yet unites them in a common creative undertaking. This can be a powerful experience for clients who are by nature isolated by strong internal boundaries.

The action method of clinical improvisation presents the following qualities of awareness and participation that are significant additions to those presented by realization:

- *Internal awareness:* The clients must be in touch with their inner creative processes—such as they are—to produce the music they will make. While in the method of realization the onset and content of musical responses come from without through visual, verbal, and aural cues, in improvisation they come to a very great degree from within.
- *Realization of individual creative impulses:* The clients must not only be aware of creative impulses, they also must express them, realizing them in some tangible, audible form, even if it is a very simple one. This has great significance, as so often hesitancy and blockage occur between the impulse to play and the actual creation of the sound itself.
- *Courage and self-esteem:* The amount of criticism, minimization, and stifling that clients such as those in this group are exposed to cannot be overestimated. All that they have not been able to do in the past produces a reluctance to do things spontaneously in

the present. Their spontaneous self-expression is, among other things, an act of courage and self-assertion and its acceptance an important step in building their confidence.

- *Awareness of the activities of others:* The tendency of such clients to become internally absorbed or preoccupied is countered by the opportunity to acknowledge the activities of leaders and peers by using them as bases for their own responses.

In return for accepting and meeting the challenges inherent in clinical improvisation, the following clinically advantageous results are achieved:

- *Directly communicative interaction:* Clients engage in spontaneous communicative interaction with peers in a way that would be almost impossible in any other circumstances. In length, intensity, relevance, and integration, the musical statements they make far eclipse anything they say. Music is not "just another way of interacting." It really presents unparalleled opportunities for this group.
- *Realism:* The parameters imposed by clinical improvisation are more those of "real life" rather than an essentially artificial structure. In ordinary social reality, one is not always told what to do or how to do it; one is not signaled when to act and when to be still. We are all improvising throughout our lives. Clinical improvisation is a training ground for reality-based responses.
- *Fundamental equality:* At the beginning of each clinical improvisation and at unforeseen and unforeseeable times within it, there are moments when all of the various characteristics and considerations that define and separate individuals, that place them in positions of power, influence, or responsibility relative to each other, disappear entirely before the one overwhelming question that challenges the creativity of all: What is going to happen next? That fundamental equality, that momentary erasure of differences, has great therapeutic potency for people who are often considered "different" and, in many senses, "inferior."

Action Techniques Used in Improvisation

The following techniques are presented sequentially to guide the passage of clients from the most circumscribed levels of awareness and participation to the broadest and most inclusive. Each technique represents a level of clinically significant participation while simultaneously laying the foundation for ascent to a still higher level.

- *Nondirectivity* designates the overall approach to the use of action techniques. The ideal in clinical improvisation is always the free, expressive, and responsive participation of the clients. This is maintained to the degree possible within the clinical context of the improvisation. Whatever action techniques are being used, the object is to support and extend activity rather than to issue directives.

- *Engagement* refers to the process of getting clients to participate musically. This is accomplished through musical intervention (vocal, instrumental) or through gesture or verbal cue to participate as continuously as possible. Often there is an alternation between the techniques of engagement and nondirectivity, as the client who needs activation to become engaged may very well cease participation without continuing attention from the leader.

- *Supportive musical coactivity* is the offering of supportive musical responses by the therapists. The therapists take the material that is generated spontaneously by the client and acknowledge it musically in such a way that the client can recognize the therapist's music as inspired by the client's own. The therapist's acknowledgment affirms the value of the client's music and encourages its continuation.

- *Aesthetic shaping* involves placing the clients' relatively brief and simple gestures—both musical and nonmusical—into a larger musical context. At the beginning of an improvisation this may be a first translation, in a sense, of what is felt and seen as well as what is heard into music, the medium of communication for the group. During the improvisation, a sequence of notes played or sung by a client can be turned into a coherent melody, a repeated rhythmic figure can become a discrete musical form, and the disparate creations of two clients can be combined into a single musical entity. The playing of the clients is not only matched, as it would be in supportive musical coactivity, but it is enhanced, and the aesthetic qualities of the music intensify the experience and increase the likelihood of further and more extensive responses. Aesthetic shaping also has particular clinical relevance when organized, musically sensitive endings are attempted. Facilitating a finishing balance— helping those who would end prematurely to sustain, while maintaining awareness of the possibility of ending in those who would perseverate indefinitely—is a final reinforcement of the awareness of what was created during the course of the improvisation.

- *Awareness and response* occurs when those participating actively are directed to the participation of others. A client whose initial response may have been nurtured through supportive coactivity and contextualized through aesthetic shaping may be encouraged through cues and gestures to awareness of, and response to, the music of the therapist at the piano. Ultimately, the goal is to facilitate awareness among group members of their moment-to-moment creative processes, to create a self-sustaining, flexible musical structure whose foundation lies in the responses of the clients to each other.

CASE EXAMPLE: GROUP 17

Group 17 is a regularly scheduled therapy group at a university-based specialty clinic ("the Center"). It is composed of four clients, ranging in age from 20 to 33 years at the time of this writing, each diagnosed as within the autistic spectrum.

Using Music to Work With Autism

The most severe deficits of many members of the special populations served by music therapy are expressive. The clients with autism in this case study can barely answer the simplest questions. Even a clear, single-word answer—"yes" or "no"—must be interpreted. Did they understand the question, or are they saying something because they know some kind of response is expected? Are they just being agreeable, because the "yes" of agreement is less likely to provoke further questions or demands for clarification? Are they repeating the last choice offered to them, or do they really mean what they say? In the year's sessions summarized by this case study, *there was not a single conversation observed that was initiated and carried on between group members.* In some sessions members do not appear to be able to respond to their own names. A grasp of the basic principle of language seems to be tentative at best. The members of the group have never communicated with each other verbally; even exchanges of the most trivial verbal pleasantries are closed off to them.

One might assume that a person who did not or could not communicate did not have an active internal world of thoughts and feelings and an interest in and understanding of the external environment. We make no such assumption. In our approach we assume that these clients possess receptive capacities and a developed personality structure, that there is an active inner life, a motivation and need to communicate to those around them. In our communication and interaction with the clients, we embrace the idea that they have receptive capacities that far exceed their expressive abilities. Any communication, musical or verbal, is made with this idea in mind.

To say, then, that music represents a tool, a device, or a technique for expressive communication in a group of adults with autism is a gross understatement. Music *becomes* the social fabric, the language, and the culture of the group. Music-making creates a world that is alive with interaction. A rhythmic/melodic statement made in unison with, at an interval with, in harmony with, or in response to other musical statements in a piece of music can, in its own way, have a clarity and an eloquence that is unique, even for a person who can speak and communicate. For someone with great deficits in these areas, the opportunity to make such statements and hear them answered, to hear one's "voice" stand out from among one's peers, or merge with others to create harmony and forms, is a rare experience of social as well as musical affirmation.

Client Profiles

To convey the features of the clients of Group 17 we present one client, Rakeem, in some detail. Because of space limitations, the other clients are profiled in lesser detail.

Rakeem, age 20, had been in therapy at the Center for 8 years. His behavior was described as "autistic-like" in early documentation received by the Center. He was in individual therapy for 4 years before starting group therapy. In addition to often-echolalic speech, Rakeem exhibits a variety of behaviors that are of concern in facilitating his involvement in music and in achieving clinical benefit from that involvement:

- *Compulsivity:* Rakeem engages in grooming (of musical instruments, clothing, and the bodies of group members and therapists) and ordering (untangling wires, placing instruments and mallets in order by size or color). These behaviors can occur before or during music-making and can be disruptive of group process and intrusive into the space of other people.
- *Impulsivity:* Rakeem leaves his chair spontaneously at any time, moves around the room at varying rates of speed, jumps directly into the air ("pogo-ing"), and vocalizes in a high-pitched or sirenlike manner ("sirening"). Clearly, such behavior has roots in the involuntary aspects of his personality. It might be shrugged off or tolerated more easily if done by a small child, but when done by a physically mature adult, it is stunning, almost shocking in its unexpectedness, its uniqueness, its grace and athleticism, and its complete departure from the realm of normal behavior. It makes participation in action methods impossible for Rakeem and more difficult for everyone else. Rakeem's impulsive behaviors may also be interpersonal responses in part to aspects of membership and participation in the group. The presence of the young woman, Tamika, and the possibility of interpersonal interaction are a source of an intensity of feeling that may be "discharged" in impulsive behavior. Likewise, the

prospect of the group beginning its musical activities can lead to exuberant running, jumping, and sirening.

- *Self-presentation* refers to those of Rakeem's behaviors that appear to stem from personal issues regarding the openness and completeness with which Rakeem wishes to present himself. Rakeem can present himself as more disabled or as less so. True, the more extreme of his behaviors appear to be beyond his conscious control. He cannot really help the jumping, running, and sirening of his most out-of-control periods; he cannot repress the spontaneous rhythmic and melodic inventiveness of his most creative musical periods. However, there is a substantial range of behavior in which Rakeem can choose how he wants to present himself and which of the aspects of his personality he wants to display publicly. It is here that the music group presents the most salient therapeutic possibilities for him.
- *Engagement:* Rakeem's ambivalence about self-presentation is reflected in his music-making. He may stop playing if his music is praised, or his playing may regress to a more "disabled" level. Rakeem often requires fairly extensive engagement to begin playing, particularly in improvised contexts: He not only needs encouragement, but he also must be given some demonstration by the therapist of a kind of playing that would work in the given musical context for him to begin. He might then not only imitate but also caricature the playing, posture, and movements of the therapist, and he might cease playing as soon as the therapist's modeling stops.

Such modeling is not necessary. Rakeem has demonstrated many times over that he can improvise spontaneously with the rest of the group. The pervasiveness and subtlety of the issue of self-presentation is at play here. For Rakeem to play spontaneously and imaginatively would reveal aspects of himself that he clearly has misgivings about showing. The exact nature of these misgivings is not clear, but is multiple in its possibilities. Is it simply not "cool" to show what one can do in this situation? Does the manifestation of such abilities open him to the possibility that more will be asked, expected, or demanded than he feels motivated to offer? Is he "getting by" with a minimum of effort, malingering in some way? Is he, despite his obvious abilities, still concerned about being "wrong," about being corrected or criticized, about being revealed as inadequate or as disabled? Is he joking, having fun at the expense of peers to whom he feels superior and therapists whose earnestness he ridicules? Is he merely being playful? All of these considerations may be parts of the puzzle. The resultant impression is of a client who is consciously withholding in significant ways, content thereby to assume a persona that is not really who he is and that substantially underrepresents his potential.

In working with Rakeem as a member of Group 17, several areas of clinical emphasis come to mind. The therapists work to help him to improve control of the compulsive and impulsive behavior described above. They work musically and interpersonally to strengthen his willingness to use the full extent of his abilities and aptitudes in the service of the group's activities, thereby presenting himself actually, openly, and honestly. Finally, they work to promote greater self-trust in his own musical impulses so that Rakeem can improvise with more spontaneity and less supervision and modeling on their part.

Tamika, age 21, had been in music therapy at the Center for 9 years. After a brief initial period of group therapy, she had 2 years of individual therapy before returning to group work, where she has been ever since. Her file contains documentation that refers to her as having "autistic tendencies," being "mentally retarded/emotionally handicapped," and as having "pervasive developmental delay."

Her language is limited, and her speech is echolalic. Tamika's behaviors of clinical concern in music therapy include rocking at times in a pronounced, almost violent way. Although rapid and done close enough to others so that it can appear dangerous, her "bobbing and weaving" never actually causes her to harm herself by coming into contact with objects or other group members. She might be smiling or singing to herself as she rocks. She does this with total absorption in or by her internal state, and it can be very difficult to get her attention, either through verbal or physical intervention, during her periods of rocking.

Another problematic behavior is "hiding," often exhibited when Tamika is overwhelmed by such musical challenges as improvising on the tambourine to a particular rhythmic pattern or holding a mallet and striking resonator bells (metal, xylophone-like bars that sound when struck and can be arranged in different melodic patterns) with some precision when directed to do so. When engaging in this behavior, Tamika hides her eyes, wraps her arms around her torso, and tucks her head toward her chest. In this posture she is literally smaller, and it is almost impossible for her to see what is happening around her or for her eyes to be seen by other group members or the leaders. This behavior differs from the rocking in that it seems less automatic and reflexive; it arises more in reaction to the particular musical situation in the group at the moment and less out of her internal physiological conditioning or the mere presence of male group members.

Another behavior, related to the hiding, is her tendency to rush through her musical activity, particularly when the action method is realization. At her turn to play, she plays rapidly, without apparent concern for tempo or accuracy, looking at neither the instrument she is playing nor the cotherapist's directions. We attribute this to the overall tension of the musical situation and the stress of being in a relatively exposed position as a member of a small musical group.

Tamika will try to end her participation in any particular musical activity, or the entire session, prematurely. She "returns" instruments and mallets while the rest of the group is still musically involved, giving them back to the leader or placing them at some distance from her. She leaves the group and walks to the door prior to the beginning of the group's goodbye song or during the song itself. This is a personal expression ("I am/want to be finished"), but it is also a separation of herself from the group and its music.

The clinical implications of these behaviors depend on whether they have substantial involuntary aspects to them or are merely habitual adaptations to the group's process. The therapists work with Tamika to help her sustain her playing for longer periods and maintain an even tempo without rushing to "get it over with." They work to help her overcome the fear of attention and doing things wrong that leads to hiding behavior, so that she can take some joy in looking, seeing, and understanding both life's processes and its products. Finally, they help her extend her awareness of the group beyond that of a setting in which the crucial moments are those in which occasional tasks or demands must be executed correctly to experiencing it as a social and aesthetic whole in which she has a valued role.

We have, at times, used the technique of aesthetic shaping in response to Tamika's rhythmic rocking, treating it as a type of musical gesture and improvising music to try to give it form so that the group as a whole could relate to what she was doing and join her after a fashion. The intent is that she might then become more attentive to what is going on beyond the sphere of her internally initiated activity and gain more conscious awareness of and control over her behavior through hearing it echoed back to her. This needs to be done in a delicate way, as there is a danger that musical stimulation and support can prolong the activity without bringing Tamika into communicative awareness.

Mitchell, age 33, has been in music therapy at the Center for 9 years. He had been placed in a group immediately on beginning his attendance and never had any individual therapy. Clearly, his deficits had their most profound impact in his socialization; he presents as shy and fearful, lacking social interactive communication skills, and seldom varying his vocal inflection. Mitchell manifests two major tendencies in music-making that are of clinical concern. One is *perseveration*, the extended repetition of notes, rhythms, or phrases almost interminably, in seeming disregard—or lack of awareness—of anything and everything that might change around it. When perseverating, Mitchell's opportunity for spontaneous, creative, interactive behavior is reduced to a series of repeated gestures, with each repetition as similar to the previous one as possible. Slowly his awareness becomes completely bound up in what has become a physical task, so that he loses all touch with what others around him are doing. He may be totally unaware of changes in the tempo, dynamics, or tonality of the music and may also be unaware that the music has ceased entirely until some strong, often nonmusical intervention is made to bring him back to awareness of people and activities in his immediate surroundings.

The other, related, problem is Mitchell's characteristic withdrawal from the possibility of spontaneous creative interaction into his projection of a continual, unchanging, essentially unresponsive and highly predictable musical "persona." Although Mitchell presents very little of the bizarre and distractive behavior that might be unnerving to others and inhibit group process, his stolid consistency of affect and paucity of expression present an issue that is of overwhelming importance to the client himself.

Thus, the area of clinical emphasis in working with Mitchell is awareness, working continually with his ongoing sense of himself and of others. The therapists structure musical and interpersonal experiences that convey and foster the sense that the musical environment in which Group 17 takes place is different from what he encounters elsewhere and that maintaining the awareness to find and realize his innate impulses to personal expression and human interaction has intrinsic rewards in music that are equally profound and not nearly so conditional as they are in the world of words.

Jesse, age 20, is very tall, heavy, and slow moving, an imposing physical presence. He had been in music therapy at the Center for 6 1/2 years. He had never had individual therapy but was placed immediately in a group. Initial Center documentation describes him as "autistic—high functioning." He is described as having far better receptive than expressive language. The latter is echolalic at times.

His family is somewhat proud of the fact the he looks "normal," having few of the mannerisms, movements, or physical features associated with disability. He appears undemonstrative in early contacts, but in fact displays a wide range of affect ranging from almost euphoric to sad and tearful. However, he can appear to be distracted, in a daze, unconnected to others in a group context.

The major problematic behaviors that Jesse presents have already been described in relation to other clients. These include difficulties in initiating interactions spontaneously and the tendency to perseverate in musical situations. Whereas in a client such as Mitchell there is a definite sense of withdrawal and detachment from others, in Jesse there is a sense of inhibition. He is reluctant to participate due to the possibility that what he does will betray the sense of normality he projects in his physical bearing.

In working with Jesse, the therapists are trying to help him organize his playing in a responsive way and cultivate the self-acceptance that will allow him to experience the rewards of spontaneous participation.

Group Format

The group meets once weekly for approximately 45 minutes. The group has been in existence, with slight changes in membership, for 3 years before the period under consideration. The clients were selected to be in Group 17 on the basis of chronological age, level of functioning, and availability. Each client is assessed musically in an individual intake session at the Center that ascertains his or her basic abilities to function in a group and the ways in which music can be of value to them in treatment.

Each therapy group is co-led by two music therapists. The person at the piano, designated the therapist, leads the group musically, and the person sitting within the group itself, designated the cotherapist, facilitates musical interactions with the therapist and among the group members themselves. The groups generally begin formally with the "hello song," a greeting song composed specifically for the group by its leaders. This song has a ritual fuction, formally marking the beginning of the group, and it may be composed with specific feeling and expectation of the group in mind. It also is an example of the action technique of *realization*, the rendering by the group in the moment of a precomposed piece. Even before the greeting song, however, music improvised by the therapist can accompany the arrival of the clients, reflecting what is perceived of their moods and energy levels. This is an initial use of *aesthetic shaping*. It captures the felt sense of the mood of the group as it enters and serves as a prelude for the group's activities, establishing the centrality of music in the group's process. The greeting song functions to orient group members to time, place, and to the presence or absence of others.

Following these events, there are two things to be accomplished before active music-making begins. The type of music the group is going to play initially must be established (realization or improvisation, the basic action methods described previously), and musical instruments must be distributed. The group is acquainted with the methods of realization and improvisation through experience and through regularly reiterated discussion of the two concepts. To the extent that they can understand the differences between them, they do.

Whenever possible, the therapists give clients autonomy in decision-making regarding choice of music and instruments. This is the action technique of *nondirectivity*, important here because it exemplifies the spirit of expression that the group's music-making implies and because they sense that the clients may have little autonomy in other areas of their lives. This is shown in the difficulty they have in actually choosing once they are presented choices. As well as being a right, choosing is a skill they need to develop.

Each client chooses from among the instruments that are made available. Availability is determined based on the requirements of precomposed pieces, the compatibility of the sounds of the instruments when played freely at all dynamic levels (as in improvisation), and the way they function musically. For example, it might be important to have both rhythmic and melodic instruments, both instruments that sustain tones and those that do not. Choosing and distribution is a fairly lengthy process, done without haste and with musical enhancement. The therapist plays during this time, reflecting the interactions, movements, and choices of the clients, creating and inter-weaving themes that may ultimately reappear (*aesthetic shaping*).

A session may include several realizations, several improvisations, or a mix of both action methods. It generally concludes with a goodbye song. The goodbye song from Group 17 was originally improvised and then retained (a transition from *improvisation* to *realization*).

Each session conducted at the Center is videotaped. Before the follow-ing week's session, the actions and interactions of the clients are noted, as well as their various musical responses, and music that is deemed significant for future sessions is notated so that it can be recreated (*improvisation* to *real-ization*). This overall process is called *indexing*.

GROUP CLINICAL IMPROVISATION: CASE PRESENTATION AND COMMENTARY

The improvisation presented here is a pivotal one in the group's overall process and in the development of several of the clients. In its entirety, the improvisation lasted 19 minutes from the distribution of instruments to the conclusion of the music. The session was indexed in detail by the therapists, as are all sessions at the Center. However, a sequential description of the interpersonal and musical interactions in their entirety would lengthen this discussion needlessly and be of little interest to those without musical back-grounds. Instead, the focus is on selected clinically significant points of in-teraction during the improvisation. These serve as illustrations of the possi-bilities of clinical improvisation as an action method and the various action techniques used to help realize these possibilities.

Setting the Stage

The improvisation takes place following the group's greeting song (*re-alization*). On this occasion, the group chooses to improvise. Each client then chooses from among the instruments that are made available. For this impro-visation the clients choose as follows: Mitchell, "big, red, drum," a large floor tom that stands on legs; Jesse, a conga drum; Tamika, a snare drum; and Rakeem, a large wooden xylophone. David, the cotherapist, has a tambou-rine and also a mallet with which he can play the clients' instruments as well as his own. Alan, the therapist at the piano, is improvising music, elevating the distribution process from a mere procedure to an overture to the group's music-making.

When the instruments are finally distributed, there is complete silence. A moment of musical and clinical significance has arrived. What is going to happen?

This is a moment of fundamental equality, one of the benefits of improvisation referred to previously. It is also a moment when the action technique of nondirectivity is used by both therapists. No musical or visual direction is provided at this point, and client responses are awaited. The clients determine, as much as possible, the course of musical events, and this is a moment to reinforce that understanding.

The improvisation that follows proceeds in a series of individually analyzable, yet thematically and clinically related movements. As each client makes his or her contribution, the music responds, expanding and contracting, using musical elements to integrate the group's sounds as one musical whole. Just as each of the movements has a form, the improvisation as a whole has a form. Clinically significant moments for three of the clients and the techniques that facilitate them are highlighted for analysis in the context of an ongoing description of the basic musical content of the improvisation.

Early Stage

In the early stages of the improvisation, the music is generally characterized by the tentativeness of the clients. If they are able to begin playing without prompting and play strongly and clearly—as Mitchell does with three strong notes on the big red drum to begin the music-making—their playing is brief. The technique of *engagement* is prominent, as David tries unsuccessfully through verbalization and gesture to get Tamika to stop rocking and then successfully through gesture to reactivate Mitchell after he has been distracted by her behavior. Rakeem paces around the room between brief sojourns at the xylophone. *Supportive coactivity* is used to attempt to extend the playing of those who are engaged, giving aural and visual cues for continuation of the music. Periods of two or more clients playing simultaneously are relatively infrequent and of short duration. *Aesthetic shaping* is used in transitional periods, creating musical links between the playing of the individuals and giving the music continuity and a forward momentum.

Significant Moment: Mitchell

Approximately 5 1/2 minutes into the improvisation, the music comes to a complete halt: Harmony resolves, and the melody, which had begun in the high register of the xylophone, descends to the low register of the piano and ceases with an emphatic bass note.

David turns to Mitchell and gestures strongly for him to begin to play. He beats the drum once loudly. Alan follows directly with a single loud chord on the piano. A total of three "beats" are done in this way, with Alan giving emphasis to the final chord in the series. There is a slight delay in Mitchell's first response, but in his second and third beats he beats the drum simultaneously with David's "conducting."

These are the action techniques of engagement, supportive coactivity, and aesthetic shaping. Mitchell responds initially to David's gesture, which re-engages him after a brief period of inaction. Alan supports Mitchell (and David), responding musically to the beating, giving impetus to the maintenance of activity. His music is nondirectional, in that no specific musical direction for further response other than what has already been done is given. By giving emphasis to the final chord, the beats are shaped into a short phrase, indicating the possibility for pausing and decreasing the likelihood of continuous, perseverative beating.

David signals Mitchell to begin a repetition of the three-beat phrase. He "conducts" Mitchell but with much more subtle gestures than he had used in the first phrase. After the second beat, he moves aside, directing Mitchell's attention toward the piano. The phrase is completed with Mitchell listening to Alan.

This is the technique of awareness and response. Seeing his alertness and anticipation, David directs Mitchell toward a musical interaction with Alan, governed not with gestures but through the music they have already begun to make together. With David's withdrawal, Mitchell is also put in the position of leadership. It is he who is initiating the music and Alan who is following.

Mitchell and Alan repeat the phrase twice more. Alan "catches up" to Mitchell, so that they are both playing simultaneously. On the last beat, Alan slows down significantly, indicating perhaps the final repetition. Mitchell beats with him in the slowing tempo, adding an extra drumbeat as the elongated phrase comes to a close.

This ability to vary tempo with Alan is very significant in that it shows a high level of awareness and attunement to another individual. The mutual creation not only of sound but also of form in closing the interaction is also significant.

In the pause after the final phrase, Rakeem vocalizes wordlessly. Alan intuitively plays the rhythm and pitches of this vocalization on the piano (*supportive coactivity*). Mitchell then plays the same rhythm on his drum.

This is also significant, because it shows the extent of Mitchell's concentration, sensitivity, and flexibility and the degree of his relatedness and responsiveness to Alan at this time. The rhythm Alan plays is in direct contrast to the way Mitchell had been beating. It is brief, rapid, light; almost fluttering. Mitchell picks it up spontaneously and immediately even though it is very uncharacteristic of the way he normally beats.

Middle Phase

The interaction between the therapists and Mitchell can be designated as a turning point in the improvisation process. During the ensuing period, there is a general increase in the spontaneity, continuity, and cohesiveness of the playing. *Engagement*, when indicated, can be accomplished with a glance or a subtle gesture, as the awareness of all is increasingly centered outside of themselves and on the musical activities of others. *Supportive coactivity* is still important, as the next analysis shows, but increasingly it is *aesthetic shaping* that is called for. The rhythmic activity of the clients is given musical definition through the creation of melody and phrases of discrete duration. This both orients and motivates the clients, and they are emboldened in their playing. There is more simultaneous playing, with *aesthetic shaping* weaving these disparate parts together and preparing the way for the possibility of *awareness and response*.

Approximately 7 minutes into the improvisation, as Alan and Mitchell are engaged in another dialog, exchanging single beats on drum and piano, Jesse enters.

Significant Moment: Jesse

As Alan and Mitchell exchange chords and drumbeats responsively, one to each beat in a slow tempo, Jesse enters spontaneously. He beats so that he is playing three notes on the conga for each note that Alan or Mitchell play on their instrument (triplets). David immediately gestures to Jesse in acknowledgment and begins to mirror his rhythm exactly, beating with a mallet on the tambourine.

Jesse's spontaneity is clinically significant, as he is usually inhibited about entering without receiving a definite cue (permission) to do so. That he is not merely mirroring the rhythm of Alan and Mitchell but still playing in a way that is consistently related is also significant. David uses supportive coactivity, *beating with him immediately in order to encourage him to sustain his playing in its individuality. He beats initially so that his beating is not only audible to Jesse but is visible as well, and he maintains eye contact as he does so.*

Alan continues his interaction with Mitchell, and their playing merges. As they beat in unison, Alan sets their beating to a series of descending melodic phrases of equal length. This melody matches the beating of Mitchell, and also accommodates Jesse who continues to beat with David's support.

Alan uses aesthetic shaping *in improvising a melody that accommodates the beating of both clients. This orients Mitchell, who begins to emphasize the beats at the end of the phrases. Jesse is able to maintain his own beating with support, even though it is much more rapid than that of Alan and Mitchell.*

Approximately 40 seconds after Jesse's entrance, Alan alters the melody. Where he previously played a melody note for each of Mitchell's slow beats, he now plays a note for each of Jesse's more rapid beats. The nature of the whole experience changes. Both clients continue to beat as they were beating.

Alan has used aesthetic shaping once again to create a more complex and interesting melody, one that fully acknowledges Jesse's beating. The duration and relative consistency of Jesse's beating at this point is clinically significant.

Rakeem, who has been wandering, seats himself at the xylophone. David immediately begins to play on the xylophone in the triplet rhythm of the melody and Jesse's beating. Rakeem responds, matching David's beating. Jesse maintains his beating.

Once again the techniques of engagement and supportive coactivity are used. At this point Rakeem is engaged immediately and is responsive to musical support, joining right in with the triplet rhythm. David plays on the xylophone so that his triplet beating is still visible to Jesse. He maintains both aural and visual supportive coactivity with both clients.

When David turns away briefly to re-engage Jesse, who has stopped beating momentarily, Rakeem rises from his chair. David immediately turns back to him, motioning him to be seated. Rakeem reseats himself and resumes playing, this time taking up the simple rhythm of Mitchell.

Rakeem is still easily pulled out of musical participation. However, he is more and more responsive to engagement, returning and reseating himself rapidly. The simple, single note rhythm of Mitchell that Rakeem adopts may be easier and less stimulating to play at this point than the more complex triplets.

Jesse recommences his triplet beating, and David sits in front of Rakeem, motionless for the moment.

Three clients are playing continuously in rhythmic synchrony, directly related to the piano and to each other, without any intervention from David.

Late Stage

The improvisation has now developed considerable momentum. Mitchell's strong beating has given it a firm rhythmic grounding, and Jesse's triplets have given it forward propulsion. They both play continuously, and Rakeem, although he continues to wander, does not go as far afield and plays more frequently. Tamika is not active, but she is rocking less. *Engagement* is no longer an issue, except with regard to Tamika, and *supportive coactivity* by David also seems somewhat superfluous at this point. Alan has shaped the musical elements into a form that is sustainable. The thrust of the improvisation is now toward *awareness and response*.

Another dialog between Alan and Mitchell begins. This time Mitchell is alert to the situation, responding rapidly and decisively. The phrases exchanged are longer and more complex, consisting of five and six notes, and there is clearly deliberation on the part of both participants concerning how to respond and what to play.

This is awareness and response *at a very high level for Mitchell.*

This time the interaction is expanded, and each client in turn is gestured to exchange a phrase with Alan. This is a sequence of *engagements*. All, including Tamika, clearly grasp the form of the musical interaction, and respond immediately to David's entrance signals. Each remains seated and attentive while others take their turns, and the responses, although simple, are also clearly related to Alan's "invitational" phrases and the music that has gone before.

This is awareness and response *on the part of the whole group in relation to Alan.*

As the expanded dialog ends, Rakeem has left the group. He has seated himself in a far corner of the room. The intermittent nature of the dialog that has just taken place, with its stopping and starting, its resting between short phrases, has caused the music to lose its rhythmic propulsion and almost all of its volume. Alan plays alone. Using *aesthetic shaping*, he creates melodic phrases based on the five-note rhythm that was prominent in the dialog just concluded. The harmonies are simple and almost pensive, encapsulating the past, holding out the possibility of transition without defining what is to come (*nondirectionality*). Turning in his chair, David gestures to the distant Rakeem, pointing to his vacant seat and the unattended xylophone (*engagement*) and gently saying his name.

Significant Moment: Rakeem

Rakeem looks at David for a moment, then proceeds rapidly and purposefully to his chair and immediately picks up his mallet to play.

At this point, despite his distance, Rakeem readily responds to engagement. *There is a sense of group connectedness—clients and* therapists, *all of the musicians— having drawn closer. To separate oneself from the group at this point in the development of the improvisation is much more significant than it was earlier in the session.*

Rakeem plays in a slow, steady rhythm. One of his notes is approximately twice as long as one of Alan's notes. Alan immediately adjusts, playing chords equal in duration to Rakeem's notes. As Rakeem plays, he smiles, grimaces, shifts in his chair restlessly, and vocalizes in a downward, sighing fashion. Alan responds to Rakeem's vocalization with a brief downward melodic phrase.

Much of Rakeem's response here has to do with efforts at calm and self-control. He chooses a slower tempo that is less stimulating to play; his body language and vocalization reflect an effort to stay in his chair and keep playing, overcoming what has hitherto been an irresistible impulse to leave. Alan uses aesthetic shaping *to further incorporate his responses into the music.*

Rakeem begins to speed up his tempo. David joins at this point, playing on the tambourine. He plays consistently, two notes on the tambourine for each of Rakeem's notes. Rakeem's excitement continues to be evident: He speeds up further, vocalizes, bounces up and down in his chair, and finally stands to leave the group. David motions him to return to his chair, and he does so immediately.

An important clinical juncture has been reached. There is a tension between the loud, propulsive, energetic music that the group had reached earlier and the quiet, almost introspective mood that Rakeem seems to require to stay involved. The therapists must contain Rakeem while continuing to acknowledge and support the group's collective energy. David uses supportive coactivity to help stabilize Rakeem's tempo, suggesting a musical outlet for his rising excitement. Rakeem ultimately attempts to leave but is immediately re-engaged. Commitment seems to be superseding excitement as a motivation.

A spontaneous shift in the music occurs. Alan's harmonies find a strong tonal center, and his playing becomes more rhythmic, taking on a more animated, dance-like form. David adapts his playing to the new dance idiom. Simultaneously Rakeem emerges from his slower tempo to play a melody that is congruent with Alan's new tempo and accompaniment.

The responses here are so synchronous it is all but impossible to discern their causal sequence. This is awareness and response of an almost extrasensory nature, rare in verbal interaction, less so in improvisation. The energized, coinitiated music can now contain Rakeem. He makes no further attempt to leave the group between this point and the music's conclusion.

As the music stabilizes at its new level of energy, Mitchell enters spontaneously. He beats loudly and regularly on his drum at a slightly slower tempo than Rakeem's. Rakeem immediately turns his head, looks at Mitchell, and assumes his tempo.

This is Mitchell's awareness and response in relation to those currently playing. As the energy level has risen close to what it was before the dialog, Mitchell is able to enter with his louder, more ponderous instrument without excessively distorting the character of the music. Rakeem's reaction, moderating his tempo to join Michael, is also awareness and response.

With the initial beats of Mitchell's entrance, the other clients begin playing spontaneously as well, in rhythms related to that of Mitchell and Rakeem.

This is awareness and response on the part of all clients. No signal or cue was given for this entrance.

Finale

With the resounding entrance of Mitchell, Jesse, and Tamika, the energy of the music quickly surpasses anything that has been heard previously.

The therapists use *supportive coactivity* to try to sustain the ensemble playing that is a major achievement for the group. David beats loudly and openly on the tambourine, making sure all can hear and see the beat of the music. Alan plays strong, dense chords to help maintain the rhythmic momentum of the music. His chord progressions foreshadow the approaching close of the improvisation.

The music maintains its energy but is slowing perceptibly. Alan's descending bass line strongly emphasizes the tonal center of the music, and he superimposes a melody that clearly brings it toward a final point of closure. Mitchell, perhaps excited by this development, begins to accelerate his beating. David uses *supportive coactivity*, giving aural and visual cues to help him reorient himself. The resulting deceleration brings the music well below its previous tempo. Once again, Alan's playing becomes mostly chordal. Emphasizing the rhythm in working for the clinically desirable result of a coherent ending, he uses *aesthetic shaping* to create a single repeated phrase: three long chords, reminiscent of the three assertive drumbeats with which Mitchell began the improvisation. After a long, held "note" of sustained beating and playing by all, the group ceases playing at David's signal.

In the silence that ensues, David asks the group a very open question, "What do you think?" He is wondering if there will be a verbal response in the wake of the intensity and exhilaration of the previous period of musical interaction. No one says a word, with the exception of Mitchell. "The drum," he says.

TREATMENT OUTCOMES

Changes During the Improvisation

The action method of group clinical improvisation offers the group a modality for expressive communication that is literally transformative. The clients' awareness of and responsiveness to the activities of others—initially the activities of the leaders but eventually of all participants—expands and becomes more refined moment by moment during the course of the music. As this refinement continues they are able to tolerate, and function creatively at, higher and higher levels of physical and emotional stimulation. The interactions toward the end of the music are clinically and musically noteworthy: the extended dialog between Alan, Mitchell, and then among all of the clients; the almost intuitive cocreativity between Alan and Rakeem; and the spontaneous entrance of the drummers near the conclusion of the improvisation. These moments exemplify communication that transcends the deficits normally ascribed to these clients.

The energy and beauty of their music and the sense of community resulting from creating it motivate the clients to challenge successfully the behavioral barriers that tend to isolate them. Rakeem literally fights with all his conscious will against the almost reflexive impulse to run, jump, and flee and ultimately succeeds in remaining with the group at its most climactic moments. Mitchell's assertive initial thematic statement, his increasingly complex and expressive engagements with Alan, his energetic, propulsive playing throughout; and his moments of subtle, perceptive imitation represent clinical and musical achievements. Rather than withdraw into mechanical, perseverative playing, his awareness and his responsiveness continually increase as the music progresses. Jesse overcomes his inhibition and enters spontaneously with rhythmically related playing that aids in musical transitions. The subtle pride these individuals take in the group and its achievements stems not only from their own hard-won gains but also from an awareness and appreciation of the struggles and gains of their peers.

Changes in Group Process Over Time

This improvisation marked a high point in the development of the group's process over time. The clients demonstrated extraordinary levels of awareness of others, spontaneity, responsiveness, independence, and organization. In previous sessions, these aspects had been observed but never for so many of the members, to such a degree, and for such a long period. The length of time during which clients participated actively was extended and the amount of stimulation they could tolerate increased. Thanks in part to the clear grounding and structure supplied by action techniques such as supportive coactivity and aesthetic shaping, they made freer and more creative choices, often initiating shifts of mood and tempo themselves.

In subsequent sessions, such a degree of cohesion was observed more frequently. Fewer interventions, particularly on the part of the cotherapist, were necessary merely to help clients sustain their participation. The degree of stimulation and excitement resulting from simply sensing themselves in intimate musical relationship with each other was less able to derail them. Likewise, less overtly stimulating music was necessary to bring response and musical cohesion. They were able to play in a broadening range of musical moods and feelings and sustain each for longer periods. Thus, in later improvisations, the transitions between "movements" would be fewer and less abrupt, and clients could more fully and subtly explore a single mood or form.

Transfer of Gains

The members of Group 17 have largely aged out of programs in which trained clinicians observe and document changes in their behavior. The best source of information on transfer of gains outside of music therapy is their parents, who were interviewed for this purpose and described significant gains in a number of areas.

- *Motivation:* Clients' parents reported an enthusiasm for attending Group 17 that contrasted strongly to their children's apathy in other areas. The group is the thing they most want to do. Mitchell's mother described him as apathetic and depressed when he started music therapy. A parent conference report from this time stated "his mother has observed that he has become too sad, that he is not interested in anything. He used to do a lot more." When interviewed, his mother described his developing enthusiasm about music therapy. A report issued during the time of this study supported her observation, stating "to see Mitchell jog into music therapy and rub his hands together in anticipation is to know that the experience is a valuable one for him." Tamika's mother reported that she has little that she likes to do and looks forward to. Music therapy is an exception. It is "at the top of the list." Jesse's mother stated that the group was a highlight of his week. He rarely displays enthusiasm for any activity, but he loves going to music therapy, and this enthusiasm has spread to other activities.
- *Musical confidence:* Each member has become confident in relating to, through, and about music outside of the sessions, using the skills acquired in the group in other situations. Tamika is able to discuss at some length with her mother the instruments she played in the session and the music the group made. Jesse discovered an old electronic keyboard in his home and insisted that his mother buy new batteries for it. "Now he wants me to play with him," she said. Mitchell is much more interested in music outside of the sessions. He is more likely to initiate musical than verbal interactions with his mother, singing spontaneously in an animated fashion that encourages her to join him.
- *Socialization:* Group members have shown an increased ability to tolerate and function in social situations. Jesse is able to work and play in cooperation with others, when previously he preferred to do things alone even when the opportunity to do them with others was available. This is something his mother never thought he would be able to do and indicates a lessening of his inhibitions and fears. Mitchell is interested in communicating and much more willing to do so. A therapist who had observed Rakeem in individual music therapy was surprised and gratified that he was able to participate productively in a group, something that she doubted he would be able to do. She observed an increase in his use of language and a decrease in compulsive behavior. Tamika's mother stated that she is calmer as a result

of group participation. Having gotten to know and feel comfortable with her peers, she can now do well in other group situations.

There has been no more eloquent acknowledgment of the group's value than that made by a parent in a rare session when parents and clients participated together. As she entered the music therapy room she exclaimed, "So this is where the miracles happen."

Dealing With Client Resistance

Addressing resistance within the context of the musical environment, given the clients' extensive personal disabilities, is a difficult task. Some of the clients exhibit behaviors that appear to be conscious and deliberate negative responses to the group's process or its intentions and can comfortably be designated and dealt with as resistance in the most common sense of that term. However, all of the clients of Group 17 display behavior that can interfere with, or supersede, any attempt at active musical participation. The clients may neither be able to control the onset of such behaviors nor may they be able to terminate them at will; hence, the formal designation "resistance" may not be entirely appropriate. Yet the appearance of these behaviors is almost certainly influenced by the intellectual, social, and emotional pressures and musical challenges that being in the group inevitably exert (Brown, 1994). Clients' resistances, like so many of their other responses to life, take uncommon forms that are not subject to their own wills.

Involuntary behaviors are relevant to the conduct of the group for two important reasons. First, they are important features of the overall personality and behavior profiles that lead to the clients' initial diagnoses and subsequent referrals to music therapy. Although the prognosis for overcoming them entirely is probably poor, alleviating them within the group and decreasing their frequency outside of the group are definitely among the attainable clinical goals.

Second, the action methods described above may be said to arise at least partially in response to just these types of involuntary behaviors and have been proven well-suited to work with them. Within the musical environment, behaviors that can clearly be interpreted as serving to resist musical participation or avoid it entirely may nevertheless be heard as musical and responded to musically by the therapist. The walking, running, jumping, twisting, banging, and flailing behaviors of resistance are often inherently rhythmic and can each be made the basis for strong, propulsive music. The talking, yelling, whining, shouting, screaming, and crying actions of resistance are often inherently melodic and can each be matched in pitch and volume by the therapist, but with the melodic extension and harmonic underpinning that creates a truly musical interaction. Resistant behavior of great intensity can suddenly and unexpectedly become "music" of equal intensity as therapist and client are linked through the unifying properties of rhythm and pitch. Thus, although certain musical behaviors are clearly indicative of conscious, deliberate responsiveness, and interactivity in the musical environment, the action methods described above may be used in response to any client action. Even no behavior at all, the only behavior that might be viewed as nonmusical and truly "resistant" in the musical environment, may be viewed as passive listening that can mark the transfer of attention from internal stimulation to events and circumstances in the external environment as part of a progression toward fuller, more overt participation.

The understanding of the potentials inherent in resistant behavior is a cornerstone of the N-R approach. Nordoff and Robbins (1977) observed that behaviors designated as "resistant"—both deliberate and voluntary—and behaviors designated as "participator" are not necessarily antithetical, but are actually dual aspects of the developing musical relationship. As its forms and modalities evolve, resistive behavior can be seen as indicating greater and greater awareness of and responsiveness to the musical process. Progress in therapy may be indicated in the quality of resistance before it is indicated by the quality of participation. In the words of Nordoff and Robbins (1977, p. 190), "To work resourcefully with each level of resistive behavior, to prevent it from regressing, *to raise the level of relationship through treating expressions of restiveness as means of intercommunication* are essential techniques of therapy."[1]

Benefits of Successive Uses of Action Methods

The alternation of the action methods of realization and improvisation improves the overall therapeutic effectiveness of N-R work in Group 17. Realization emphasizes the awareness, perceptions, and behaviors that enable the clients to make precomposed musical statements at prescribed times. Improvisation uses the prerequisites for realization and further expands awareness and perception to enable the clients to make spontaneous, self-expressive yet relevant musical statements when they themselves feel them to be appropriate. Full participation in realization is a developmental step in the process that leads to full participation in improvisation.

The group is often more comfortable with precomposed pieces and enjoys the process of learning them and the clear sense of accomplishment that arises from their realization. Realization brings assurance and reassurance.

---

[1]Scale I, a scale designed by Nordoff and Robbins (1977) to evaluate the client–therapists relationship in musical activity, measures both levels of participation and qualities of restiveness. For each level of participation that the scale describes, there is a concomitant and equally valued quality of restiveness.

As clients gradually become acquainted with and master their parts, their sense of assurance grows. As the various parts are woven together, they become aware of the interrelation of the parts and the resultant whole, and their assurance grows still further. As they change parts and recreate the piece several times, they are reassured with each realization of their own abilities as individuals and as a group. Ultimately, however, the vitality of the experience dissipates as its novelty fades. At such a juncture, the clinical choice is often to use improvisation.

Although realization may become stale, it usually has a favorable effect on the music that is subsequently improvised. The experience of realizing carefully crafted melodies and consistent rhythms leads to coherence in the freely created music that is immediately noticeable. At times, clients will insert melodic and rhythmic material from a recently realized piece into an improvisation, a time-honored technique among both composers and improvisers. Again, their recollection of a past event and their description of it in the present are also of clinical significance. They are rarely able to access the past and describe it verbally with the coherence and accuracy they can display in music-making.

Improvisation is clearly a strain at times. It is also a risk, in that it can turn out unsatisfactorily for one reason or another. The volume of sound being created can isolate clients; some are moved by the lack of structure back into internal preoccupation. Also, impulsive and preservative behaviors may increase. There is no way to remedy these derailing results through practice or rehearsal. There is no guarantee that a second improvisation will be any better than the first.

When it is considered clinically beneficial to continue with improvisation, there are ways to make it a less-destabilizing experience. Instruments may be chosen that are smaller, quieter, and of different timbres. They can necessitate more concentration and coordination to produce a sound and assure that the sounds produced are not so loud as to isolate one client from another. The musical choices of the therapist in *supportive coactivity* and *aesthetic shaping* can reflect the need for clearer, simpler structures that facilitate group stability. It is truly because of the clinical possibilities and therapeutic opportunities that the therapists remain committed to improvisation. And we suspect that clients continue to choose improvisation when they do because of its musical possibilities; a sense of freedom; and the possibility of unexpected and unique musical fulfillment.

It will also be considered beneficial to return to realization at some point. This reinstates all of the assurances and reassurances that structured music and specific direction can supply. In this alternation between the two action methods lies the essence of the clinical strategy for Group 17: the balance of freedom and structure leading to continuous musical and personal development.

THERAPIST'S USE OF SELF

Therapists as Models

The most easily observed aspect of the therapist's use of self in Group 17 is as a model of behavior in the musical–therapeutic environment. The therapists serve as models for musical activity. Aspects of playing music such as listening, responsiveness, and instrumental techniques are modeled by the therapists for and with the clients. Clients learn a great deal of what they know of playing music from watching and listening to the therapists play.

Therapists also model a constructive, conscientious, involved attitude toward music-making itself. By bringing commitment and enthusiasm to their own playing and singing, they convey the idea that music is not about "going through the motions." Rather, music is about investing those motions with the inner fire of creative expression. Therapists also model the appropriate ways of receiving and responding to the creative efforts of others. By applying no strict critical or aesthetic standard, by encouraging and praising all sincere efforts, the therapists model the attitude that the group must have in order to create together and that each individual must have toward their own personal efforts to continue to challenge the barriers to their development.

Finally, the therapists model teamwork. They do this both musically and interpersonally. The listening, responsiveness, and creativity that typify the group creation of music are also aspects of interpersonal relationships that assure longevity, mutual gratification, and success. At any moment, whether it is a time of relative relaxation or a time of creative intensity, clients look to the interactions of the therapists as examples of how to treat others and how to expect that they will be treated.

Therapists as Creators

When the music therapists improvise in a session, it is necessary that they tap into their own inner creative resources. There is no prescription, no preconceived plan as to what exactly will happen. Even before considering their relationship to the clients, the therapists carry with them into the session their own musical preferences, tendencies, and skills. Although the therapists may have conscious intentions to create music in a particular way to facilitate and enhance the client's development, the exact nature of what and how they create reflects both their conscious and unconscious life. To enter into a genuine and responsive musical relationship with clients, the music therapist has to use his personal relationship to music. To be effective, the therapists, both at the piano and on the floor with clients, must allow themselves to be absorbed in the musical event. It is during these times that new developments for the group can occur.

Because improvisation is such an integral part of the N-R approach, the use of self is seen as vital to creating the conditions for change within the client. If two similarly trained therapists use the same action method, the music that results may be quite different. Thus, even when therapists use *realization*, their distinctive use of self will be evident in the resulting music. Even a written-down piece is not predetermined in performance, because it becomes improvisational as the individual responses of the group members are integrated into the event. Moreover, a piece would be played and led differently if another group were doing it. In improvisation, the personal interpretation of the thematic and formal possibilities of the playing of the clients leads to a unique shaping of these musical responses.

In a previous publication (Turry, 1998), musical countertransference was discussed as a way of examining the personal musical responses that the music therapist may have to a client. Becoming aware of a particular musical response to a client can give the therapists more awareness and understanding of the therapeutic relationship and of the client's musical–clinical needs.

EMPIRICAL SUPPORT

The relative paucity of empirical research to support the manifest benefits of music therapy is not limited to the N-R approach.

> The claim that music therapy can help individuals with autism still rests mainly on the profession's own substantial and rigorous clinical documentation, and on the recognition of its benefits by parents, carers, and other professionals. A common criticism by those without direct experience of the efficacy of music therapy is that the improvements reported to arise from improvisational music therapy and their generalization to other settings have not been substantiated by controlled research studies. In response, experienced practitioners point out that while each child's (or client's) individuality and the subtle aspects of emotional expression and creativity within the dynamics of relationship are paramount considerations in music therapy, these features do not lend themselves readily to measurement by scientific research methods that are designed to compare treatment groups and to make "blind" assessments of behaviors defined a priori. (Robarts, 1996, p. 138)

Despite the fact that Nordoff and Robbins documented their work extensively and in minute detail, they never published the results of any effort to evaluate their work quantitatively. They did, however (Nordoff & Robbins, 1977), develop evaluation scales to aid in the understanding and interpretation of behavior within sessions, between sessions, or over an entire course of therapy. The scales associate various qualities of premusical and musical interaction to quantified levels of interpersonal relatedness and communication. These scales are used currently by trained therapists to assess clinical situations and define clinical goals. How applicable they would be in studies comparing the effectiveness of the N-R approach to other methods or to control groups is unclear, as this has never been attempted.

In recent years, quantitative and qualitative research concerning the efficacy of N-R music therapy with clients with autism has begun to emerge. Edgerton's (1994) study of the effects of improvised music "based on Nordoff and Robbins (1977) Creative Music Therapy approach" (p. 31) concluded that "improvisational music therapy is effective in eliciting and increasing communicative behaviors in autistic children within a musical setting." Aldridge (1996, p. 56), in his study of N-R music therapy with children diagnosed as developmentally delayed, reached a more expansive conclusion:

> We can say that children, when they partake in improvised creative music therapy, achieve significant developmental milestones in comparison to those children who are not treated. Later, when a comparison group of children are treated, they too rapidly achieve developmental goals. (p. 268)

An extensive qualitative research study of N-R group music therapy with clients with autism was undertaken by Aigen (1997). He found that music had a role in facilitating transitions and meeting individual and group needs and helped to enhance emotional expression. The approach gave the clients the tools to relate in a way not possible through verbal means. In a further study (Aigen, 1998), the same author examined several cases of individual music therapy conducted by Nordoff and Robbins, some of which involved children with autism. One of the core findings was that each course of therapy evolves uniquely which, we feel, occurs in groups as well.

As music therapy research methods are tested and refined, it is expected that more empirical support for the N-R approach will be offered. Some combination of qualitative and quantitative methods may well be necessary to encompass the broad range of phenomena that occur during music-making and result from the process.

REFERENCES

Aigen, K. (1997). *Here we are in music: One year with an adolescent, creative music therapy group* (N-R Music Therapy Monograph, Series 2). St. Louis, MO: MMB Music.

Aigen, K. (1998). *Paths of development in N-R music therapy*. Gilsum, NH: Barcelona.

Aldridge, D. (1996). *Music therapy research and practice in medicine*. London: Jessica Kingsley.

Brown, S. (1994). Autism and music therapy—Is change possible, and why music? *Journal of British Music Therapy, 8*, 15–25.

Bruscia, K. (1987). *Improvisational models of music therapy*. Springfield, IL: Charles C Thomas.

Bruscia, K. (1998). *Defining music therapy*. Gilsum, NH: Barcelona.

Edgerton, C. L. (1994). The effect of improvisational music therapy on the communicative behaviors of autistic children. *Journal of Music Therapy*, *31*, 31–62.

Nordoff, P., & Robbins, C. (1977). *Creative music therapy*. New York: John Day.

Robarts, J. (1996). Music therapy for children with autism. In C. Trevarthen, K. Aitken, D. Papoudi, & J. Robarts (Eds.), *Children with autism: Diagnosis and intervention to meet their needs* (pp. 134–160). London: Jessica Kingsley.

Turry, A. (1998). Transference and countertransference in music N-R music therapy. In K. Bruscia (Ed.), *The dynamics of music psychotherapy* (pp. 161–212). Gilsum, NH: Barcelona.

RECOMMENDED READING

Aigen, K. (1995). The aesthetic foundation of clinical theory. In C. B. Kenny (Ed.), *Listening, playing, creating: Essays on the power of sound* (pp. 233–257). Albany, NY: State University of New York.

Aigen, K. (1995). Cognitive and affective processes activated in music therapy: A preliminary model for contemporary Nordoff–Robbins practice. *Music Therapy*, *12*, 16–39.

Aigen, K. (1996). *Being in music: Foundations of Nordoff–Robbins music therapy*. Nordoff–Robbins Music Therapy Monograph Series 1. St. Louis, MO: MMB Music.

Aigen, K. (1996). *Improvised song in group music therapy* [videotape]. Available through the Nordoff–Robbins Center for Music Therapy at New York University.

American Music Therapy Association. (2001). *Effectiveness of music therapy procedures: Documentation of Research and Clinical Practice* (3rd ed.). Silver Spring, MD: Author.

Ansdell, G. (1995). *Music for life: Aspects of creative music therapy with adult clients*. London: Jessica Kingsley.

Bruscia, K. (Ed.) (1991). *Case studies in music therapy*. Phoenixville, PA: Barcelona.

Forinash, M. (Ed.) (1991). *Music therapy supervision*. Gilsum, NH: Barcelona.

Forinash, M. (1992). A phenomenological analysis of the Nordoff–Robbins approach to music therapy: The lived experience of clinical improvisation. *Music Therapy*, *11*, 120–141.

Hibben, J. (1999). *Inside music therapy: Client experiences*. Gilsum, NH: Barcelona.

Lee, C. (1996). *Music at the edge: The music therapy experiences of a musician with AIDS*. New York: Routledge.

Nordoff, P., & Robbins, C. (1977). *Creative music therapy*. New York: John Day.

Nordoff, P., & Robbins, C. (1983). *Music therapy in special education*. St. Louis, MO: MMB Music.

Pavlicevic, M. (1997). *Music therapy in context: Music, meaning, and relationship*. London: Jessica Kingsley.

Ritholz, M., & Robbins, C. (1999). *Themes for therapy*. New York: Carl Fischer.

Ritholz, M., & Robbins, C. (2003). *More themes for therapy*. New York: Carl Fischer.

Robbins, C. (1993). The creative processes are universal. In M. Heal & T. Wigram (Eds.), *Music therapy in health and education* (pp. 7–25). London: Jessica Kingsley.

Robbins, C., & Forinash, M. (1991). A time paradigm: Time as a multilevel phenomenon in music therapy. *Music Therapy, 10,* 46–57.

Robbins, C., & Robbins, C. (1980). *Music for the hearing impaired and other special groups*. St. Louis, MO: MMB Music.

Stige, B. (2002). *Culture-centered music therapy*. Gilsum, NH: Barcelona.

Turry, A., & Ritholz, M. (1994). The journey by train: Creative music therapy with a 17-year-old boy. *Music Therapy, 12,* 58–87.

8

NARRADRAMA: A NARRATIVE ACTION APPROACH WITH GROUPS

PAMELA DUNNE

Editors' Introduction: Narradrama, which features the integrated use of various creative arts techniques in the service of narrative therapy, stands in the humanistic tradition of personal growth as therapy. Using many of the same constructs and techniques as the family psychodrama approach featured in chapter 2, narradrama aims at change of the individual rather than of the family system. Its practice is thoroughly improvisational, both for the therapist (who makes choices in the moment without prior planning) and for clients (who are encouraged continually to follow their initial impulses). The evident success of these methods with this group appears to be the result of the confluence of clients with ample psychological resources; a multimodal action approach that encourages clients' exploration and expression of their nascent and emergent solutions; and a warm, respectful, innovative therapist who creates a mutually supportive context for the realization of clients' goals.

This chapter introduces narradrama (Dunne, 1992, 1997a, 1997b, 2000), a method of implementing narrative therapy using action techniques from drama therapy and other creative arts rather than solely verbal techniques. The case example featured in this chapter is that of a small group of professionals who work collaboratively toward removing obstacles to attaining their personal and professional goals.

NARRATIVE THERAPY AND NARRADRAMA

Narrative therapists point out that story, or narrative, provides the conceptual framework for understanding the meaning of our lives. Story provides the basis for organizing and patterning life experiences into forms the human consciousness can comprehend. Stories demonstrate how lives change and determine which aspects of our life experience are expressed, understood, and valued. Our internal self-narrative shapes our understanding and expression of our life experience.

If we accept that persons organize and give meaning to their experience through the storying of experience, and that in the performance of these stories they express selected aspects of their lived experience, then it follows that these stories are constitutive—shaping lives and relationships. (White & Epston, 1990, p. 12)

People are seldom aware of the role story plays in their perceptions of meaning and value and rarely consider how story can be explored to reveal discoveries about life and the choices life entails. Most people are unaware of their internal stories or how they automatically find meaning in the events in their lives by interpreting them as elements of our internal self-narratives. Often, people think themselves into a sort of paralysis. As clients, they usually come into therapy with convoluted, problem-saturated stories, feeling their lives are stuck and that they have few options. Through narrative therapy clients become aware of the role story plays in the interpretation of their lives, challenge the assumption that there is only one possible interpretation of events and these internal narratives, and open themselves to new interpretations and stories.

Narradrama (Dunne, 1992, 1997a, 1997b, 2000) combines narrative therapy with drama therapy and other creative arts methods. It borrows freely from psychology, sociology, anthropology, experimental theatre, music, dance, and poetry. Narradrama evolved from techniques developed in my own practice and teaching over the past 20 years at California State University, Los Angeles, and at the Drama Therapy Institute of Los Angeles. Narradrama consists of a therapist interacting collaboratively with a group of participants, using a variety of action methods to help participants experience alternative solutions by experimenting with narratives derived from the participants' own lives. These methods freely incorporate any of the various creative arts: music, drawing and painting, poetry, dance, and drama. All of these forms of expression may at times be helpful to clients in expanding their awareness of their internalized narratives or in considering alternatives to the problem and possible solutions. Whereas traditional narrative therapy uses only language, narradrama draws from all the creative arts, thereby tapping the wisdom not only of the mind but also the wisdom of the senses and body. Incorporating other creative arts methods allows participants to express themselves through their most natural modes of expression. For example, dancers or athletes might be accustomed to communicating with their body, while painters might be more comfortable communicating visually.

Narradrama retains the basic advantages of traditional verbal narrative therapy (i.e., externalization, nonexpert position, focus on alternative rather than problem-saturated stories) and also reflects essential theories of drama therapy and belief in the importance of the role and the power of drama to transcend and transform human experience. Landy (1996) said, "by reducing a role to its essential actions and feelings, the actor/client opens up a universe of possibilities" (p. 107). Narradrama also makes use of the interrelationships among the arts and the ability of one art form to expand and enhance another. According to Rogers (1993),

> Art modes interrelate in what I call the creative connection. When we move, it affects how we write or paint. When we write or paint, it affects how we feel and think. During the creative connection process, one art form stimulates and nurtures the other, bringing us to an inner core or essence which is our life energy. (p. 8)

Although narrative therapy and narradrama are both story-centered, narradrama offers the opportunity to expand the story from exclusively verbal into verbal and nonverbal communication through enactment. While traditional narrative therapy uses the technique of externalization (described below) to help a client sever his identification with their problem, narradrama takes externalization one step further by letting participants identify their problems with objects and people distinct from themselves. Action techniques foster understanding and empathy among group therapy clients as they explore and discover new possibilities together. In playing multiple roles (audience member, player, observer, or auxiliary), participants are removed from their own single vantage point and so can observe the problem from different points of view. To summarize, the basic tenets of narradrama are as follows:

1. All people have the innate ability to create.
2. The creative process is inherently healing and transformative.
3. Expressive activity in each of the arts stimulates, nurtures, and expands expressive activity in each of the others.
4. Narradrama centers on story and aims to life experience.
5. Narradrama uses action techniques inviting participants to respond through intellect, emotions, body, and spirit.
6. Narrative emphasizes and expands unique outcomes and occasions when the problem was overcome.
7. Narradrama derives its effectiveness from collaboration rather than the authority of the therapist.
8. In narradrama, the therapist believes, accepts, and respects all people.

Narradrama requires a safe, supportive environment and a therapist who is warm, empathic, honest, and vulnerable. The therapist works with the client to create an atmosphere that encourages spontaneity and the opening of psychological space. Whenever possible, narradrama sessions make use of a reflecting team whose comments and inquisitive observations help open space for new possibilities and alternative stories.

Through action methods it becomes possible to reexamine or redefine one's own internal self-description. The conscious use of dramatic narrative can help therapy participants transform the outcome of experience by activating imagination in the mode of Stanislavski's (1936) "As If." By looking behind and beyond the surface of reality to the stories through which reality is interpreted, participants can transcend the illusory limitations of immediate reality and even transport themselves in time and space: either backward, to the time of an important event, or forward, to visualize the completion of a life's dream. Participation in these sorts of transcendent experiences opens the door to the exploration of wish fulfillment, experimentation, and alternative stories. By functioning in the As If, participants can initiate personal transformations that allow them to "restory" their lives, thereby granting themselves a new sense of power and agency in shaping their self-identities.

BENEFITS OF NARRADRAMA AS GROUP THERAPY

While narradrama can be practiced as an individual therapy, more possibilities are available when it is practiced with a group. In narradrama groups, members enjoy being a part of a process-centered approach, focused on unique outcomes and alternative solutions that enable them to help each other find new solutions and overcome their problems. As group members recall exceptions to problems, they realize that there have been times in their lives when their problems were less significant. As each member hears others making discoveries and moving forward, a kinship develops within the group that engenders an atmosphere of hope and trust. Group members begin putting their life scenes into action and learn from each other's perceptions, actions, and successes in changing their relationship to a given problem. They become active participants in the therapeutic process and expand their roles from clients to peer helpers. Narradrama participants thus not only accelerate and facilitate their own inner growth but also promote the growth and well-being of their fellow participants. This normally results in the formation of close relationships with the other members of the group. In a group led by a qualified therapist, narradrama can foster an atmosphere of love and trust along with a level and quality of creativity that most artists associate with solitude. Narradrama thus offers a uniquely rewarding and transforming experience.

This approach to therapy is quite different from approaches such as psychodynamic therapy in which members reveal their issues, express their problems, confront others, and search for insights in past events that might lead to new behaviors. In such groups, members describe themselves and their lives with a problem-saturated focus or pathological diagnosis. These descriptions can reinforce their own existing beliefs about themselves, often keeping them stuck in their old actions.

Most of my clients have continued to participate in narradrama sessions because narrative therapy facilitates inner exploration and growth. Psychotherapy, including traditional psychotherapy, has always been not only a tool for healing but also a venue for personal growth. Jung (1981) noted that many of his more affluent and better-educated clients chose to continue therapy long after their original problems had been solved, in a quest for personal knowledge. In my own practice, I have found that narradrama invites participants to open themselves to new possibilities in which they question whether they want to continue in the same relationship to the problem. Many narradrama clients participate because they want to enhance their quality of life and realize their maximum potential.

NARRADRAMA ACTION TECHNIQUES

In narradrama, the therapist uses several action techniques, described below, to achieve the following goals:

1. Keep the group nonpathological by externalizing the problem through drama and creative arts and by teaching group members to redescribe the problem and consider additional possibilities.
2. Explore unique outcomes (times when group members do not give in to the problem) to restory each member's life and discover resources and strengths.
3. As group members demonstrate improved competency and changed directions in their lives, mark these moments by using techniques such as life paths, journeys, and rituals to encourage their commitment to these new directions.
4. Enable group members to acknowledge each other's actions through a reflecting team, which honors and affirms participants' newly discovered resources, abilities, and wisdom.
5. Cultivate respect for all group members, reaffirming their competence and potential for growth rather than seeing them as pathological or sick.

Numerous narradrama techniques fall under the rubric of action methods and may serve as tools for the therapist. Using such techniques stimulates fresh ideas about ways people can work together to integrate the emotions, body, mind, and soul, as well as resolve problems. These action methods, described in detail below, include (a) externalization, (b) dramatizing or sculpting unique outcomes, (c) role expansion, (d) action environments, (e) rituals, (f) action maps and journeys, (g) action monologues and inner monologues, (h) deconstruction and reconstruction, and (i) reflecting teams and Greek chorus.

Externalization

In traditional narrative therapy clients are empowered to separate themselves from the problem and adopt new perspectives on its influence in their lives. This process, termed *externalization*, serves as one of the principal keys to narrative thinking which emphasizes that the person is not the problem; the problem is the problem. Externalization involves naming the problem, identifying its characteristics, attributing to it actions and intentions, and exploring the client's relationship with the problem. Externalization enables clients to actively investigate how they have been influenced by and (particularly important) have on occasion been able to overcome or be free of a particular problem. This is termed *finding exceptions*, a prelude to identifying *unique outcomes* (an alternative to the problem-saturated story from the past).

Dramatizing or Sculpting Unique Outcomes

A unique outcome may become apparent through externalizing a problem utilizing objects, masks, or art or reexamining a previous exercise that was helpful. White and Epston (1992) reported that,

> As persons separate from the dominant or totalizing stories that are constitutive of their lives, it becomes more possible for them to orient themselves to aspects of their experience that contradict these knowledges. I have referred to these contradictions as unique outcomes. (p. 127)

Verbally described unique outcomes can be expanded, through narradrama, into a "unique outcome scene." Enacting this scene sometimes has a rippling effect that leads to the discovery of additional unique outcome scenes. Sometimes these scenes may be real-life re-enactments and at other times hypothetical or imaginary scenes that help put the client in touch with relevant inner resources. Using narradrama techniques to act, dance, sculpt, or mime different story possibilities further expands the range of options available to the client. Conceiving and enacting or sculpting unique outcomes enables clients to restory their lives and choose new and more attractive alternatives. White and Epston (1990) commented that, "as unique outcomes are identified, persons can be encouraged to engage in performances of new meaning in relation to these. Success with this requires that the unique outcome be plotted into an alternative story about the person's life" (p. 41).

Role Repertory Expansion

At the core of the dramatic experience, whether expressed in dramatic play, creative drama, improvisation, or any other kind of theatrical activity, is the principle of *impersonation*, which refers to the ability of the participant to take on a role. The simultaneous experience of "I am me and not me" illustrates this paradoxical union of engagement and separation: I take on a role, and then I separate from it. Taking on and playing roles serves as the single most significant distinguishing feature of dramatherapy and differentiates dramatherapy from other forms of psychotherapy and healing. According to Landy (1996), "role becomes the container of those qualities of the individual that needs to be enacted in drama therapy. Story is the verbal or gestural text, most often improvised, that expresses the role, naming the container" (p. 100). Landy, along with other drama therapists (Emunah, 1994), believed that the more roles one is able to play, the better one should be able to deal with a variety of circumstances. It becomes important, then, for the therapist using narradrama to expand the role repertory of the client. By playing and creating roles, participants step through the looking glass into that magical land of imagination—the land of As If. There, participants and observers can envision different perspectives, gather new insights, and challenge the problems in their lives.

Action Environments

Action environments are action exercises that assist participants in defining and creating new environments. Any concept can be represented within a physical space that has been transformed by the imagination of the participants, using a limited number of simple props. Whenever a verbal description is offered in therapy, the option exists to create or re-create an action environment. Through drawing, enacting, and creating narradrama environments, participants can learn how real experiences and predicaments can be surmounted or transformed once these are changed into environments. The preferred environment is a useful form that invites the participant to imagine a more desirable outcome that can be explored and evaluated.

Rituals

Rituals are defined as ceremonies that help narradrama participants clarify, mark, celebrate, and commemorate important events, decisions, and moments in their lives or to make transitions. A *marking ritual* emphasizes an important change of direction in a person's life (i.e., saying goodbye to the old and embracing the new). A *transformational ritual* affirming personal growth might consist of a player assuming a cocoonlike posture among group members who symbolically nurture growth within the pupa, followed by enacting the emergence of a newly hatched adult. A *transitional ritual*, perhaps to celebrate an adult child's departure from home to go to college, might be portrayed by having each group member present the client with an object that embodies spiritual significance (e.g., a heart for love, a rock for strength).

By creating and actively participating in such rituals, usually with an audience of invited guests, participants together with other significant characters and personalities symbolically enact the choices they have made. The symbolic and cognitive value of a transitional ritual in celebrating real-world milestones and achievements should be evident. Transitional rituals and related ceremonies can be repeated to celebrate the cultivation of new skills as well as the acquisition of new levels of competence (Imber-Black, Roberts, & Whiting, 1988).

Action Maps and Journeys

A "map" or "journey" helps equip a client with the skills necessary to formulate and enact a plan. *Mapping* involves the creation of a life map that represents (in drawings rather than language) where the client's life is and where the client wants his or her life to go. Clients usually begin by drawing possible pathways and then create a life-sized representation of the paths that can often fill the entire room. The client can select and use other members of the group, any available objects, and furniture to represent different characters, obstacles, and choices encountered along the pathways. Participants can visit different pathways, examine possibilities at various points, and make decisions based on their newly discovered options.

A *journey* is similar to mapping but depicts a single path rather than several different paths that might be taken. Both mappings and journeys offer participants the opportunity to safely formulate strategies to successfully overcome a real or hypothetical problem. Just as with mapping, a journey is often enlarged to full size with fabrics, props, chairs, and whatever else can be used to convey the intent of the imagination.

Action Monologue and Inner Monologue

An *action monologue* involves creating a scene in which one person enacts an important moment, for instance, an imaginary encounter with allegorical characters. An *inner monologue* occurs when the client takes on the inner voice of one of the characters (or his or her own inner voice), revealing what is really going on beneath the surface. Developing an action monologue or inner monologue can help clients gain greater awareness of their ideas and feelings, illuminating and defining different circumstances and choices.

Deconstruction and Reconstruction

Deconstruction involves taking an externalized problem such as anger and examining its various components, perhaps through construction of a mobile. Looking at these deconstructed elements can enable the client to analyze them dispassionately and reveal their interactions. *Reconstruction* begins when clients feel empowered to choose the components they wish to keep or restructure (if applicable) and throw away those elements they do not wish to keep. This can be accomplished by adding to or changing the mobile to change its meaning.

Reflecting Teams and Greek Chorus

Reflecting teams originated in family therapy and have been adapted for use in narrative therapy by such therapists as Tom Andersen (1991), Karl Tomm (1990–1991), and Michael White (1995). A two-way observation room can be used as a reflecting team environment. A two-way observation room is equipped with two-way mirrors, positioned between adjacent rooms so as to permit viewers in the darker room to see into the better-illuminated one while remaining out of sight. First the client, therapist, and other group members are observed as they interact with each other in the brighter room, while the reflecting team remains invisible in the semidark room. When the scene ends, the lights come up on the reflecting team, who then talk to each other. The members of the reflecting team formulate questions and express their curiosity and observations about particular issues, events, and ideas. This expression of curiosity leads to new questions in which the members are asked to avoid analysis or judgment but instead to adopt a stance of honest curiosity, wonder, and appreciation. Reflecting team members "situate" each remark by indicating what about their own personal experience, education, or thinking has informed it rather than interpreting the client's experiences.

The client observes this interaction, but the reflecting team does not speak to the client. If a two-way mirror is not available, the reflecting team can sit slightly away from the client but talk to the other members of the reflecting team without speaking directly to the client, just as if there had been a real two-way mirror. After the reflecting team finishes its observations and comments, the focus shifts back to the client, who comments on his own experiences and ideas, as well as the ideas expressed by the reflecting team. The therapist might ask the client, "What struck you about the observations made by the reflecting team?" Anderson (1991) noted that "people stuck in a problem-saturated story invariably repeat the same questions over and over again, so the best approach is to bring forth new energy, questions, and possibilities" (p. 39).

The technique of the *Greek chorus*, a group standing off to the side of the stage from the protagonist, punctuates the dialog of a scene with commentary (Papp, 1985). It can also be used to provide ideas or to double for the protagonist, providing alternatives and insights. The Greek chorus (as in Greek tragedy), while in some ways similar to a reflecting team, functions more as a knowledgeable observer and often verbalizes insights that would not occur to the protagonist. The reflecting team, on the other hand, is much more tentative and inquisitive. The reflecting team avoids making assumptions, does not play the role of the expert, and focuses on stimulating inquiry and curiosity.

CASE EXAMPLE

The offices of the Dramatherapy Institute of Los Angeles are located in what was originally a large home that was converted to offices and classrooms. The institute is less institutional than a modern office building and has amenities such as a kitchen where we can prepare herbal teas and whatever else we want, providing a homelike and nurturing environment. I usually arrive earlier than the participants and spend a few minutes in prayerful meditation and making necessary preparations before the session begins. As participants arrive, we spend our time together before the session talking and catching up with each other.

The group featured in this case presentation is composed of five individuals who come from various professional backgrounds. There is an engineer, a teacher, a vocational counselor, a businessman, and an actress. All of the people in this particular group have experienced a roadblock in their lives (e.g., dissatisfaction with a career but unable to make changes; an unfulfilled personal relationship).

All of these clients have previously been in individual therapy (including Freudian, Jungian, and other forms of traditional "talk" therapy) for between 6 months and 2 years. This is their first experience in group psychotherapy. The group has agreed to meet once every 3 weeks for 3 hours, and all of the members have committed to continue in group psychotherapy for a minimum of 6 months. At the end of the 6 months, the group will decide whether to continue for an additional 6 months. At certain transitional points (e.g., at the end of the first 6 months), other members may be added with group agreement.

Sessions

Session 1

The first person to arrive is Julie, age 28, a bright, energetic actress who moved to Los Angeles to pursue her career about 2 years ago. There seems to be a space in Julie's life that is unfilled. Acting had once filled that empty space but is no longer doing so. Julie wants to move forward but feels frozen and too frightened to move. Even so, it is significant to note that she did make it to Los Angeles (a major move and life change), which demonstrates her capacity to persevere and to accomplish specific goals. She is seeking a clear direction and new ways to accomplish her goals. Most of all, she wants to conquer her fears, which are negatively affecting her personal relationships, her work, and her ability to create.

Ann arrives next. Ann is 38, works for the county as a vocational counselor, and wants to become a licensed family counselor. She has always dreamed of being an actress, but her family did not support her dream and urged her to graduate from college with a useful, marketable degree. For years Ann has buried her dream of acting but has felt increasingly frustrated with her life. Whenever Ann had the opportunity to act (even at a party, playing charades), she experienced joy and fulfillment, but she has never dared to even consider that she might become a professional actress.

Then Max arrives. Max, a 35-year-old engineer, is overworked, shows symptoms of stress, and is having a difficult time moving forward in his life or defining what he wants. Max feels uncomfortable in social situations and uneasy about communicating with people and engaging them in conversation. He spends much of his time alone and experiences feelings of loneliness and sadness because of his lack of connection with others.

Rosanna and Harold arrive last. Everybody is on time tonight, which is the norm for this group. Rosanna, age 45, is a teacher and loves her work. Rosanna recently divorced her husband of 20 years, feeling the relationship had been stifling her. Because of her ex-husband's high expectations and demands, she felt she could never please him. She constantly faced intensive criticism, which led to feelings of depression and hopelessness that began to affect her ability to teach and engage in healthy social relationships. After a serious emotional breakdown, she decided that she needed to leave the marriage to save herself. With everything in her life changing, Rosanna needed clarity about her life direction, what was important to her, and what she had to offer.

Harold, age 43, is the manager of a small business. He was divorced 4 years ago and is outgoing and charismatic. He has been unable to decide how to meet his career goals, which demand more and more out-of-town travel, and still maintain the kind of daily contact he would like to have with his five children, of whom he has joint custody. In addition, he is disillusioned with his job and wonders whether he should go back to school and pursue a different career.

The first task is to create a nurturing, collaborative atmosphere in which everybody can feel comfortable and inspired, an environment conducive to the sorts of changes and experiences we are seeking. Arranging the room casually with comfortable large pillows and easily accessible creative materials like art supplies, puppets, fabrics, and musical instruments, assists in evoking a positive working atmosphere that facilitates our objectives. Often, I play peaceful environmental sounds (i.e., ocean gentle waves) or music in the background (i.e., single flute) to set the mood and suggest a nurturing place.

One activity that I like to do in first working with a group is to help individuals become aware of their preferred environment. Experience has taught me that when individuals become more aware of their preferred environment and begin to re-create this environment in their daily lives, the changes in their environments stimulate positive changes in other aspects of the participants' lives.

Therapy begins with inviting the participants first to conceptualize their ideas and then draw them on paper to communicate their ideas to the other members of the group. "What we need to do is to conceive of an environment that is very special for you and then to place yourself in it. As you conceive your environment, do your best to draw your ideas so that you can explain them to the other members of the group."

This exercise is designed to "physicalize" an imaginary environment. Experienced practitioners would refer to this activity as *physicalization* and *acting out of environments*. Each participant then introduces his or her preferred environment to the group. After the environment is introduced, the other participants are invited into each other's environmental spaces to experience the spaces for themselves.

Julie begins by drawing a picture of her preferred environment. Her drawing is filled with the color blue, which she experiences as restful. Wind blows through Julie's environment. To illustrate the sound of the wind blowing, Julie asks the group to make the sounds of the wind, which she likens to the music of her soul. Julie depicts this environment by unfolding swaths of different blue fabrics and constructing a womblike structure, into which each group member has the opportunity to enter. Julie says, "My eyes are drawn to the blue form; it is so inviting. Energy is there, and I can feel the wind coming in."

Adding to and enlarging Julie's concept, Rosanna draws a picture of a person diving into the water. This dive is then ritually performed using puppets who voice their thoughts and experiences as they dive into the water. Everybody joins in, and experiences the rush of excitement as each of us jumps into the water (the unknown) to begin swimming (creating). Rosanna says, "I like to dive into opportunities and just go for it. Taking risks is a part of who I am."

Ann draws an altar and describes her environment as a place of rest and rejuvenation, a place of peace and stillness (see Figure 8.1). Lighting a candle within her fabric altar, she invites us to join her in a long moment of stillness. After doing the exercise, Ann reflects, "Being still helps me to get centered. I thought everybody was like this. When I light a candle in my home, it is centering to me. I put my hand to my chest honoring myself."

Harold's drawing features starlike explosions that trace spirals as the tendrils of the explosion burst outward. His environment is filled with bursts of energy, representing, as he says, "countless opportunities for self-fulfillment." The group improvises a vocal background to express the feelings Harold's drawing evokes. There is an undercurrent of collective awareness punctuated by soft vocal explosions. As we give voice to our feelings, we are infused with energy and join in a spontaneous dance.

Max paints a forest and a beach scene of tall trees and majestic waves. He prefers to have others enact the environment and expresses that he is uncomfortable with getting up in front of others. Group members, at his

Figure 8.1. Preferred Peaceful Environment

direction, enter the scene draped in green, flowing fabrics, which transition into large billowing waves. Creating an environment of blue fabric, at Max's direction from his seat, they recreate the sounds of the ocean and seagulls. Suffused by the color blue, the group invites Max to join them (he does so, still feeling some discomfort), and all experience running through the ocean and over the waves, thereby becoming local manifestations of energy accumulating over vast distances.

To the uninitiated or inexperienced this sort of exercise might seem trivial or even silly. Not everyone is immediately receptive to entering into the empathic and creative frame of mind necessary to experience this sort of collaborative experience.

Some individuals need more warm-up time for physicalizing and acting-out activities (like Max, who did not want to join in the enactment until the very end). If Max had decided to stay out the entire time and direct the scene from his seat that would have been fine, too. Different individuals might even perceive the same experiences differently.

But all the members of this group were willing and able to open their minds to conceive and enter the new space established within the group's collective imagination.

At this point in the session, about 2 hours in, I feel each person has been strengthened and inspired and think it might be helpful to talk to each other about the experiences we have just shared.

Group members voice observations and perceptions of their own preferred environments as well as the environments of others. Ann describes Rosanna's environment as "the opposite from mine, but it had a deep impact on me. I discovered what it was like to jump right in and try something without procrastinating about it. I really discovered a sense of freedom through doing this that I have not felt before." Max said, "I really liked the environment that I painted, but I felt uncomfortable with movement. At first I did not want to join in, but with the encouragement of the others, I decided to try."

To close the session, I contemplated several possibilities: (a) Closure could involve each group member taking something special from their environment into a brief ritualized group ceremony, (b) group members could write in their journals what they had found most helpful in tonight's experience, or (c) group members could work in pairs writing poems to express their feelings about what they have done and each partner could write a letter to the other reflecting and appreciating the strengths and competencies of the other. I decided to collaborate with the group to make this decision, and the group selected the third option.

A poem and letter from each partner would be shared with the whole group, an idea to which group members responded with enthusiasm. Max, who felt very comfortable with language, wrote the following poem based on his environment experience.

Heart, what are you doing?	Mind, what are you doing?	Soul, what are you doing?
I'm beating,	I'm thinking	I'm fearing,
and beating,	And thinking,	And fearing,
and beating	And thinking	And fearing
because that's my job:	Because that's what	Because that's what
to keep you alive.	I do best.	I have learned.
That was yesterday.	That was yesterday.	That was yesterday.
Tomorrow you will feel	Tomorrow you will be quiet	Tomorrow you will love
And feel	Quiet, Quiet.	And trust
And feel.		And know.

Julie wrote the following letter to Max:

> Dear Max,
>   I see you walking from the deep green darkness and confusion of the forest into a clearing. I see you looking up and seeing through the trees

an opening where the sun and wind washes through you and over you into you bringing you coolness and clarity and reminding you each time the waves and wind touches your face that you choose your friend strength. Strength was so happy and felt released and acknowledged when you spoke to him/her today. Strength seemed to feel better and understood and appreciated what you said today. This letter is from the wind opening to you Max and your beautiful strength. One can be clothed in many ways, but the pureness of essential being really boils down to how you feel.

    Love,
    The Wind

The group leaves the therapy space inspired and full of ideas for bringing the magic of their imaginary environments into their daily lives.

I believe in inviting the group to focus and reflect on a creative assignment between meetings. In designing these assignments, I often ask group members what they found most useful in a session and build on that. In past experiences, I have found that, when individuals begin introducing more of their preferred environments into their daily lives, this creates ripples that sometimes result in profound changes. I also believe it is important to expand the preferred environment. Often, group members discover other aspects of their environment by continuing to make drawings in their journals.

I leave the group with the following creative assignment: "Write or draw reflections in your journal about this session. Choose one or more aspects of your preferred environment to bring into your life on a daily basis. Record in your journal the effect of introducing this new part of preferred environment into your life. Draw other aspects of your preferred environment in your journal. At the next group session, be prepared to share your experiences and observations with the group."

Session 2

At the next meeting, energy fills the room as group members share how the environment exercise has had an impact on their lives. Julie has painted part of her apartment blue and reports feeling much more centered and alive in her home environment. Max brings in a cushion that he has dyed blue and describes his plan to bring more of the color into his environment. Ann talks about lighting a candle in her home in a ritual that helps her center herself and feel at peace. Throughout the next meetings, these environments will further influence the group as they continue to introduce more of their magical and creative environments into their daily lives.

After we have shared our experiences with our environmental changes, I invite each participant to create an externalized problem mask or drawing to objectify the externalized problem.

I believe some form of externalization is important at this point to separate the person from the problem and clearly delineate the problem. While my suggestion here was to create a mask, other ideas that might have been just as useful might have been to create a clay figure or a painting to show the externalized problem.

Julie speaks of feeling paralyzed, afraid to move forward. She creates a one-dimensional flat mask (Figure 8.2a), a face covered with strips of black yarn, that she calls "fear and confusion about moving forward." Julie, taking the role of "Fear," says, "I'm afraid, I can't see. I feel paralyzed. I don't want to see. There's danger ahead." I interview "Fear," asking questions such as, "When have you had the most power over Julie? When have you had the least power over Julie? Fear, try to remember when you have had the least effect on Julie. At those times what was she doing?"

Later, Julie creates a personal agency mask that she calls "Seeing." This is a three-dimensional tissue paper mask with puffed pieces of bright green and blue tissue depicting nature's cleansing and the healing effect of the wind (Figure 8.2b). Julie, assuming the role of Seeing, says, "In the forest there is a clearing. I walk toward it head up. The cold, clean, crisp wind and sunlight on my face, I can see. From into the light I come. It is still, and always will be, where I draw my inspiration."

Julie, further exploring the role of Seeing, moves to music and sounds that she teaches and instructs the group to make. I interview Julie's personification of Seeing: "How can Julie find you when she needs to? How can you occupy more of Julie's life? When was Julie most aware of you?" When she finishes the exercises, Julie reports, "I physically had the sensation in my body of opening. I felt changed." (Figure 8.3).

Working in pairs or triads, each group member then externalizes a problem with a mask. Some group members really enjoy this exercise, while others express frustration in trying to create a mask that they believe falls short of the idea in their mind. They abandon the project quickly, leaving very little detail on the mask. I try to reinforce the idea that the finished art or quality of art is not the focus but rather the process of creating it. I encourage group members to tear tissue paper (not cut it), using shape, color, or even finger paints (rather than doing intricate work with pencils or scissors). I tell them, "I am very curious what you mean by 'X' (the externalized problem) because in my mind I visualize 'X' in many different ways. I would like to be able to see how you see it." We work with externalized masks for a while, and then the person's relationship with the problem becomes clear.

Next, curious about how the externalized problem might influence life decisions at choice points, depicted as crossroads, I suggest that each person draw a simple crossroads in their life. To assist in focusing on this activity, I offer a mapping exercise in the form of a pathway drawing (a much simpler and easier art activity).

Most people find the drawing part of the pathway exercise easy; the harder part concerns deciding on what the paths represent. I hope that the pathway drawing will help participants see how their externalized problem affects their life decisions.

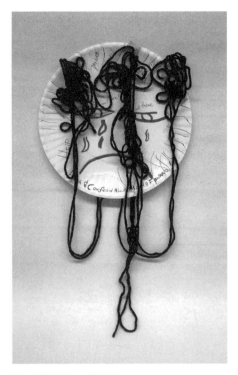

Figure 8.2a. Externalized Problem Mask

Figure 8.2b. Externalized Personal Agency Mask

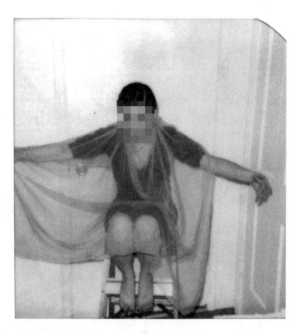

Figure 8.3. Moving as Seeing

Later, we physicalize each other's maps and reproduce these locales life-size in the therapy space (*mapping and physicalization*). Physicalization of the pathway drawing allows group members to intensify their focus on their life path.

Ann creates a drawing that illustrates two paths (see Figure 8.4). One path leads to acting, and the other path leads to becoming a licensed family counselor. Ann physicalizes the scene by using group members to first create the world of acting and then the world of family counseling. Ann enters both scenes and experiences what it feels like to be in each. In the acting space, she becomes more in touch with a feeling of strength, of having honored the part of herself that had wanted to become an actress. "This led me to consider whether I have been under the influence of a self-limiting belief (externalized problem), which has been restraining me."

I considered two possible options, wondering which would be most helpful: (a) to assist Ann to externalize her self-restraining belief by being interviewed in that role and thereby gain insight through acting the role and (b) to encourage Ann to cast one other group member as "self-restraining belief" and a second group member as herself and set up a "sculpture" that showed their relationship. Ideally, by assembling the sculpture, she would feel empowered, and by viewing the sculpture from a distance (a technique called mirroring), she would discover what she wanted to do with respect to the problem.

I discussed these options with Ann. She chose to cast one group member as self-restraining belief and another as herself, then direct the group members in the scene as she sat back and watched it. This proved to be a very empow-

Figure 8.4. Pathway Choices

ering choice. Ann was enabled to see that she no longer wanted to give this self-limiting belief so much power. "I walk down both paths, the path of acting and the path of family counseling. When I started the drawing I thought that I needed to choose between the two paths, but why couldn't I walk down both paths simultaneously?" Later she commented, "This took a huge weight off my shoulders." This important realization proved to be a breakthrough for Ann.

I next considered how we could mark and celebrate this moment. I considered whether we should (a) paint a drawing of the moment, (b) create a strengthening dance, or (c) develop a celebratory ritual to signify the importance of this moment.

After I consulted with her about this decision, Ann chose to create a ritual involving movement that would celebrate the joy of acting. She showed the other group members some ideas for dance structures and movements that would be personally meaningful to her and then gave musical instruments to each of the members of the group. She began the ritual and the rest of us joined in, expanding her dance and movement ideas. It turned out to be an especially wonderful and joyous ritual and became one of the most important moments of our shared adventure.

Then it was Julie's turn. Julie showed us a drawing that illustrated several possible paths, each emanating from the center of the drawing. All paths seemed equally important. One led to writing a book of monologues and sending out a proposal to a publishing company. Another path led to developing and advertising classes at a professional theater company for teenagers.

A third path led to increased trust, participation in a relationship, and more social activity. Julie had considered each of these as viable alternatives.

To help her decide, Julie's different paths were physicalized by placing group members, fabrics, chairs, and so forth to represent the different directions (*journeys*). Julie's drawing was different from Ann's in that she wanted to explore all the paths and felt no particular conflict as to which path to pursue.

I pondered four options that could lead to different scenarios: (a) A group member could be chosen to represent each of the paths, and each path could be interviewed so that Ann could become familiar with its possibilities and importance; (b) Julie could explore one path at a time, without choosing any path as being better than the others; (c) Julie could choose which path she prefers to explore, either because she feels less familiar with it or because it has more importance to her at this moment; or, finally, (d) Julie could choose to explore a path in which she feels blocked.

After discussing the possibilities with me and the group, Julie knew immediately that she wanted to explore the path of writing, because she had been feeling blocked and unable to move forward on that path. To explore this path she wanted to create an action monologue in which she expressed her inner thoughts. After enacting this monologue, Julie stated, "I feel that something has shifted. I believe I can do this. I can break this down into simple steps that I can complete."

Considering possible options, I wondered which might be more helpful: (a) collaboration with Julie to break down the task of writing a monologue book into simple steps or (b) enacting an imaginary "Ritual of Book Completion," so that she could experience the possible satisfaction that might come from finishing her book. Faced with these sorts of options, participants usually find it easy to choose one.

Julie knew right away and said, "I want to do a ritual of completion" (*action ritual*). Julie considered the possibilities and then enlisted the other participants to create a chorus of voices as part of the ritual. The chorus of voices, representing the readers of her book, would welcome Julie's book of monologues and celebrate their completion.

The ritual Julie enacted was of her writing a letter to the publisher, sealing the letter, and then mailing it. All of these moments were heightened, imbued with the magic of ritual. As the letter was mailed, the chorus of voices came in, quietly but joyously expressing the good energy and hope with which Julie's dreams were received: "Let it flow." "The stories are inside of you." "You have lots of support." "There's wind behind you." "We are there with you." "It's already being done. You just need to do it." "You can do it." Julie's demeanor showed that this ritual had brought her hope and lifted her spirits. Then she told the group that she wanted to set a deadline for completing the first 15 monologues and mail the proposal to the publisher. Julie came up with the strategy that she would audiotape the supportive voices of the chorus from the previously described exercise, put this tape in a box with a blue ribbon, and put the box and tape in a visible place at home in case she needed it.

Rosanna concluded the session with a drawing (see Figure 8.5). While a pathway occurred in her drawing, that was not the primary focus, but rather a "Banner of Love."

Sometimes other group participants may be working on an exercise that doesn't have the same relevance for another member or they may want to spin the exercise differently. Often in those situations a participant may come to me and ask if they can do something different. I really appreciate a person being so in touch with themselves and sensitive to what they need to be doing.

Rosanna's drawing was an example of this, as the focus of her drawing was on the "Banner of Love." This she defined as the world of the spirit, God's wisdom, and also containing a portrait gallery of characters from the Bible who have been examples as well as famous individuals from history who have been an inspiration. Rosanna wanted this past wisdom to inform her present and she drew nourishment from authors of special poems and meaningful quotes and books which were important to her. She referred to the wisdom she gained from these sources as "soul talk."

As the session was coming to a close, I contemplated what would be the most appropriate creative assignment to give the group. Because most group members had differentiated two or more paths, I considered whether it might be preferable to encourage them to (a) write an "Effects Story" for each path in their drawing, to clarify the effect of choosing each different path; (b) research a specific historical event in which the choices made greatly influenced the future of particular people or countries; (c) paint additional drawings showing the results of taking the specific path chosen; or (d) take photographs of objects, people, events, or other meaningful objects that help them to celebrate or clarify their chosen paths. I thought it might be fun to integrate some of my thoughts about this into a creative assignment.

In discussing my ideas with the group, the following creative assignment emerged: "Reflect on the path drawing that you have completed, and picture in your mind what it would be like to choose either path. Imagine a story to go with Path 1. This story needs to show the effects of choosing that path. Then do the same for Path 2, and write an "Effects Story" about choosing Path 2. For the path drawing or support drawing (Rosanna's Banner of Love picture), photograph objects, people, nature images, animals, and so forth that celebrate or clarify your chosen path or support group."

Session 3

At the beginning of this meeting, Ann announced that she had painted a drawing of her dance ritual of celebrating acting and put it on her dresser. This drawing and movement ritual of celebrating acting would greatly affect

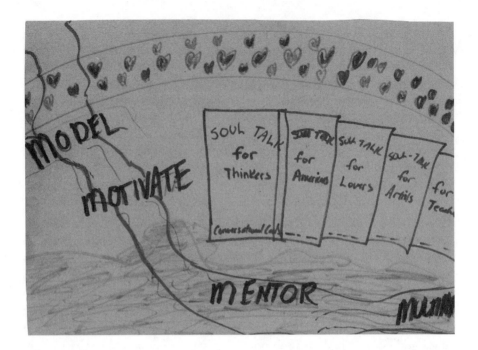

Figure 8.5. Banner of Love Drawing

her life in the weeks to come. Ann said, "I wanted to honor my joy of acting. My picture shows this. My purple dancing figure shows my being free and creative. I'm existing in something much bigger than myself." Rosanna said she had put her Banner of Love drawing in the medicine cabinet, where it invites her reflection each day. Harold disclosed that he was still working on his path drawing in an effort to gain more clarity about a current decision. Julie brought in 15 completed monologues and proudly informed the group that she had met her first deadline. She also reported that she had a photograph taken of herself with a blue envelope representing mailing the monologues to the publisher and another picture showing the deposit of this envelope into a mailbox near her house. She put this picture on her refrigerator to remind her daily of this commitment. Julie said, "For me to be witnessed by the group shifted many things. I had a magnificent month." Julie then read us one of her monologues, to the sincere appreciation and applause of the group. Next, to continue the idea of physicalizing a drawing, everyone was asked to complete a picture of a journey, drawing in his or her own way. These journeys are to contain certain specific points on them (i.e., shoreline, ocean, island, and destination). I thought that this exercise would assist the group to explore further where they wanted to be in their lives and what roadblocks might confront them.

Everyone completed this assignment in a different way (ranging from representational drawings to symbolic ones). At this point, Max has his first encounter with a symbolic golden entity he refers to as "The Shiny Golden

Me" (see Figure 8.6a). Max's golden entity appears at the destination point of his journey, next to a palm tree (note arrow 1). The Shiny Golden Me also appears as "golden lights," (note arrow 2) over the boat. The Shiny Golden Me appears at the end of the journey as bright sunlight shining down (Figure 8.6b; see arrow 1) on the island shore. Max imagines himself sitting next to the Shiny Golden Me, which Max refers to as the "highest me," "full of potential," and "at peace." Other aspects of Max's drawing (Figure 8.6a) involve jumping into some deep and treacherous water, a challenge for which Max needs to be prepared (note arrow 3). Next he enters a boat that carries him to a place of rest (note arrow 4), on the way to his destination point. The resting place is important because the rest nurtures Max and allows him to continue on his journey. When traveling in the boat, the Shiny Golden Me shines down on him, strengthening him to complete the final leg of his journey. This is a particularly fascinating example of a journey drawing that demonstrates many imaginative possibilities. After first explaining with a paper sketch, Max depicted locales from his journey drawing in life-size by placing objects, people, and fabrics within the room (*physicalization of journey*). Max's path takes him to different points in his journey. At important moments, Max speaks about his feelings at each point.

To continue further, Max could (a) explore the deep and treacherous water as an independent entity by creating scenes that suggested this, (b) experience a role reversal with the deep and treacherous water, and (c) become more familiar with the resting place and how to get there. Going from sketch to life size, Max could depict his "resting place" by positioning people, objects, and fabrics within the environment, (d) take the role of the golden figure and develop a dialogue between himself and the golden figure using different physical positions to delineate each charcter.

All these ideas seem very useful to Max, and at some point he wants to explore all of them, but the attraction today is Max's relationship to and with the golden figure. Max places himself on the island, re-created by group members with vocal environmental sounds, placement of fabrics, and soft recorded music. Max role-reverses with the golden figure, and I interview him as the golden figure (*role reversal* and *externalization interview*). I learn through this interview about Max's desire for more spiritual focus and balance in his life. This is only one aspect of the golden figure that begins speaking inwardly to Max. Later in the session Max wants to experience what it would feel like to arrive at his destination. He enacts his arrival at that location, with the golden figure at his side. In his role reversal as the golden figure, Max becomes tearful. One group member suggests that this is "an honoring of Max's soul."

Before introducing the "Journey" exercise, I suggested that two or three of the group members become members of the reflecting team. From the first session I have been working up to this by giving creative assignments and some in-group short assignments that invite participants to appreciate, wonder, and reflect curiosity. Reflecting teams reflect about what they have just

Figure 8.6a. Journey Drawing

Figure 8.6b. End Point Journey

witnessed by wondering and asking questions that pique their curiosity. They also notice special things to appreciate about the person and the session and share points of connection with the scene. The group expressed excitement about the reflecting team but were at the same time anxious about actually trying it. Two members finally volunteered to be the team and placed themselves away from Max so that they could begin observing the scene. Reflecting team members switch back to being participants when they share and enact their own journey drawings. Members of Max's team were surprised about their first experience. They were feeling less anxious than they anticipated and made such comments as "Being on the reflecting team puts me in a wonderful space of not having to have an answer." "I love the way we all piggyback on each other's thoughts." At the conclusion of the exercise Max himself comments, "It woke me up to some things I couldn't have otherwise noticed. . . . It helped me to get to a much deeper place. . . . I got a lot out of it."

To keep the energy flowing as the session neared its end, I began wondering about the creative assignment. I don't like to set the creative assignment in advance but rather to work spontaneously and collaboratively with the group in considering what might be most helpful.

My own curiosity about the journey drawings inclined me to suggest this creative assignment: "Place your journey drawing in a highly visible location. Reflect on it during the week, and write a story about it or design an illustrated picture book that describes your journey story. Find two things that you can appreciate about how you approached the journey. Continue expanding your preferred environment."

Session 4

At the next meeting the group members again shared their experiences. Max said that he had put the golden figure on his refrigerator door, and the presence of this figure had been having an amazing centering effect on him. He also brought in a vinyl cushion for a kitchen table, which he had spray painted a salmon color in an effort to surround himself with more color in his home, bringing it more in line with his magical environment. Rosanna and Harold indicated that they were still adding to their journey drawing. Ann, eager to speak, announced that she had been cast in a small role in an educational film promoting a family counseling center. Ann had learned about the film at work and tried out for it, thinking she could get a small part, but instead had been offered a much larger role. This outcome clearly integrated Ann's two paths (acting and family counseling) because she had become an actress in an educational film about family counseling.

During this session everyone created a mobile to represent significant things in their lives. Members not sharing at the time about their mobile served as members of the reflecting team. I wanted the positive energy about the team from the previous session to continue into this session. Group members showed less signs of anxiety this session and were looking forward to being on the reflecting team. Each group member introduced his or her mobile through an interview. I asked questions such as, "What surprises you most about this mobile?" "What part of the mobile strikes you as the most important at this time?" "If that part could speak, what would it say to you?" Then the reflecting team commented about what happened during the interview.

Max's mobile was striking (see Figure 8.7) in its use of color, symbols, and style. I find creating a mobile a very easy way to assist group members to explore how they can make specific decisions about deconstructing and reconstructing their lives. Deconstruction is the breaking down of something into its component parts to enable the individual to decide which parts they want to keep and which they want to discard. The beige and brown paper pieces of yarn (note arrow 1) hanging from Max's mobile represented "ordinary day-by-day and bland existence." In the center of the mobile was a striking cobalt blue yarn thread that holds a red shiny birthday whistle and a gold fuzzy cloth together (see arrow 2). "I'm curious about this shiny whistle, and that fuzzy bright gold hanging part, and the cobalt blue threads. What do those mean to you?" Max replied, "The red shiny whistle means 'fun'; the bright, golden hanging part is 'fuzzy'; and the whistle is 'funky.' I want my life to be more in balance. There is too much beige and brown right now. There needs to be more fun, fuzziness, and funkiness. The cobalt blue center part shows creativity and holds everything up. I want it to be that way in my life with creativity taking a larger part." I asked Max to deconstruct creativity. He said, "finding creative solutions, taking time to have fun, taking a risk."

When you observe Max's mobile, it shows his life in the balance he prefers. To assist Max to expand this image further I invite him to physicalize his preferred life picture by creating a living sculpture with group members playing each part of his restoried mobile (i.e., the party whistle, the cobalt blue threads, the beige everyday life square and the fuzzy golden cloth). In that restoried picture, I asked him to consider the following questions: How large would creativity be? Where do fun, fuzzy, and funky belong? Where is the cobalt blue and how does it relate to the other parts? This activity offers many role options to Max: director (through creating the sculpture), player/ participant (through becoming creativity or another part), or audience (through observing and contemplating the finished sculpture). Experiencing each of these roles creates possibilities for insight and change.

The reflecting team discussed the mobile and expressed curiosity about the hanging blue yarn holding up the center. "I notice that the color blue keeps reappearing. I wonder what would happen if Max continued to experience more of the color blue?" "I identified with that, too. I notice in my own life I prefer people, and when I experience that color I feel peaceful." "I wonder how Max feels when he experiences the color blue?" "I also wonder what would happen if that red party whistle took over more space—how would that affect Max's life?"

Julie's mobile contained different hanging "threads of fear," with the single exception being a heart in the middle of the mobile that was free of fear. In deconstructing fear, Julie discovered that most of her fears were about

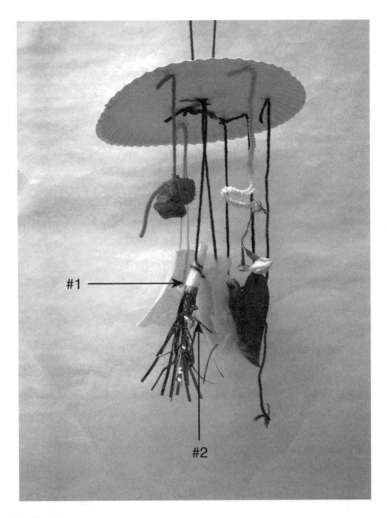

Figure 8.7. Mobile

things that had never occurred. She also found that she felt less fearful when she was alone but was more threatened and frightened in social relationships. To reconstruct her relationship with fear, Julie imagined a balloon that was filling up (representative of the heart) and pushed the other pieces away, pushing aside fears. Group members assisted in being the balloon. Julie held onto the color blue. In interview, she discovered that, to her, blue represented truth and strength, purity and love. I wondered how Julie could assess the color blue. What would be most helpful? Perhaps she could role reverse and take on the role of the color. She might express her ideas artistically, exploring different art forms with blue. She might imagine and create a bridge to the color blue. I asked Julie, "What is the bridge to the blue? How do you get there when you need to?" Julie thought it would be helpful to create and perform a monologue (she often chose this dramatic form because it had been so helpful to her). She began the scene searching in a shop for a handful of small objects which, she discovered later, were blue beads. As she touched these beads, her head cleared, and she connected with truth, strength, purity, and love. She said, "When I let fear overwhelm me, I can't move. It is as if I am holding my breath and not breathing. That is part of my old pattern. I can't move forward because I am paralyzed with fear." The reflecting team wondered, "I wonder what the blue beads might say to chase away the fear?" "What ways could the balloon assist Julie in achieving what she wants?" "I loved the strength of the balloon." Julie observed, "I found the reflecting team so incredible. I really started wondering. They held all the energy up."

Ann wanted to explore her relationship to money but seemed embarrassed to do this in front of the group. I proceeded very tentatively and slowly, respectful of her feelings. I noticed that the mobile (*action mobile, interview*) contained different parts of that relationship (i.e., casualness, looseness, spending under stress, poor organization). I wondered if Ann was ready to clarify a new relationship with money or whether she needed to continue to think about it. Ann took a long time but decided to identify certain parts of the mobile as more significant. She indicated that she really wanted to try to find a different perspective or way of looking at money. I thought the reflecting team would help Ann see additional options. In response to Ann's mobile and interview the group reflected, "I wonder what would happen to Ann's world if she changed her relationship to money?" "I appreciate her openness to explore the topic even though see seems embarrassed about it. I know in my own life when I have been willing to look at something that I was already changing." "I wonder if she is experiencing that change, too?" Ann, in responding to the reflecting team said, "I felt really listened to and honored. I did not feel I was being judged for feeling embarrassed or uncomfortable. I really liked the spirit of the thing. I was surprised at how so many of the statements were meaningful to me. I wondered how so many different points of view could give me such clarity. The experience was very affirming." The reflectors commented, "I felt that I respected each person more. I so enjoyed it because there was a safety net" and "I saw pockets of myself in the mobile."

With reconstruction, group members have begun to restory their lives in positive ways.

In this session, with the presentation of such significant scenes and rituals, I wondered about finding a way group members could be invited to reflect deeply about what they had just sculpted, created, and enacted. In reflecting on my own experiences, I remembered that each time I relive a significant scene, I often discover something new. So repeating or playing back a scene (i.e., a videotape) can become a wonderful reflective tool. Also, expanding a scene through a different art form may sometimes bring forth new discoveries and a deeper awareness.

Accordingly, I gave the following creative assignment: "Focus on the most important aspect or idea of your mobile that you discovered in the group. If you developed a ritual in relationship to your mobile, repeat it during the week. If you developed a sculpture or scene, expand it by writing or drawing about it in your journal. Write a poem or future scene inspired by your mobile."

Session Some Months Later

Several months later, the group met. Before this meeting they were asked to bring in significant examples of art (drawings, paintings, masks, photos, mobiles) and written material (poems, prose, journal entries) that were especially meaningful to them. They were invited to draw from the resources of their previous discoveries, images, colors, shapes, and figures to create a collage of symbols (from previous works or new ones) that continue to influence their lives in significant ways.

I am preparing clients to move from novice to veteran and from client to consultant. While they continues to serve as an audience for each other until the end of therapy, I often invite nongroup members who (along with group members) witness progress, authenticate change, and legitimatize alternative knowledge.

Julie created a collage by placing on a large flowing blue cloth on the floor significant pictures, empty picture frames, and objects. To help nourish the scene she brought in a special incense, saying, "Smell brings me back to what I love, and I am beginning another part of my journey." Julie began a monologue, starting from the time 2 years ago when she left New York to the present. "I couldn't decide whether to stay in New York or leave. I'm in my apartment and wondering what I should do. I've been offered a part in a play in California. Should I take it? Then I look at the pictures on my mantle, and I realize these are just pictures with smiles. The reality is that I don't have very close relationships in New York." Julie took all the pictures out of the frames and stared for a long time at the empty pictures. She saw her face in the reflection of the empty glass of the picture. "That's real. I left everything behind. I surrounded myself with the wisdom of the blue. I know I'm going to expand the light. I'm going to put it in my heart. I want to put my fear in that closet over there (she does so). I want to commit to three things. I want to live bigger and move away from my fears. I want to complete my monologue book, and I want to let my boyfriend close to me and risk intimacy." At another moment she says, "I'm in a forest, and I see a clearing. I walk toward it heading uphill. I feel the cold, clean, and crisp wind and the sunlight on my face. I can see everything vividly. I feel the wind across my face. I am the King of my own Kingdom. I am the King of my own Kingdom." The group repeats this line back to her and variations of the line: "You are the King of your Kingdom." "You decide what to do." "You are the King of your Kingdom, and you have great wisdom." We all honor the King with different gestures showing respect (bowing, looking up to). This monologue shows the importance of thinking about selected past moments in a progression that leads Julie to the realization that she is the king of her kingdom. With the fear in the closet, Julie embraces her future, taking in the wind and light (her sustenance), the color blue, and her determination to take risks and accomplish her goals.

Julie summarized her experience with narradrama: "I have found narradrama to be very helpful, especially the experiential part. It seemed when I experienced something with all of me (mind, body, and spirit) that the result was more immediate. I found that I can deal with things in the present and that I don't have to keep reliving the past (like in previous therapies), which would have made me feel more despondent. You don't have to go back into the past. You don't have to feel stuck in mire. You can move forward." Julie wanted very much to continue in the group, to confront her "fear of moving" and fulfill her desire for autonomy.

Rosanna brought in a collage of photographs she had created of important events and people that helped to relive her history. She also brought her treasured Banner of Love picture. She had been reflecting on her picture for the last 6 months every time she opened her medicine cabinet, drawing daily inspiration from it. As we all looked at her picture again, stillness filled the room. Everyone was astonished to see the words "Soul Talk" on the picture. In recent weeks Rosanna had published a series of inspiration cards, which she called Soul Talk. These were cards with inspirational quotes and questions that were being sold and distributed in bookstores. When the Banner of Love picture was completed months earlier, Rosanna had not even thought of publishing Soul Talk cards. With wonder and astonishment, we all (even Rosanna) realized in the same moment that in this picture, created months before, Rosanna's future was starting to be realized. One of the cards in Rosanna's Soul Talk aptly stated, "Each and every one of us has a champion deep inside us. It is up to ourselves to bring that champion out" (Amaginomics, 2002).

Drawing from earlier imagery (Figure 8.8a), Ann created a picture (see Figure 8.8b) in which the most important symbol, a purple dancing figure, moved in synchronicity with other key symbols. Reflecting on this picture, Ann decided to create a ritual in which group members blessed the continuation of her journey. In preparation for this ritual, Ann set up her first environment and lit a single candle. Ann placed herself close to the candle, taking in the stillness and peace. After centering herself she went around to every person in the group, each of whom in his or her own way blessed her. Ann stated, "I realized how important it was for me to revisit my history and how, revisiting it, my experience deepened. I felt so supported by the group and optimistic about my future."

In reflecting on their therapy experiences through narradrama, Ann said, "I start feeling uneasy when I think I have to sit and talk about something (like in my previous therapies), but when I draw or write or enact something, it is freeing. It brings me back to myself. It helps me to play with the images that I've got. And when I feel more comfortable, then I feel more empowered. I am relating to something within me rather than to an expert. One thing I noticed that is different from talk therapy is the use of space. In talk therapy you sit and talk to a therapist, and that is your world, but in our group the whole room is your space. When I move in that space it feels like I have more space in my life." When asked about her future goals in therapy Ann said, "What I want to continue to work on is 'claiming my own space.' It's like when you go on an audition. This is your time. Fear sometimes gets in the way of me claiming my space, and I want to find a ritual to defeat fear." In reflecting about her ideas of therapeutic space and opening to new possibilities, Ann wrote the following poem, which reflected much of her group experience:

A candle lit
A chime rings
Stillness
Opening to the Inner Light
Breath
Heartbeat
Dropping down
Finding the resting place
in the substance of the body
The quiet one
finds her voice
her body
She begins to move from that inner knowing
Pressing toward the known and the unknown
Opening to possibility
Flowing through impossibility
In joy and freedom she dances
The door swings open
The path widens
Being
Body
Voice
Trust
Action

Concluding the Group

The experiences of Julie, Max, Rosanna, Ann, and Harold in the narradrama group helped them achieve the new focus and direction they had sought and continued to affect their lives more than a year later. Ann has begun to follow the dream career path she had abandoned for more than 20 years while still continuing her studies to become a licensed family counselor; Julie overcame her fear of writing and self-revelation and is meeting the deadlines for her book of monologues. Max is actively incorporating more color, emotions, and people into his life and experiencing life more vividly

Figure 8.8a. Earlier Dancing Figure

Figure 8.8b. Current Dancing Figure

PAMELA DUNNE

and deeply. Rosanna is choosing the way she wants to live and who she wants to become. Harold plans to experiment with living in New York and Los Angeles, thereby meeting some of his career and personal goals. By exploring their stories through narradrama, these clients changed their lives for the better.

Therapy for this group concludes with an invitation to members' significant others to attend a special meeting (i.e., celebration) to witness the changes and new realizations group members are embracing. Group members will be asked to serve as future consultants to others and to the therapist as they continue to experience themselves as authorities on their own lives, their problems, and solutions to these problems. This authority is a kind of expertise that is recorded in some kind of creative format (videotaping, audiotaping, autobiographical account or montage, interview, videotaped enacted diary or scroll, or living newspaper—snapshot sculptures of restoried life scripts, videotaped with voiceover headlines) so that it is accessible to the therapist and other potential group members. During the special meeting, the therapist will ask each group member to give an account in some creative form of their process of overcoming their problems. Group members may show and describe their artwork, enact scenes, create sculptures, and use any other helpful techniques. The therapist may ask such questions as, "Imagine that I was meeting with a person or group who was experiencing a problem like you used to have. From what you know, what advice do you think I could give that person or group? Just imagine that someone found out that you were a veteran of this sort of problem and that you had freed your life from it. If he or she decided to consult with you, how would you help him or her?" At the end of the meeting, certificates or awards tailored to each individual are given.

Resistance

In narradrama, the term *resistance* would not typically arise, as it implies pathology or negative labeling that disempowers or marginalizes clients. If a group or individual member seems reluctant to move past the initial warm-ups (which are used to relax, imagine, and explore) into a deeper exploratory phase, that reluctance could suggest that they need more time to warm themselves up to the process or the issue. If a group member is not following through on goals developed during sessions then the direction or medium (i.e., art, drama, movement, or poetry) is deemed unsuitable. By showing cooperation with the client and saying, "I've noticed that the goals and ideas we discussed in group last time did not seem to work for you. Can you tell us what we need to know about working with you so that together we can come up with ideas and goals that work better for you?" the therapist establishes and models a collaborative, respectful stance. Narradrama group members are invited to pass on any intervention, activity, and so forth in which they are unwilling to engage by just saying "pass." There is no stigma for wanting to pass, and a client is fully respected for his or her honesty.

Dealing With Crises

In a crisis, accompanying increased vulnerability are also opportunities for growth and change. Narradrama action techniques help in externalizing the problem and collaborating with the family or client to explore management of the current crisis and prevention of future ones. Using a spectrogram (see chapter 2 for a description of this technique) readily reveals the influence of the problem. Sculpting a pivotal problem moment or exploring strategies for change through behavioral rehearsal invite individuals to examine their preferred life strategies. It may be helpful to meet extra times or increase the time of therapy as well as to collaborate with the individual or family to implement specific tasks between sessions. These tasks may be "noticing tasks," which ask the individual to become aware of times and ways the problem is being handled better. As the client or family makes decisions to move in positive directions, inviting significant individuals from the client's social network to witness a simple ritual or ceremony may be meaningful to the individual or family. Also, it is very effective to use a reflecting team to notice the client's preferred development or what might occur as unique outcomes. Reflection team members can recall that they are helping the client make meaning in response to preferred developments; they are not simply noticing or commenting on "positives." The presence of the reflecting team is particularly important for an individual or family in crisis, as the team often becomes a kind of helpful support structure, opening space and generating new ideas.

Dealing With Potential Conflicts Within the Group

Participants entering narradrama group therapy learn that the focus is on abilities, not on deficits. The relationships among the therapist, client, and other group members develop as ones of partners engaged in discovery. In the safety of this setting, individuals are less likely to engage in disruptive and competitive behavior. Should disruption or competition occur, it may be helpful for the therapist to ask questions (or stage a role reversal), which brings the group back to supportive functioning.

A related potential problem is that of advice-giving or judgmental remarks directed toward other group members. To counter the negative effects of this behavior, group members agree to "situate the remark," meaning that all remarks are to come from their own personal experience and connect to something specific in their life. Whether or not such remarks are helpful to another member, the one hearing it will not experience it as judgmental.

"Stuckness"

Another group problem involves group members who commiserate and get stuck in talking about problems. The therapist may then ask, "Is talking about the problem over and over again producing new life strategies? On a scale of 1 to 10, how helpful is continuously talking about the problem?" A therapist using narradrama recognizes that people often become stuck in a habit or are restrained by a belief that has temporarily disabled and negatively influenced their lives. A habit is an act that is repeated so often that it becomes automatic. By viewing habits not as born with people but rather as developing over time, group members discover whether they want to continue a particular habit by externalizing it through a living sculpture, drawing, or improvised conversation with that habit. Group members experiencing stuckness may be temporarily unaware of the strengths that they have and the resources they have to get unstuck. Empowering clients to discover, deconstruct, and challenge constraining beliefs may be effected by having them enact different parts of the belief with other group members or, using the multiple-ego technique used in psychodrama (Blatner, 1999), staging a chair sculpt (with different chairs representing the parts). In the tradition of solution-focused therapy, the narradrama therapist might ask, "Dream with me for a minute. Suppose tomorrow morning you woke up, and this event that has troubled you was less influential in your life. How would you know? How would others know? What regrets would you have 5 years from now if you stayed stuck with your current issue versus taking a risk and doing what you sometimes dream about? What rewards would you imagine having if you took the risk and it worked out? How would you begin doing this on a very small scale for the next week, so that the chances of having regrets 5 years from now are less?" (Metcaff, 1998, p. 52).

Role of the Therapist

Narradrama therapists do not think of themselves as leaders so much as collaborators, facilitators, codiscoverers, or coconstructors of solutions. When therapists take on more directive roles, clients have less chance of seeing themselves as competent. Therapists often need to take a back seat, assisting group members to step out of their pathology by watching for competent behaviors and potential unique outcomes at every moment. Therapists may want to write down things about each group member to document that client's strengths and competencies, to be shared or reflected on at the end of the group. It is important to assist a group to stay on their track, moving toward their goals by using clients' skills and abilities, not those of the therapist. Transparency (in process), openness, and willingness to be vulnerable are preferred qualities of therapists using narradrama.

CONCLUSION

To an outsider, the work of the narrative therapist might look easy. The session participants apparently do most of the work, while the therapist serves as their facilitator, audience, collaborator, and mentor. But, just as being a qualified doctor or schoolteacher involves preparation and effort that may not be superficially evident, the work of the therapist is complex, and the skills and specialized knowledge must be learned over years.

For centuries the power of drama and the arts to illuminate and define human experience has been a part of human experience, although drama and the arts are rarely considered therapy per se. The therapeutic value of ritual and magic has always been a component of both therapy and the arts, although hardly ever harnessed and used by traditional therapists. Narradrama enables participants to separate themselves from their problems and to explore possible solutions and clarifications through both verbal and nonverbal communication. Max, Rosanna, Ann, Julie, and Harold have begun a continuing process of positive change. By examining their life stories and making new discoveries, these participants made new choices that better reflect their real desires and values, choices that will undoubtedly change their lives. Some of these new attitudes and choices were nonverbal but could nevertheless be felt on an emotional or physical level and manifested in changes as distinct as a more confident posture or a new freedom of expression and movement. Using the reflecting team was undeniably helpful in opening space for new alternatives, and many of the observations of the reflecting team were embraced and adopted by the clients.

Narradrama is unique in its ability to incorporate different means and methods of expression from across all the creative arts. As a form of action therapy, narradrama invites and empowers clients to examine their present circumstances, decide where it is they want to go, experiment with alternatives, and ultimately decide to implement positive changes in their lives.

REFERENCES

Amaginomics Publishing. (2002). *Soul Talk*. West Covina, CA: Amaginomics.

Anderson, T. (1991). *The reflecting team: Dialogues and dialogues about the dialogues*. New York: W. W. Norton.

Blatner, A. (1999). Psychodramatic methods in psychotherapy. In D. J. Wiener (Ed.), *Beyond talk therapy: Using movement and expressive techniques in clinical practice* (pp. 125–143). Washington, DC: American Psychological Association.

Dunne, P. B. (1992). *The narrative therapist and the arts*. Los Angeles, CA: Possibilities Press.

Dunne, P. B. (1997a). Catch the little fish: Therapy utilizing narrative, drama, and dramatic play with young children. In C. Smith & D. Nyland (Eds.), *Narrative therapies with children and adolescents*. New York: Guilford.

Dunne, P. (1997b). *Double-stick tape: Poetry, drama, and narrative as therapy for adolescents*. Los Angeles, CA: Possibilities Press.

Dunne, P. (2000). Narradrama: Narrative approach in drama therapy. In P. Lewis & D. R. Johnson (Eds.), *Current approaches in drama therapy* (pp. 111–128). Springfield, IL: Charles C Thomas.

Emunah, R. (1994). *Acting for real. Drama therapy: Process and performance*. New York: Brunner/Mazel.

Imber-Black, E., Roberts, J., & Whiting, R. (Eds.). (1988). *Rituals in families and family therapy*. New York: W. W. Norton.

Jung, C. G. (1981). The aims of psychotherapy. In H. Read, M. Fordbam, & G. Adler (Eds.), *The archetypes and the collective unconscious* (Collected Works of C. G. Jung, Vol. 9, Part I). Princeton, NJ: Princeton University Press.

Landy, R. J. (1996). *Essays in drama therapy: The double life*. London: Jessica Kingsley.

Metcaff, L. (1998). *Solution-focused group therapy*. New York: Free Press.

Papp, P. (1985). *The daughter who said no* (VHS, B&W, 70 minutes). New York: Ackerman Institute.

Rogers, N. (1993). *The creative connection: Expressive arts as healing*. Palo Alto, CA: Science & Behavior Books.

Stanislavski, C. (1936). *An actor prepares*. New York: Theatre Arts.

Tomm, K. (1990–1991). Live taped therapy sessions with reflecting team. Calgary, Alberta: University of Calgary.

White, M. (1995). *Re-authoring lives: Interviews and essays*. Adelaide, South Australia: Dulwich Centre.

White, M., & Epston, D. (1990). *Narrative means to therapeutic ends*. New York: W. W. Norton.

White, M., & Epston, D. (1992). *Experience, contradiction, narrative, and imagination: Selected papers of David Epston and Michael White, 1989–1991*. Adelaide, South Australia: Dulwich Centre.

RECOMMENDED READING

Blatner, A. (1988). *Foundations of psychodrama: History, theory, and practice* (3rd ed.). New York: Springer.

de Shazer, S. (1991). *Putting difference to work*. New York: W. W. Norton.

Epston, D. (1989). *Collected papers*. Adelaide, South Australia: Dulwich Centre.

Fox, J. (1987). *The essential Moreno*. New York: Springer.

Freedman, J., & Combs, G. (1996). *Narrative therapy: The social construction of preferred realities*. New York: W. W. Norton.

White, M. (1989). *Selected papers*. Adelaide, South Australia: Dulwich Centre.

Zimmerman, J., & Dickerson, V. (1996). *If problems talked: Narrative therapy in action*. New York: Guilford.

CONCLUSION

DANIEL J. WIENER AND LINDA K. OXFORD

Although the case presentations in this book show the immediate
and sometimes profound impact of the use of their featured action methods, such effects should not be equated with pervasive and lasting therapeutic change. Action methods, although they may be accompanied by
marked, even dramatic changes, do not typically effect therapeutic results
independently of other curative factors. It should neither be assumed that
action methods are inherently curative nor that mastering action techniques is a substitute for sound clinical judgment or cultivating an appropriate relationship with clients.

SELECTION OF APPROPRIATE METHODS

All action methods of therapy are designed to mobilize the client's creativity and spontaneity, facilitate discovery of new solutions by providing
new perspectives on the problem, and encourage risk-taking and skill development in a low threat setting. Yet specific action methods are neither equally
accessible to nor effective with all clients. Which of these methods is most

likely to rapidly engage the particular client, efficiently and effectively promote therapeutic change, and equip the client to more successfully meet future life challenges? Can we learn from case presentations what makes action methods generally effective, or how they may be selected to produce favorable outcomes for the populations to which they are applied?

Although the therapists in each of the cases featured in this book work in distinctly different ways, their approaches share certain common theoretical tenets that characterize most action methods of therapy. Therapists who use action methods of conjoint treatment believe that direct experience is superior to verbal description of events, interactions, and relationships; that here-and-now experiences are more vital than recollections of the past or expectations of the future; that enhancing spontaneity and creativity facilitates health and growth for both client system and therapist; and that healing power exists in human encounters and relationships. Action-oriented therapists participate actively and personally in therapy sessions rather than maintaining clinical detachment. They are more available and vulnerable as coparticipants when they lead their clients into direct experiences of life and relationships rather than simply helping them deconstruct and make meaning of their reported experiences.

However, the various action methods featured in the chapters in this book arise out of distinct, even contrasting, theoretical rationales and diverse positions on the role of the therapist; the utility of client insight; and the centrality of developmental constructs used in the selection, sequencing, and timing of interventions. Specialists of all kinds, with intensive training and experience in one particular modality, typically apply that approach in their clinical work without considering whether a different modality might be more appropriate. Even were they to do so, there is little empirical evidence to guide such a choice. Psychotherapy outcomes research provides few instances in which the superiority of one treatment approach over another has been demonstrated. Within the community of creative arts therapies, however, it is believed that particular creative arts modalities are differentially effective for clients functioning at specific developmental levels (Johnson, 1999).

While acknowledging that differently abled populations are likely best reached by specific approaches, we contend that clinical outcomes are not solely the result of technique but of craftsmanship, an applied art that requires the effective use of self of the therapist. The craftsman's development of expertise and attainment of recognition as a "master craftsman" result from a synthesis of talent, training, and experience. Just as the level of craftsmanship at playing a musical instrument, painting a picture, or writing a novel are not equally manifested in any one individual, therapists' craftsmanship likely is related to their affinity for and mastery of a preferred therapeutic modality. The sort of craftsmanship required for the highly active and expressive practice of developmental transformations (featured in chapter 5) may not be found in a skilled practitioner of the nurturing-yet-directive type of art therapy featured in chapter 6, or vice versa. By exploring different modalities while working under the supervision of skilled, experienced mentors and teachers, clinicians may discover that their personal talents find fuller expression in other therapeutic approaches than in their present, familiar work.

The prime directive of improvisational theater, "accept all offers," also provides the foundation of effective therapy. Characteristic of master therapists is their mastery of improvisation; their ability to spontaneously develop and implement interventions specific and unique to the person, setting, and situation "in the moment." Their exceptional ability to integrate creativity, craftsmanship, therapeutic use of self, and what particulars each client system offers them infuses their work with an elegance and artistry that is difficult to analyze, challenging to teach, and almost impossible to replicate.

LIMITATIONS OF APPLYING ACTION
METHODS ACROSS MODALITIES

Action interventions that are safe and effective with individuals and groups (nonaffiliative therapies) may work poorly with couples and families (affiliative therapies) and may even have an effect entirely opposite to that intended by the therapist. These differences arise from differences in the relational contexts of treatment. Clients in individual therapy or in nonaffiliative therapy groups present their situation from an individual and personal perspective, as sole protagonists in their unique dramas. The therapist is concerned with validating and shifting the individual client's subjective reality rather than influencing a consensual reality that other real-life players in the client's social world share. Members of the individual's own real-life social system are not present in individual or group therapy to contest, modify, expand, or support any one person's perceptions.

By contrast, couples or family therapy requires that the phenomenological truth of each member of the system equally be recognized and validated (Seeman & Wiener, 1985). The therapist serves as the advocate and supporter of all members of the system rather than of one particular member (protagonist). When members of the protagonist's family system are actually present, each member of the system is a client in his or her own right, with unique feelings, experiences, and perspective on reality that the therapist is required to validate. In work with families, the audience no longer is a group of empathic others connected to the protagonist and his or her issues through projective identification but are actual participants in a real-life drama who have a vested interest in both its process and outcome. The interests and agenda of the protagonist may often be seen to be in serious conflict with those of other family members as actual relationships and interaction patterns replace the unilateral description of these relationships presented by any one member of the system. The therapist must therefore shift from championing the interests of one particular family member to advocating for the entire family system. To this end, the therapist must help members relinquish their adversarial or antagonistic positions and adopt a collaborative stance in overcoming a common problem.

Further, the power and intensity of evocative action methods can quickly escalate the emotional intensity of here-and-now family interactions, relationships, and experiences. Action methods, because they appear to bypass ego defense mechanisms, can rapidly intensify group affect in interactions between relative strangers; even more volatile, then, is their use with couples and families, whose interactions are fraught with far greater emotional significance due to their investment in their relationships to one other. For these reasons, action techniques in affiliative therapies generally are modified to reduce the likelihood of inadvertently escalating conflict or polarization in couples or family systems. Action sequences are also interspersed or alternated with verbal processing to promote cognitive integration of action exercises. Without such cognitive integration, experiential "action insights" rarely are translated into lasting cognitive and behavioral change.

As examples of the differences between affiliative and nonaffiliative applications of action methods, consider the application to relationship therapy of role reversal and doubling, psychodramatic techniques developed to work with nonaffiliative therapies, to relationship counseling. Full role reversals call for two people engaged in an encounter to step out of their own roles, enter the role of the other, and continue their interaction. If encounters are orchestrated between family members, such full role reversals risk escalating hostility, polarizing antagonistic positions carried into therapy from real-life interactions, magnifying fixed and inflexible roles, or facilitating the creation of new weapons to be used against one another as insights into the other's vulnerabilities are gained or power imbalances are exploited.

Doubling, the speaking for one person by another who seeks to express the unstated, underlying feelings and perceptions of the one spoken for, is a useful technique in nonaffiliative therapies. Through creation of an empathic bond, it engenders affirmation and support for the protagonist being doubled, validating this protagonist and lending additional ego strength that promotes motivation and initiative. However, doubling of family members by one another may produce regression to a more fused or undifferentiated state, where the boundaries between their own inner and outer worlds, as well as between self and other, become blurred and confused. This loosening of boundaries may obscure problem ownership, inhibit individuation, and promote overinvolvement of family members with one another. Doubling is also contraindicated in therapy with couples and families in which one person is already speaking for or interpreting another and in situations in which power imbalances might allow one partner or family member to use the role of the double to manipulate or coerce another.

Some action methods are useful in both affiliative and nonaffiliative therapies but generate distinctive client responses in each. One example of this is the Rehearsals for Growth exercise "Presents" (described in chapter 4). Typically, when Presents is conducted with a pair of nonaffiliated group members, the primary focus of the receiver's response is on his or her own reactions to the content of the gift that his or her own imagination has supplied and a diffused awareness of gratitude toward the giver. By contrast, marital couples enacting this exercise usually are first aware of how both the gift received and the manner of giving and receiving impact their marital relationship in the present moment, coupled with often quite strong associations and memories of historical events in their spousal relationship that have been triggered by the enactment. Therapists thus need to attend to the context in which an action method might be used as well as to the technique itself as they seek to match the technique to the desired outcome.

CONCLUDING THOUGHTS

We live in an era in which the demand for cost-effectiveness and accountability of mental health services, the proliferation of seemingly new methods, and the cross-fertilization of psychotherapeutic approaches are accelerating, resulting in an increasing number of mental health practitioners seeking training in specific techniques rather than in broader clinical approaches. These practitioners are becoming de facto eclectics, for whom theoretical coherence is of lesser concern than is the utility of the methods they use, utility typically being measured by the efficacy and efficiency of visible and rapid symptom reduction. Thus, the value of learning an approach or acquiring a technique is assessed by pragmatic considerations: Are there populations for which it would be (more) effective? Can I acquire it relatively rapidly and cheaply? Does it have a visible "brand name" with which I can claim expertise? In such an era the current anecdotal claims made for the efficacy of an approach or technique are likely to exceed any eventual results obtained by empirical testing of its actual worth. Moreover, the technique itself may assume primacy over the experience, judgment, and skillful application of the practitioner's art.

QUANDARIES OF RESEARCH

We have mixed reactions to the initiatives of both the American Psychiatric Association (2000) to establish practice guidelines for mental disorders based on expert clinical consensus and the American Psychological Association to identify and approve so-called "empirically supported" treatments that have demonstrated their effectiveness through controlled, replicable studies (Chambless et al., 1998). On the one hand, the psychotherapy field has long been vulnerable to accusations of "peddling snake-oil" to the unwary public in the form of permitting faddist treatments to flourish unchallenged and for making unsubstantiated claims regarding the benefits of mainstream approaches. On the other hand, an imprimatur for certain empirically justified psychotherapy approaches appears likely to lead health maintenance organizations and government regulatory agencies to the eventual conclusion that approaches not scientifically demonstrated to be broadly effective are valueless and that their use is tantamount to professional malpractice. If the burden of proof of efficacy is applied in this way, the ethical and legal practice of psychotherapy may become confined to the formalized application of a limited number of scientifically validated (currently, mostly cognitive–behavioral) techniques.

Such a result would have a devastating effect on the use of action methods generally, because, as noted above, there is little current empirical support (of the sort that would convince skeptics) for the efficacy of action methods. This situation would be both unfortunate and unfair, because the major sources of public funding for mental health research (the National Institute of Mental Health and National Institute on Drug Abuse) appear to fund outcomes research only on approaches that may be implemented with fixed protocols and already have been the subjects of empirical outcome studies. Thus, action method approaches, which generally entail improvised (nonstandardized) therapist responses that vary with the unique demands of the moment and may not focus on their clients' diagnoses (let alone prescribed interventions), appear unlikely to become candidates for research grants awarded in accordance with these institutes' current policies.

In contrast to approaches researched within university-based clinics and hospitals, action methods are predominantly practiced in private practice and within agencies. As has been noted by several authors writing in the mid-1990s (cited in McCollum & Stith, 2002, p. 5), therapy as conducted for research purposes not only differs considerably from therapy as conducted in an agency setting but also appears to produce outcomes not replicated in typical clinical practice.

We believe that clinical innovation may stimulate the development of effective treatment methods rather than passively following from new developments in research, so that science follows the lead of clinical practice and not vice versa (Davison & Lazarus, 1995). However, innovative practitioners should temper their enthusiasm for creative techniques with clinical wisdom, especially when claims of the effectiveness of these techniques appear unsupported by or incompatible with well-established scientific and theoretical principles. Anecdotal reports cannot replace the need for properly designed and controlled studies of outcome or validity. By supporting and integrating into their clinical practice research studies that examine outcomes and the differential effectiveness of treatment, practitioners can assume an important role in influencing standards of mental health treatment. Through adopting a willingness to study their own practices, therapists have an opportunity to effect change rather than merely react to it.

Application of outcome research to any clinical approach should focus on relevant clinical questions—Is it effective? Under what conditions is it effective? And, How can already effective therapy be enhanced? Science can provide an invaluable means by which practitioners learn which treatment works best under what circumstance, what constitutes appropriate quality of care, and which treatments are cost-effective. Emphasis in integrating research into the culture of the creative arts therapy professions should be placed on methods to access research and to provide a pragmatic model of the relationship between research and practice. The aim is a useful model that can be used by practitioners to incorporate research information into clinical decision-making.

Fruitful pursuits for future investigations include retrospectively analyzing treatment failures and attempting to identify factors that might predict, and ultimately enhance, outcome, including client characteristics, treatment parameters, and therapist variables (e.g., experienced vs. inexperienced). Discrepancies in treatment outcome may be affected by the varying levels of training, experience, and competence of the therapists involved. Still another critical issue revolves around how therapists' morals, values, and personal style overtly and covertly influence treatment goals, interventions, and outcome.

We believe that the use of action methods has been tested over time by considerable clinical experience. We look to our readers to join us and others in obtaining further necessary training in action methods, integrating them into their clinical practice, finding ways to satisfactorily demonstrate their efficacy and efficiency, and sharing the results within their professional networks.

REFERENCES

American Psychiatric Association. (2000). Practice guidelines for the treatment of psychiatric disorders: Compendium 2000. Washington, DC: Author.

Chambless, D. L., et al. (1998). Update on empirically validated therapies II. *The Clinical Psychologist, 51*, 3–16.

Davison, G. C., & Lazarus, A. A. (1995). The dialectics of science and practice. In S. C. Hayes, V. M. Follette, R. M. Dawes, & K. E. Grady (Eds.), *Scientific standards of psychological practice: Issues and recommendations* (pp. 95–120). Reno, NV: Context Press.

Johnson, D. R. (1999). Refining the developmental paradigm in the creative arts therapies. In D. R. Johnson (Ed.), *Essays on the creative arts therapies: Imaging the birth of a profession* (pp. 161–181). Springfield, IL: Charles C Thomas.

McCollum, E. E., & Stith, S. M. (2002). Leaving the ivory tower: An introduction to the special section on doing marriage and family therapy in community agencies. *Journal of Marital and Family Therapy, 28,* 5–7.

Seeman, H., & Wiener, D. J. (1985). Comparing and using psychodrama with family therapy: Some cautions. *Journal of Group Psychotherapy, Psychodrama and Sociometry, 37,* 143–156.

APPENDIX

INFORMATION PROVIDED BY AUTHORS REGARDING THEIR APPROACHES

DYNAMIC FAMILY PLAY (CHAPTER 1)

Key Journals

Journal of the Arts in Psychotherapy

Professional Associations and Author Contact Information

International Association for Play Therapy
2050 North Winery Avenue, Suite 101
Fresno, CA 93703
a4pt@sirius.com

National Association for Drama Therapy
733 15th Street, NW, Suite 330
Washington, DC 20005
202-966-7409
NADT@dmg-dc.com
www.nadt.org

Steve Harvey, PhD
PSC 824, Box 587
FPO AE 09623
saharvey1@yahoo.com

275

Educational Requirements

Dynamic family play should be used only by professionals with experience and training in expressive-oriented family therapy who are licensed as mental health providers and specialize in work with children and families. Additional training in expressive arts therapies is highly recommended, including continuing education or advanced work in art, drama, dance, or play therapy. Supervised training in dance and movement therapy is especially useful.

Training Programs

At the present time no formal training program is offered in dynamic family play on a regular basis. Dr. Harvey does present workshops in this modality through training institutes sponsored by the IAPT and the NADT.

FAMILY PSYCHODRAMA (CHAPTER 2)

Key Journals

Family Process
Journal of Marital and Family Therapy
International Journal of Action Methods
Journal of Psychodrama, Sociometry, and Group Psychotherapy

Professional Associations

American Association for Marriage and Family Therapy
1133 15th Street, NW
Washington, DC 20005
202-452-0109
www.aamft.org

American Society of Group Psychotherapy and Psychodrama
301 North Harrison Street, Suite 508
Princeton, NJ 08540
609-452-1339
609-936-1659 Fax
www.asgpp.org

American Board of Examiners in Psychodrama, Sociometry, and Group Psychotherapy
P.O. Box 15572
Washington, DC 20003
202-483-0514

Educational Requirements

Specialized training in marriage and family therapy at a graduate level and licensure as a mental health provider are necessary prerequisites to the effective, responsible practice of this therapeutic approach. Competence in using narrative/constructivist and solution-focused therapies and psychodrama is required.

Training Programs

Information about marriage and family therapy graduate and postgraduate programs endorsed by the AAMFT is available through AAMFT. Information about psychodrama training is available from the ASGPP. Certification as a practitioner of psychodrama is offered by the ABEPSGP.

CEREMONY IN MULTIPLE-FAMILY GROUP THERAPY (CHAPTER 3)

Key Journals

Family Process
Journal of the Arts in Psychotherapy

Professional Associations

International Society for Traumatic Stress Studies
60 Revere Drive, Suite 500
Northbrook, IL 60062
847-480-9028

American Association for Marriage and Family Therapy
1133 15th Street, NW
Washington, DC 20005
202-452-0109

Educational Requirements

No specific requirements.

Training Programs

Post Traumatic Stress Center
19 Edwards Street
New Haven, CT 06511
203-624-2146

REHEARSALS FOR GROWTH (RfG) (CHAPTER 4)

Key Journals

International Journal of Action Methods

Professional Associations and Author Contact Information

Rehearsals for Growth, LLC
Daniel J. Wiener, PhD, Director
2306 Berlin Turnpike, Suite 101
Newington, CT 06111
860-490-3337
growth@rehearsals.com
www.rehearsals.com/RfG This website contains an annotated bibliography of writings on the practice of RfG in various clinical contexts as well as current information on training opportunities.

Educational Requirements

RfG is intended for use by professionals who are licensed as mental health providers having experience and training in RfG and moderate experience with theatrical improvisation.

Training Programs

A 68-hour certificate training program is available to mental health practitioners and graduate students within 1 year of their terminal degree. Preparation for competent use of RfG requires moderate additional practice of theatrical improvisation. RfG is an adjunctive modality that can be combined with virtually any treatment approach.

DEVELOPMENTAL TRANSFORMATIONS (CHAPTER 5)

Key Journals

Journal of the Arts in Psychotherapy

Professional Associations and Author Contact Information

National Association for Drama Therapy
733 15th Street, NW, Suite 330
Washington, DC 20005

202-966-7409
NADT@dmg-dc.com
www.nadt.org

Educational Requirements

Master's degree in drama therapy; postgraduate certificate in developmental transformations.

Training Programs

Institute for Developmental Transformations
526 West 26th Street, Suite 309
New York, NY 10001
212-352-1184

ART THERAPY (CHAPTER 6)

Key Journals

Art Therapy: Journal of the American Art Therapy Association
American Journal of Art Therapy
Journal of the Arts in Psychotherapy

Professional Associations

American Art Therapy Association
1202 Allanson Road
Mundelein, IL 60060-3808
888-290-0878
arttherapy@ntr.net
www.arttherapy.org

Art Therapy Credentials Board
PO Box 30428
Charlotte, NC 28230
877-213-2822
atcb@nbcc.org
www.atcb.org

Educational Requirements

Master's degree in art therapy; certification by AATA. There are four routes to becoming registered with AATA through the ATCB. The most common is a master's degree in art therapy by an AATA-approved program, followed by 1,000 hours of paid clinical experience with 100 hours of clinical art therapy supervision. For other options, please see www.atcb.org or contact the ATCB.

Training Programs

All approved master's degree programs are listed in the AATA Web site, www.arttherapy.org. Post-master's training is available at the Institute for Expressive Analysis in New York City.

MUSIC THERAPY (CHAPTER 7)

Key Journals

Journal of the Arts in Psychotherapy
British Journal of Music Therapy
Journal of Music Therapy Perspectives
Musicing

Professional Associations

American Music Therapy Association
8455 Colesville Road, Suite 1000
Silver Spring, MD 20910
301-589-3300
301-589-5175 Fax
info@musictherapy.org

Nordoff–Robbins Center for Music Therapy at New York University
The Steinhardt School of Education
82 Washington Square East, 4th Floor
New York, NY 10003
212-998-5151
212-995-4045 Fax
Nordoff.robbins@nyu.edu
www.education.nyu.edu/nordoffrobbins

Educational Requirements

Master's or doctoral program in music therapy, certification by the Certification Board of Music Therapists; Nordoff–Robbins Certification Training (post-master's, competency-based)

Training Programs

Seventy-eight programs at universities in the United States offer degrees in music therapy (BA, MA, PhD).

Certification Board of Music Therapists
506 East Lancaster Avenue, Suite 102
Downingtown, PA 19335
800-765-2268
info@cbmt.org
www.cbmt.org

NARRADRAMA (CHAPTER 8)

Key Journals

Journal of the Arts in Psychotherapy

Professional Associations and Author Contact Information

National Association for Drama Therapy
733 15th Street, NW, Suite 330
Washington, DC 20005
202-966-7409

Drama Therapy Institute of Los Angeles
310-478-7188
310-589-0209 Fax
pamdunne@dramatherapyinstitutela.com
www.dramatherapyinstitutela.com

Educational Requirements

Master's degree in drama therapy. Specific narradrama training is available through the Drama Therapy Institute of Los Angeles, which enables the drama therapist or other mental health professional to practice from a narrative perspective.

Training Programs

The Board of Examiners for the National Association for Drama Therapy recognizes two levels of competence: the registered drama therapist (RDT) and registered drama therapist–board certified therapist (RDT-BCT). In either case, the practitioner's credentials must have been earned through a combination of academic coursework, study, and supervised practice.

AUTHOR INDEX

Numbers in italics refer to listings in the references.

SUBJECT INDEX

Abuse
   in dynamic family play case, 37
   and family play, 41–42
Acting out of environments, in narradrama,
   240
Action environments, in narradrama, 235
Action maps, in narradrama, 236
Action method(s), 3–5
   advantage of, 5–6
   assumptions behind use of, 268
   covert made overt in, 6
   cross-modality limitations of, 269–271
   dynamic family play, 19–21 (see also
      Dynamic family play)
   for emotional catharsis, 104
   empirical support for, 6–7, 272 (see also
      Empirical support; Outcome research)
   family narrative therapy, 45
   in family therapy, 15–16, 49, 75–77 (see
      also Family therapy)
   and group affect, 270
   and group therapy, 103, 138, 139 (see
      also Group therapy)
   and humanistic psychology tradition,
      15, 103–104
   and internal self-description, 232
   limitations and cautions on, 7
   in narradrama, 231, 233–237 (see also
      Narradrama)
   in Nordoff–Robbins approach to music
      therapy
      group clinical improvisation, 201–
         204, 211–218
      realization, 199–200, 210, 211, 222–
         223, 225
   and other curative factors, 267
   and patients' difficulties,164
   promise of, 12
   in psychotherapy, 4
   and research vs. clinical practice, 271–
      273
   selection of, 267–269
   and self-destructive individuals, 169
   for substance abuse problems, 108–110,
      133–134 (see also Rehearsals for
      Growth)

successive uses of, 222–223
Action mobile, 256
Action monologue, in narradrama, 236
Action ritual, 248
Activity group, 103
Address the Telephone exercise, in Rehears-
   als for Growth, 128–130
Adolescents (teenagers), play methods for,
   20
Aesthetic distance, 78
Aesthetic shaping, in music therapy (N-R
   approach), 203, 208, 210, 211, 212,
   213, 214, 216, 218, 219, 223
Affect(ive) expression, in group therapy, 139
   and case study of homeless mentally ill
      (developmental transformations),
      144, 146, 152
Affiliative systems, and nonaffiliative sys-
   tems, 10, 269–271
Agency, in family case history (over Sadness),
   57
Agenda, hidden, 47, 53–54
Alienation of parent and child, in family
   drawing, 22
"Altered States" exercise, 119
Ambiguity, in group therapy, 138
   and case study of homeless mentally ill
      (developmental transformations),
      143, 144, 148, 151, 152, 156
American Art Therapy Association, 194, 279
American Association for Marriage and Fam-
   ily Therapy, 276, 277
American Board of Examiners in Psycho-
   drama, Sociometry, and Group Psy-
   chotherapy, 276
American Journal of Art Therapy, 279
American Music Therapy Association
   (AMTA), 197, 280
American Psychiatric Association, 271–272
American Psychological Association, 272
American Society for Group Psychotherapy
   and Psychodrama, 276
Anderson, Tom, 237
Anxiety(ies), 164, 167
   automatic, 167
Approaches to Art Therapy, 190

287

Cognitive–behavioral group treatment, 104

Communicative interaction, from music therapy (N-R approach), 202

Communion, as ceremony, 78

Community, from music therapy (N-R approach), 200, 218–219

Competition
in group art therapy, 175–176
in narradrama, 262

Complexity, in group therapy, 138
and case study of homeless mentally ill (developmental transformations), 143, 144, 147, 152

Compulsivity, of autistic client in music therapy, 205

Concretization, 51, 52

Conflicts within group, in narradrama, 262

Conjoint therapy (treatment), 4
action methods for, 3, 4, 5, 10 (see also Action methods)
psychodramatic methods of, 49 (see also Psychodrama)

Conserved roles, 48

Core scene, 23
in dynamic family play, 27–28
in case presentation, 38–39

Countertransference
in developmental transformations approach, 137
with group therapy for homeless mentally ill (case example), 150
musical, 225

Couples therapy
as conjoint therapy, 3, 4
vs. individual therapy, 269–270
and psychodrama, 45

Courage, and music therapy (N-R approach), 201–202

Creative arts therapists, 16, 76, 104. See also Art therapy

Creative expression
in group art therapy, 176
in music therapy (therapist as model), 224

Creative family play, pace and timing of, 28

Creative music therapy, 198. See also Nordoff-Robbins approach to music therapy

Creativity
and dynamic family play, 20
and "environmental mother," 165
and sense of self, 166

in spontaneous interactive play, 21

Creators, therapists as (music therapy), 224–225

Crises
and narradrama, 262
and psychodrama, 48–49

"Crossing-over" ceremony, 91

Cross-training, 7

Dance ritual, 249

Dance therapy, 76, 104

Death, coping with, 10
and dynamic family play, 29, 35, 38

Deconstruction, in narradrama, 236, 254

Defining, in group therapy, 140

Developmental transformations approach, 135–136, 137, 161
educational requirements for, 279
embodiment in, 136–137
encounter in, 137
in group therapy, 138–140
with homeless mentally ill (case example), 140–161
information sources on, 278
playspace in, 136
training programs for, 279
transformation in, 137

Diagnostic Drawing Series, 194

Difference, news of, 56, 62

Directives, in group art therapy, 176

Directive therapy, 23

Displacement, in Rehearsals for Growth, 128

Distancing, in ceremony, 78

Doubling, 270–271

Drama therapy, 104
empirical support for, 161

Drama Therapy Institute of Los Angeles, 281
and narradrama, 230, 238

Dramatic enactment, 72, 103. See also Psychodrama
for substance-abuse clients, 109

Dramatic methods, 16

Dramatizing, in narradrama, 234

Duhl, Fred and Bunny, 46

Dynamic family play, 19–21, 23
case presentation in
core scene, ritual and termination of treatment in, 38–39
evaluation play in, 30–33
individual and dynamic play in, 34–38
initial games, 33–34

presenting problem, 29–30, 40
core scene in, 27–28
discussion of case
  engagement and resistance, 39–40
  successive uses of similar methods,
    40–41
educational requirements for, 276
empirical support for, 41–42
free play in, 28
information sources on, 275
initial evaluation in, 24–26
initial games in, 26–27
integration of verbalization and play
  activity in, 28
and interactive family play, 23
setting of, 23
termination in, 28
therapist's use of self in, 24
training programs for, 276

Educational requirements
  for art therapy, 279–280
  for developmental transformations, 279
  for dynamic family play, 276
  for family psychodrama, 277
  for multiple-family therapy, 277
  for music therapy, 280
  for narradrama, 281
  for Rehearsals for Growth, 278
Egocentricity, and role reversal, 51
Ego psychology
  and anxieties, 164
  and art therapy, 163
Elaboration, in dynamic family play, 41
Embodied encounter, in developmental
  transformations approach, 135
Embodiment, in developmental transformations approach, 136–137
Emotional catharsis, and group therapists, 104
Emotional expressiveness, for substance-
  abuse clients, 109
Emotional growth, from play experiences, 22
Empirical support
  for action methods, 6–7, 272
  for art therapy, 7, 194
  for ceremonies in multi-family treat-
    ment, 98
  for drama therapy, 161
  for dynamic family play, 41–42
  for music therapy, 7, 225–226
  for psychodrama in family therapy, 72
  See also Outcome research

Emunah, Renee, 111, 128
Encounter, in developmental transforma-
  tions approach, 135, 137
Encounter groups, 103, 104
Engagement
  behavioral, 76
  in dynamic family play, 39–40
  in music therapy (N-R approach), 203,
    206, 212, 213, 214, 215, 216
Entry ceremony, for foster children, 82–84
"Environmental mother," 165, 173
Epston, David, 46
Equality, from music therapy (N-R ap-
  proach), 202, 212
Evaluation, initial, 24–26
Evaluation play, in dynamic family play, 30–
  33
Experiential interactive play, 20–21
Experiential therapy, 4
  therapist's vs. client's drama in, 65
Expressive momentum, 26
Expressive play, 20–21
Externalization, 51, 52, 76
  in narradrama, 230, 231, 234, 244
Externalization interview, in narradrama, 251

Family narrative therapy, 45
Family play, dynamic. See Dynamic family play
Family Process, 276, 277
Family rituals, 16
Family roles, 48
  in family dramatic play, 32
Family scripts, 46–47
  in family case history (Hudson family),
    53, 70
    replication of, 70
    rescripting of, 58, 69–72
  and roles, 48
Family sculpting, 15
  in case history, 60–61
  in Rehearsals for Growth, 126–128
Family therapy
  action methods in, 15–16, 49, 75–77
  as conjoint therapy, 3, 4
  dynamic family play, 19–42, 275–276
    (see also Dynamic family play)
  vs. individual therapy, 269–270
  multiple-family (ceremonies), 75, 79–
    98 (see also Multiple-family therapy)
  psychodrama in, 45–73, 76, 276–277
    (see also Psychodrama)
Farewell ritual, in dynamic family play, 38

Initial games, in dynamic family play, 26–27
  in case presentation, 33–34
Inner monologue, in narradrama, 236
Institute for Developmental Transforma-
  tions, 279
Integrated treatment approaches, and empiri-
  cal support, 72
Integration of verbalization and play activ-
  ity, in dynamic family play, 28
Integrative approach, to therapeutic family
  play, 19
Interactive lecture, for foster families, 85–87
Interactive play, in dynamic family play, 39–
  40, 41–42
  experiential, 20–21
  natural, 21–23
Interactive style, in dynamic play therapy, 32
Internal awareness, and music therapy (N-R
  approach), 201–202
Internal family systems therapy (IFS), in
  Rehearsals for Growth, 112–115
International Association for Play Therapy,
  275
International Journal of Action Methods, 276,
  278
International Society for Traumatic Stress
  Studies, 277
Interpersonal demand, in group therapy, 139
  and case study of homeless mentally ill
  (developmental transformations),
  143, 144, 145, 148
Interpersonal relationships, in music therapy,
  224
Intimacy, and Mirrors exercise, 119, 120, 121

Journal of the Arts in Psychotherapy, 275, 277,
  278, 279, 280, 281
Journal of Marital and Family Therapy, 276
Journal of Music Therapy Perspectives, 280
*Journal of Psychodrama, Sociometry, and Group
  Psychotherapy*, 276
Journals
  on art therapy, 279
  on ceremony in multiple-family group
  therapy, 277
  on developmental transformations, 278
  on dynamic family play, 275
  on family psychodrama, 276
  on music therapy, 280
  on narradrama, 281
  on Rehearsals for Growth, 278
Journeys, in narradrama, 236

Kelley, George, 4
Kempler, Walter, 46
Kinetic Family Drawing, 194

Language, vs. action methods, 5
Leader role, in interactive lecture, 87
Lecture, interactive (foster children), 85–87
Letter ceremony, for Vietnam veterans, 87–
  91
Lowen, Alexander, 104

"Magic Shop, The," 62
Mapping (narradrama), 236, 246
Marking ritual, 235
Masks
  in group art therapy, 187–188
  in narradrama, 244, 245
Master player, 24
Meaning, attributed to play, 22
Media of expression, 138, 145, 147, 165
  switching of, 37
Mental health practitioners
  as eclectics, 271
  see also Therapist(s)
Mentally ill homeless persons, developmen-
  tal transformations approach for
  (case example), 140–161
Metaphorical object, 16
Milan school or group, 16, 76
Minuchin, Salvador, 15, 46
Mirroring
  in art therapy, 166, 193
  in narradrama, 246
  in psychodrama, 63–64, 68, 72
Mirrors exercise, in Rehearsals for Growth,
  114, 119–121
Mobiles, in narradrama, 253–57
Modeling, by therapist for autistic client
  (music therapy), 206, 224
Momentum, expressive, 26
Monologue
  action, 236
  inner, 236
"Monster" game, 35–37, 40, 41
Mood disorders, of substance-abuse clients,
  108–109, 122
Moreno, J. L., 45, 49, 103
"Mother, environmental," 165, 173
Motivational enhancement therapy, 108
Multimedia art project, 11
Multimodal play, 76
  in family therapy, 16

child as narcissistic extension (art therapy), 184
    See also Family therapy
Parts language, in IFS, 114–115
Pathway exercise, in narradrama, 244, 246–248
Peer testimonial, in Rehersals for Growth, 115
Perseveration, of autistic client in music therapy, 208
Personal agency mask, 244, 245
Personal growth
    and narradrama, 229, 233
    See also Humanistic psychology tradition
Personification, in group therapy, 140
    and case study of homeless mentally ill (developmental transformations), 145–146
Physicalization, in narradrama, 240, 246, 248
Physicalization of journey, in narradrama, 250, 251
Plasticene, in art therapy group, 177, 178–179
Play
    attuned, 160
    evaluation, 30–33
    individual and dyadic, 34–38
    multimodal, 16, 76
    therapeutic, 165
    use of terms and examples from, 31
    See also Dynamic family play
Play breaks, 26
    in case presentation, 34
    in dynamic family play, 36–37
    in observed example, 41
Play flow, 26
Playspace, in developmental transformations approach, 136
    in case example (group therapy with mentally ill homeless), 142, 144, 157
Poet's Corner game, in Rehearsals for Growth, 121–124
Posttraumatic stress disorder (PTSD)
    and ceremonies for women, 98
    and graduation ceremony for Vietnam veterans, 95–96
    interactive psychoeducational group therapy for, 85
    lecture on (daylong ceremony), 96
    and therapeutic ceremony, 79
Pragmatics
    in acquiring technique, 271

of group art therapy, 173–174
Prescribed family rituals, 16
Presents exercise, in Rehearsals for Growth, 124–126, 271
"Pretend" activity, 16, 77
Previewing, 61–62
Primal-scream groups, 104
Problem mask, 245
Professional associations
    for art therapy, 279
    for developmental transformations, 278
    for dynamic family play, 275
    for family psychodrama, 276
    for multiple-family therapy, 277
    for music therapy, 280
    for narradrama, 281
    for Rehearsals for Growth, 278
Projection, in group therapy (case example with homeless mentally ill), 152, 153
Project Reachout, 141
Psychodrama
    covert made overt in, 55
    dependence on therapist minimized in, 72
    emotional purging in, 104
    in family therapy, 16, 45–46, 72–73, 76
        case study in (Hudson family), 49–72
        educational requirements for, 277
        and empirical support, 72
        information sources on, 276
        integration problems in, 67
        theoretical foundations of, 46–49
        training programs for, 277
    mirroring in, 63, 72
        in case study, 63–64, 68
    and Moreno, 49, 103
    vs. talk therapy, 4
Psychosocial development, during art therapy, 174–175
Psychosocial functioning, and Rehearsals for Growth program, 132–133
Psychotherapy, 4
    and personal growth, 233 (see also Humanistic psychology tradition)
    and scientific validation, 272
Psychotherapy outcomes research, 268. See also Outcome research
PTSD. See Posttraumatic stress disorder

Realism, and music therapy (N-R approach), 202

Realization, in Nordoff-Robbins approach to
    music therapy, 199–200, 210, 211,
    222–223, 225
Reconstruction, in narradrama, 236–237,
    254, 255–256
Reflecting teams, in narradrama, 233, 237,
    251–252, 264
Rehearsals for Growth (RfG), 107–108
    case example of, 110–112
        Address the Telephone exercise in,
            128–130
        family sculpting in, 126–128
        internal family systems therapy in,
            112–115
        Mirrors exercise in, 114, 119–121
        Poet's Corner game in, 121–124
        postgroup functioning of members
            in, 131
        Presents exercise in, 124–126, 271
        warm-up exercises in, 116–119
    changes in participants in, 131–132
    educational requirements for, 278
    improvement from, 132–133
    information sources on, 278
    situation and outcomes of, 130–131
    training programs for, 278
Rehearsals for Growth, LLC, 278
Reich, Wilhelm, 104
Relationships, and conjoint therapy, 4. See
    also Conjoint therapy; Couples
    therapy; Family therapy; Group
    therapy
Repetition, in dynamic family play, 41
Rescripting, 58
    in family case history (Hudson family),
        69–72
Research
    needed on interactive play, 42
    quandaries of, 271–273
    and unconventional designs, 6
    See also Outcome research
Resistance
    in dynamic family play, 39–40
    in music therapy group, 221–222
    in narradrama, 261–262
Restructuring, 76
RfG. See Rehearsals for Growth
Rites of passage, action methods for, 6
Ritual(s), 16, 77
    action, 248
    action methods for, 6
    as analogic, 77

dance, 249
in dynamic family play, 27–28, 38–39
in family therapy, 16, 76
marking, 235
in narradrama, 235–236, 247, 248, 258
therapeutic value of, 264
transformational, 235
transitional, 235, 236
witnessing in, 76
Robbins, Arthur, 190
Robbins, Clive, 198
Rogerian psychology, 103. See also Human-
    istic psychology tradition
Role(s), 48
    conserved, 48
    and de-roling, 157
    of therapist
        in ceremony, 81
        as "coach's coach," 33
        in interactive lecture, 87
        in narradrama, 263
        and playspace (developmental trans-
            formations), 136
Role crisis, 48–49
Role-playing
    structured, 140
    for substance abusers, 109
    unstructured, 140
Role relationships
    action methods as dramatizing, 6
    as scripted, 48
Role repertory expansion, in narradrama,
    234–235
Role reversal, 47, 51, 72
    and affiliative vs. nonaffiliative thera-
        pies, 270
    for conflicts within groups, 262
    in family case history, 58–59, 67
        with room, 65
        with Sadness, 51–54, 63
    between family members (risk in), 67
    in narradrama, 251
Role-training techniques, 48
Roth, Sallyann, 46

Satir, Virginia, 15, 46, 75, 111, 126
Scheff, Thomas, 78
Scripts
    and action methods, 6
    See also Family scripts
Sculpting
    with chairs, 263

in group art therapy, 182–184
in narradrama, 246
of unique outcomes, 234
Sculpting, family, 15
in case history, 60–61
in Rehearsals for Growth, 126–128
"Self," the, in internal family systems therapy, 112–113
Self, sense of, 166
Self-esteem, and music therapy (N-R approach), 201–202
Self-harm, in family drawing, 22
Self-injuring patients
art therapy for, 168–170, 191–192
case presentation on, 165–166, 170–193
theoretical framework for understanding of, 167–169
Self-presentation, of autistic client in music therapy, 206
Sensitivity and encounter groups, 103
Sharing
in group art therapy, 177–178
in psychodrama, 69
Silver Drawing Test, 194
Skill improvement, and Rehearsals for Growth program, 132–133
Slavson, S. R., 103
Socialization, from music therapy (N-R approach), 200, 220
Social milieu therapies, 4
Sociometric exercises, 103
Spectrogram, 56, 57, 58, 262
Spontaneous family play, pace and timing of, 28
Stages-of-change transtheoretical model, 108
Stanislavski, Konstantin, 232
Story(ies)
and action methods, 6
in dynamic family play, 31
vs. scripts, 46
Strategic therapists, 15–16
Structural Family Therapy, 15
Structured role-play, in group therapy, 140
Structured transition, out of role-play, 157
"Stuckness," in narradrama, 263
Substance abuse therapy
action methods for, 108–110, 133–134
group approaches to, 108
through Rehearsals for Growth, 107–108
case example of, 110–131

changes in participants in, 131–132
criteria for improvement from, 132–133
educational requirements for, 278
information sources on, 278
situation and outcome of, 130–131, 133
and self-esteem, 116
Suicidal patients, 168
in art therapy group, 171, 172
Supportive musical coactivity, in music therapy (N-R approach), 203, 212, 213, 214, 215, 217, 218, 219, 223
Switched media, 37
Symbolic events, ceremonies as, 77

Talk (verbal) therapy, 49
and action methods, 4, 5, 7
and children, 51
in conjoint therapy, 4
and questions of truthfulness, 109
and Rehearsals for Growth, 110
and self-injuring patients, 169
Teenagers, play methods for, 20
Telephone exercise (Address the Telephone), 128–130
Telling scarf or ball game, 26, 27, 28
Termination, in dynamic family play, 28
Theater, and ceremony, 77
Theater games, improvisational, 11
The Other Place (TOP), 141
Therapeutic ceremonies, 78–79
therapist's use of self in, 97–98
See also Ceremony(ies)
Therapeutic play, 165
Therapeutic rituals, 16
Therapist(s)
characteristics in success of, 269
as craftsman, 268
cross-training of, 7
pragmatic eclecticism of, 271
role of
in ceremony, 81
as "coach's coach," 33
in interactive lecture, 87
in narradrama, 263
and playspace (developmental transformations), 136
as using self, 24, 97–98, 190–192, 224–225
Therapy, experiential, 4
therapist's vs. client's drama in, 65

Tomm, Karl, 237
Training programs
    for art therapy, 280
    for developmental transformations, 279
    for dynamic family play, 276
    for family psychodrama, 277
    for multiple-family therapy, 277
    for music therapy, 280–281
    for narradrama, 281
    for Rehearsals for Growth, 278
Transactional analysis, 103
Transference
    in art therapy, 190
    in dramatic enactment, 72
Transfer of gains, in music therapy group for
        autistic clients, 219–221
Transformation, in developmental transfor-
        mations approach, 137
Transformational ritual, 235
Transformation of relationship, and thera-
        peutic ceremony, 79
Transition, out of role-play, 157
Transitional ritual, 235, 236
Trauma, psychological
    action methods for, 6
    family treatment of, 79–81
        for Vietnam veterans, 88–96
Traumatization, secondary, 79

"True Confessions" exercise, 118

Underdistancing, in ceremony, 78
Unique outcomes, in narradrama, 234
Unison movement and sound, in group
        therapy, 140
Unstructured role-play, in group therapy, 140

Verbal description, as inadequate, 49
"Verbal Mirrors" game, 120
Verbal therapy. See Talk therapy
Vietnam veterans, ceremonies in program for,
        87–96
Visualizations, in group art therapy, 186–187

Wadeson, Harriet, 190
Warm-up exercises
    in group art therapy, 174
    in Rehearsals for Growth, 116–119
Welcoming ritual, in dynamic family play,
        38–39
Whitaker, C., 15
White, Michael, 52, 237
Wiener, Daniel J., 107
Winnicott, D. W., 165
Witnessing, in family therapy, 76
    Writing, arising from art therapy, 181–
        182

ABOUT THE EDITORS

Daniel J. Wiener, PhD, is a professor in the Department of Counseling and Family Therapy at Central Connecticut State University in New Britain. He is licensed both as a psychologist and a marriage and family therapist and is a diplomate in marital and family psychology, an American Association for Marriage and Family Therapy approved supervisor, a certified group psychotherapist, and a registered drama therapist. He has 34 years of experience in academic teaching, psychotherapy practice, postgraduate clinical training, and organizational consulting. Since founding Rehearsals for Growth in 1985, he has been applying theater improvisation techniques to relationship skills training and has presented his work nationally and internationally at over 100 professional conferences.

Linda K. Oxford, MAR, MSSW, is licensed as both a marriage and family therapist and a clinical social worker. She is an adjunct instructor in the Counseling Program at Harding University Graduate School of Religion, and clinical director of Agape Child and Family Services in Memphis, Tennessee. Ms. Oxford has more than 20 years of experience as a therapist, trainer, and consultant with special interests in action methods of couples and family therapy. She specializes in brief solution-focused therapy and professional and organizational training and regularly presents at regional and national professional conferences.